POVERTY ARCHAEOLOGY

POVERTY ARCHAEOLOGY

*Architecture, Material Culture and
the Workhouse under the New Poor Law*

Charlotte Newman and Katherine Fennelly

berghahn
NEW YORK • OXFORD
www.berghahnbooks.com

First published in 2024 by
Berghahn Books
www.berghahnbooks.com

© 2024 Charlotte Newman and Katherine Fennelly

All rights reserved. Except for the quotation of short passages for the purposes of criticism and review, no part of this book may be reproduced in any form or by any means, electronic or mechanical, including photocopying, recording, or any information storage and retrieval system now known or to be invented, without written permission of the publisher.

Library of Congress Cataloging-in-Publication Data

Names: Newman, Charlotte (Curator and archaeologist), author. | Fennelly, Katherine (Historical archaeologist), author.
Title: Poverty archaeology : architecture, material culture and the workhouse under the new Poor Law / Charlotte Newman and Katherine Fennelly.
Description: New York ; Oxford : Berghahn Books, 2024. | Includes bibliographical references and index.
Identifiers: LCCN 2023020654 (print) | LCCN 2023020655 (ebook) | ISBN 9781805391098 (hardback) | ISBN 9781805391104 (ebook)
Subjects: LCSH: Architecture and archaeology—Great Britain—History. | Social archaeology—Great Britain. | Poor—Great Britain—History—19th century. | Workhouses—Great Britain—History—19th century. | Poor laws—Great Britain—History—19th century. | Public welfare—Great Britain—History—19th century. | Material culture—Great Britain—History—19th century.
Classification: LCC DA533 .N4426 2024 (print) | LCC DA533 (ebook) | DDC 941.081—dc23/eng/20230614
LC record available at https://lccn.loc.gov/2023020654
LC ebook record available at https://lccn.loc.gov/2023020655

British Library Cataloguing in Publication Data

A catalogue record for this book is available from the British Library

ISBN 978-1-80539-109-8 hardback
ISBN 978-1-80539-377-1 epub
ISBN 978-1-80539-110-4 web pdf

https://doi.org/10.3167/9781805391098

Contents

List of Figures — vi
Preface — viii
Acknowledgements — xi

Introduction. Introducing the Workhouse — 1
Chapter 1. Poverty Archaeology — 14
Chapter 2. The Sick — 29
Chapter 3. The Elderly — 61
Chapter 4. The Young — 83
Chapter 5. The Mad — 109
Chapter 6. The Workers — 130
Concluding Thoughts — 145

References — 153
Index — 159

Figures

1.1. Pie chart illustrating condition of workhouses in the north of England in 2007. Demolished 33%; partial demolished/use still related 12%; partial demolished/redeveloped for alternative use 28%; largely complete/use still related 19%; largely complete/redeveloped for alternative use 8% (drawn by Charlotte Newman). 15

1.2. Plan of West Yorkshire workhouse locations (drawn by Charlotte Newman). 16

1.3. Ripon Workhouse, north-west elevation (photographed by Charlotte Newman). 21

1.4. Wharfedale Workhouse, principal north-east elevation (photographed by Charlotte Newman). 22

2.1. Pateley Bridge Workhouse, principal south-west elevation (photographed by Charlotte Newman). 33

2.2. Great Ouseburn Workhouse infirmary, north-west elevation (photographed by Charlotte Newman). 34

2.3. Great Ouseburn Workhouse, principal south-east elevation (photographed by Charlotte Newman). 35

2.4. Skipton Workhouse, north-east elevation (photographed by Charlotte Newman). 38

2.5. Skipton Workhouse plan (1930), part 2 (after National Monuments Record, reference unknown, digitised by Charlotte Newman). 39

2.6. Bramley Workhouse second infirmary, south-east elevation (photographed by Charlotte Newman). 43

2.7. Plan of Phase 5 development of Leeds Workhouse (drawn by Charlotte Newman). 47

Figures • vii

2.8. Bradford Workhouse infirmary (1906), principal eastern elevation and sanitary towers, East (photographed by Charlotte Newman).   55

3.1. Plan of Phase 3 development at Great Ouseburn Workhouse (drawn by Charlotte Newman).   67

3.2. The Phase 3 and Phase 4 development of Bramley Workhouse (drawn by Charlotte Newman).   68

3.3. Leeds Workhouse, principal elevation (digitised by Charlotte Newman).   71

3.4. Bradford Union Workhouse, principal elevation of New Poor Law workhouse (photographed by Charlotte Newman).   76

4.1. Leeds Moral and Industrial Training School, north-east elevation (photographed by Charlotte Newman).   96

4.2. Leeds Moral and Industrial Training School, ground- and first-floor plans (digitised by Charlotte Newman).   98

5.1. Leeds Workhouse lunatic ward (1862), north (photographed by Charlotte Newman).   118

6.1. Bradford Workhouse nurses' home, principal western elevation (photographed by Charlotte Newman).   139

6.2. Bradford Workhouse nurses' home plan, ground floor (digitised by Charlotte Newman).   140

6.3. Leeds Workhouse nurses' home, L-plan extension, north-east (photographed by Charlotte Newman).   141

6.4. Leeds Workhouse nurses' home, ground-floor plan (digitised by Charlotte Newman).   142

Preface

The book that you are reading is the culmination of a collaborative effort that began as a conversation between two doctoral students. This book is the consequence of discussions over glasses of conference wine and biscuits between sessions, of long drives between train stations and archaeological sites, and, from March 2020 to mid-2022, of phone and Zoom chats as the authors found themselves on opposite sides of the country, watching a global health crisis play out with the rest of the planet. It is interesting that many of the conversations that surrounded the expansion of the buildings discussed in this book – the need to meet unprecedented demand, the state's response to public health concerns, the problem of movement around the country – were repeated (albeit in different ways) around the COVID-19 pandemic: conversations about how and why we build hospitals and institutions for the health and accommodation of the public.

The research on workhouses in Yorkshire that forms the core discussion of this book began as the research of Charlotte Newman. The data collected here and for the purposes of the project resulted in a substantial body of research on regional workhouses in the United Kingdom. Though some of the research conducted for this study was published in journal articles, in the pages of *Post-Medieval Archaeology* and the *International Journal of Historical Archaeology*, the whole research project remained unpublished until now. From 2012, the annual conferences of the Theoretical Archaeology Group, the Society for Historical Archaeology and the Society for Post-Medieval Archaeology led to some detailed conversations with Katherine Fennelly about common research interests. When the two authors met, Katherine was writing up her own research on lunatic asylums and architecture, and common research findings drove collaborations on conference papers. A small research project on a rural almshouse in Rutland in England – the Lyddington Bedehouse – followed, which eventually led to the drafting of a co-authored article in the *International Journal of Historical Archaeology* on the archaeology of institutions in the United Kingdom, and eventually to the collaborative development of this book. What started as a brainstorm on a whiteboard has led to this thematic book on the different inmate classes of workhouses in Yorkshire.

Over the course of the last decade and a half, as both authors engaged in the archaeology of later historical institutions in the British Isles, certain themes and questions emerged from conferences, particularly with our American colleagues, on how our work constituted an archaeological approach to institutional confinement. Though these questions have been circulating in the discipline of historical archaeology for nearly half a century, every new discourse or research avenue seems to recall them, and we are still no closer to consensus. Given that most of the notable archaeological approaches to institutions from the early twenty-first century were carried out in North America and Australia, a British approach seemed marginal when Charlotte first began her research on workhouses and Katherine first approached lunatic asylums for study. This is surprising given that many of the ideas that underpin or heavily influenced the construction of these institutions had early expression in government reports and advisory documents, in policy and in the writings of reformers in the British Isles. It seemed, a decade ago, that we needed to take a regional approach even then, considering the ideas that were developed here using examples that were built here. As such, we put our own research into practice by each developing an interdisciplinary method for assessing and researching institutional buildings that were still standing, still in use, or completely demolished and built over, which addressed the needs of our own fieldwork on sites here in Britain and Ireland.

Regionality was a theme that emerged from both of our studies. Though the overall area studied is small (geographically limited to the north of England), and despite government efforts in the nineteenth century to standardise the ways in which state institutions were constructed, the architecture and built heritage of institutions for social confinement in Britain and Ireland varies considerably by region. That there are differences between the four nations is unsurprising given the different administrative bodies that were, variously, responsible for welfare and healthcare provision. What is more surprising is how individual counties, cities and even parishes applied the wider ideas of institutional control, improvement and management that much of the discourse on poverty and psychiatry has traditionally treated as homogeneous. As each individual Union or hospital adapted to state recommendations in their own way, different kinds of buildings emerged. Though they were similar to each other in overall form, and though many bore the handiwork of a handful of architects whose designs dominated the institutional architecture of the nineteenth century, the ways in which each individual institution responded to demands on their space emerged as highly variable.

It is this discussion of regionality and variability that underlay many of our early conversations. Though books about workhouses and workhouse architecture have been published before, we were concerned that our own views on the ways in which institutions *differed* were not represented. An archaeological approach that focused on the materiality of individual sites was needed, and we have offered the results of our approach here. Furthermore, the variety of inmate types in these institutions was also underplayed, and we have attempted to rectify that in this volume. This is our contribution to the discipline and to the conversation on institutional archaeology and methods in historical archaeology. This book is also the culmination of a decade of research, conversations, collaborations and writing, and (we hope) evidences the value of researchers working together to formulate answers to some of the questions in our discipline.

—Katherine Fennelly in Lincoln and
Charlotte Newman in Cornwall, May 2023

Acknowledgements

This book is the product of a collaborative effort, not just between the authors, but also with the other archaeologists and historians and researchers of the history of poverty who advised and contributed to the discussions that built it. We are grateful to Professor Harold Mytum for his support, for chairing sessions to which we contributed and asking interesting questions of our work. The Society for Historical Archaeology, Theoretical Archaeology Group and Society for Post-Medieval Archaeology annual conferences were places where we assembled ideas, and we thank these learned societies for providing a venue for sessions and discussion. Deirdre Forde and Suzanne Lilley contributed their research and interest to conference sessions and to our previously published work, and were invaluable as both colleagues and friends – not to mention excellent company during unexpected snowstorms in Texas.

Katherine would like to express her gratitude to her colleagues and students at the Department of Archaeology at the University of Sheffield for continued support and encouragement to pursue interesting research in heritage and archaeology. She would also like to thank her former colleagues at the University of Lincoln and particularly at Lincoln Conservation, where she was working when she began contributing to this book. Much of this work was assembled during the COVID-19 pandemic, so the support of online communities on Discord has been invaluable in helping to maintain social and creative spaces even while we were all confined to our homes. Special mention to the Splendid Isolation Slack Group – to Cassie, Zi, Alys and Karen – who have been a patient sounding board, and a well of inspiration and help throughout the writing process. Parts of this book were made possible thanks to their Zoom-based co-working sessions. Katherine needs music to write, and she would like to express her thanks to EXO for accompanying many long hours of writing and revision.

Collaboration is valuable in our discipline and finding a person with whom we can work is priceless. Katherine is immensely grateful to Charlotte for always being an enthusiastic collaborator and good friend, and for meetings that never feel like work. She looks forward to their next collaboration. The Fennelly family are an ongoing support and Katherine is especially grateful to her father Sean, who has never complained when his daughter has raided his book collection. She would also like to express her particular thanks to Hannah for always answering the phone to her sister. Finally, Katherine owes more to James Greenhalgh than can be expressed in this short acknowledgement section. To him and to the feline company of Edward and Ripley she is immeasurably grateful.

The research that formed the basis of this book has benefited from the input, intellectual and emotional, of various people and organisations. Charlotte is deeply indebted to Dr Kate Giles, for giving the original work direction and purpose and for her support and motivation. She would also like to thank the Department of Archaeology, University of York. She is grateful to all her friends and colleagues – Amritesh, Hartley, Suz, Sarah, Ashley, Gemma, Graham, Jen – who have shared her enthusiasm for this project and accompanied her on fieldwork. The MA Buildings Archaeology students of the year 2008–9 deserve a special mention for all their help. Charlotte would especially like to thank the staff at Leeds, Bradford, Northallerton, Skipton, Wakefield and Keighley archives and at the National Monuments Records for sharing vital resources for this research with her. Gratitude is also due to Ripon Museum Trust, Campbell & Plenty, Nidderdale Museum, English Partnerships, Leeds Primary Care Trust, Bradford Teaching Hospitals NHS Foundation Trust and Thackeray Medical Museum for allowing her to access workhouse sites. The writing of the original work owes a lot to Charlotte's academic writing tutor at the University of York, Steph, and her passion for words. As a dyslexic academic Charlotte often struggles to convey the complexities of her ideas in words. This book would not have seen the light of day without the determination and perseverance of Kat, who always championed this work and generously crafted this final contribution. Charlotte is very thankful to her parents, who believed in her and made this research possible. Finally, she would like to thank her husband Mark and all her friends for their unwavering support and commitment to this project.

Introduction
Introducing the Workhouse

That large loud Clock, which rolls each dreaded Hour,
Those Gates and Locks, and all those Signs of Power:
It is a Prison, with a milder name,
Which few inhabit without dread or shame
—George Crabbe, *The Borough: A Poem*

The workhouse has a notorious historical reputation. They were called prisons 'with a milder name' or 'Bastilles for the Poor' by their contemporaries, and considered to be an escalation of the problem of poverty, rather than a solution to it. As with their material representatives, the laws that surrounded the workhouse are equally infamous. The eighteenth- and nineteenth-century Poor Laws left a built and material legacy of over two centuries of legislative provision for the poor and infirm. Workhouses represent the first centralised, state-organised system for welfare, though that legacy is somewhat lost behind their notorious historical reputation. This reputation is drawn from the work of contemporaries like the poet and surgeon George Crabbe, and later critics of the system of poor relief such as the Fabians Sidney and Beatrice Webb, whose scathing history of the Poor Laws (1929) led to their repeal in England and Wales in 1930. Workhouses were intended to be specialised institutions, with dedicated subdivisions for the management of different categories of inmate. An inmate is anyone who was resident in the workhouse, and this broad definition includes both staff and patient. The term inmate is used here primarily to refer to the poor whose management was the subject of the mission of the Poor Laws, except where explicitly stated. Among the varied missions of New Poor Law workhouses – constructed after the 1834 Poor Law Amendment Act – were the management of the long-term ill and infirm, the containment of contagious disease and the care and treatment of inmates who could not be catered for in other institutional contexts, like children and mentally ill who were considered incurable.

The workhouse as an idea and the workhouse as a material individual institution are very different. Since the late 1990s, archaeologists approaching institutions for the management of poverty (such as Lucas 1999; Piddock 2001) have clearly identified the idiosyncratic nature of these institutions, which vary in form and mission according to where they were built, who they were built by and the frameworks that shaped their make-up. To say that a workhouse constructed for a city, a town or a rural area will vary in architecture and management practice is almost a truism. Despite this, workhouses are relatively homogenised in their historical reputation, much of which is also bound up with press coverage of scandals in the 1840s and 1850s. Press coverage and anti-Poor Law supporters called for welfare reform in the interwar period. The reason behind the uniformity and relative formlessness of the historic workhouse in scholarship and in the popular imagination is probably the scale of the workhouse system. Workhouses were built in every region and locale of England and Wales in the mid-nineteenth century alone. In our previous work we have both attempted to address regionality in public institutions for welfare and the management of poverty (Newman 2015; Fennelly and Newman 2017; Fennelly 2019), and will apply a regional, critical means analysis to the architecture of individual institutions to account for wider practice here. Like our predecessors, we are also limited by the scale of examples available and will thus focus solely on the north of England to address our questions on spatial organisation and material management.

In 1834, the Poor Law Amendment Act, which provided formally for a standardised system of poor relief in England and Wales, dictated that workhouses be constructed 20 miles apart, so that a network of closely linked institutions could cater to an increasingly populous landscape. As such, workhouse buildings were to be found in every major village and hamlet, and they have left a significant legacy of built heritage (Morrison 1999, 1). It is probably for this reason that the workhouse as a built institution has been generalised, the experience of individuals in one workhouse equated with the experience of others in workhouses, despite significant variation in management practice on an almost case-by-case basis. The conditions uncovered during the much-publicised Andover Scandal of the 1840s (described later in this chapter), for example, where inmates were reported to be gnawing on bones they were tasked with crushing, contributing to an overhaul of workhouse management from the top down in the 1840s (Shave 2018, 340), has come to popularly typify the experience of workhouse inmates, even as Andover was considered in its own time as an exceptional case. This book aims to build a social archaeology of poverty and health in workhouses in just three English counties, illustrating the diversity of experience and the heterogeneous nature of these buildings, even as they shared architects, plans and a common legislative framework.

This book will be an archaeologically informed examination of the historic workhouse – a singular institution in writing on poverty and welfare in the nineteenth century, but one with nearly two thousand individual sites before the Poor Law Amendment Act of 1834. After this Act, commonly referred to as the New Poor Law, 583 individual Poor Law Unions were established to manage their workhouses, each Union catering to several parishes (Fowler 2007, 28). The workhouses serving the Unions catered for large numbers of people with many varying needs, including poor relief, as well as medical care or other kinds of care. An increasing number of sick and infirm inmates over the course of the nineteenth century led to the establishment of dedicated infirmaries and medical facilities, which gave former workhouses purpose after the abolition of the workhouse system in 1930. Many workhouses became hospitals. Looking specifically at the groups involved in driving the need for increasingly specialised medical care in workhouses, leading ultimately to the conversion of many into hospitals, this book will address the heterogeneous nature and regional needs of different workhouses. The situation of 'the inmate' in the workhouse site is the central theme of this work. In his work on the 'total institution' – an institution to cater to all aspects of life without much contact with the outside world, such as a workhouse – sociologist Erving Goffman (1961, 18) draws a distinction between the inmate and staff: the inmates as a 'large managed group' and staff whose job it is to supervise. However, his designation of staff as separate is contingent on the idea that staff leave the institution and are integrated into the wider world. In a nineteenth-century workhouse, this distinction is less clear, as staff of all hierarchical levels lived on site. As such, the inmate here is both the recipient of the management strategies laid down in the New Poor Laws of 1834, and the staff who are responsible for that management.

Before tackling the nuances of the workhouse system, it is first necessary to outline the background to poverty and welfare reform in England and Wales in 1834. Workhouses as institutions are often discussed in the same context as prisons and asylums (see, for example, discussions of almshouses and destitute asylums in the 2001 special issue of the *International Journal of Historical Archaeology* on institutions). Like prisons and asylums, workhouses formed part of a wider drive towards social and civic improvement that underpinned significant changes in law, in architecture and in the organisation of the English economy in the late Georgian period. The similarities between these institutions architecturally are largely superficial, however (Morrison 1999, 53), as the architecture of workhouses was so varied that the ideologies of the period that informed other institutions had less impact on the day-to-day running of workhouses than the management strategies of individual Boards of Guardians. Historical archaeologists have identified the drive towards civic improvement, materially articulated in institutions like workhouses, as part of a consolidation of a capitalist economy, both driving and driven by the Industrial Revolution and an expansion of mercantile trade in the Atlantic World in the late modern period (Leone 1995; Johnson 1996). The 'non-productive body' that could not or would not contribute to an increasingly industrialising economy became a problem (Lucas 1999, 135). French historian Michel Foucault (1989, 46) refers to the exclusion of the non-productive body and its institutionalisation as being driven by the 'imperative of labour' inherent in the capitalist economy of the industrial West. Sarah Tarlow (2007, 16) goes further to suggest that this drive was part of the 'improvement' and rationalisation of English society, identifying improvement as a 'cross-cutting ethic, directed not only at the improvement of agricultural production . . . but also at the moral, intellectual and physical improvement of the self, of the labouring people, of society, of production and of the human environment'. Part of this all-encompassing drive towards improving the people was on the one hand a consolidation of a messy and disparate network of charity and welfare institutions and sources – dubbed by historian Olwen Hufton (1974) the 'economy of makeshifts' – and the execution of the ideals of utilitarian reformers like Jeremy Bentham by imposing improvement on people through their material environment on the other. Unfortunately, much archaeological scholarship on the management of poverty during the emergence of a global capitalist economy (including this book) is focused on the anglophone world. Even so, workhouses are still generalised as expressions of an idea and rarely examined critically as individual or regional institutions.

Much of the historical reputation of workhouses comes from sensationalist and fictional accounts of workhouse life penned by authors like Charles Dickens, most notably in books like *Oliver Twist*, and from anti-Poor Law reportage in the popular press after a series of scandals in the 1840s. While much of this reputation is unearned or limited to a number of notable examples, workhouses at the end of the eighteenth century were not pleasant places. Privation was a general order in workhouse management, and cost-cutting measures were commonplace. A notable example that reads as particularly offensive to the late modern reader is the burial of an illegitimate child with another unrelated dead inmate at the parish workhouse of St Paul, Covent Garden in 1791 (Richardson 2012, 79). The idea of *improvement* in the New Poor Law workhouse extended to not just people, therefore, but the buildings themselves. By the third decade of the nineteenth century the mishmash of old parish buildings, charitable institutions, almshouses and other buildings that made up provision for the poor in England were deemed unacceptable by a Whig government under Earl Grey, riding a wave of reform after their success with parliamentary reform in 1832. As such, the New Poor Law had the material effect of transforming the built environment of poverty and redefining institutional provision for welfare. For the people for whom the reform of the Poor Laws was intended to benefit, however, the New Poor Laws changed their social and material landscape irrevocably.

It is important to point out that at the start of the nineteenth century, most people in England were poor. Those suffering under serious poverty were the target of reformers and institutions, but even then, serious poverty was not always constant, as some people were only significantly worse off for a season or in light of circumstances such as the death of a breadwinner. From the establishment of the first Elizabethan Poor Laws in 1601, the business of welfare and charity was shared among many different groups and institutions. The workhouse – such as it was – was a last resort for most. People *got by* through the charity of their neighbours, on out-relief (alms, charitable donations, goods) distributed by their local parish Poor Law overseers, or through religious groups such as the Society of Friends. These 'patchy, desperate and sometimes failing strategies of the poor for material survival' (King and Tomkins 2003, 1) often involved multiple institutions and charitable groups. Engagement with varying levels of welfare could be seasonal or year-round. Workhouses in which the able-bodied could be put to work sprang up around England and Wales throughout the seventeenth and eighteenth centuries with varying degrees of success, and often dependent on the resources of whichever parish built them. This drove some parishes to bond together in 'Unions', the first notably successful example of which was the Bristol Corporation of the Poor in 1696 (Brundage 2002, 11). Subsequent Acts and Poor Laws encouraged Unions to share the burden of institutional poor relief. The idea was codified into law with Gilbert's Act in 1782, which proposed a 'system' of workhouses, in which the vulnerable could be housed and the idle put to work. Gilbert's Act was written and championed by Member of Parliament Thomas Gilbert, whose various Bills on the employment and relief of the poor brought the problem of an unconsolidated Poor Law system to the frequent attention of parliament throughout the 1770s and 1780s. Workhouses established during this period are referred to in this book as Gilbert Unions. Despite its popularity, Gilbert's Act was not universally taken up, and there is some discussion among historians as to what kinds of parishes adopted the policy. Uptake of the Union system in the eighteenth century and early nineteenth century was inconsistent, varying from area to area. Historians debate the extent to which the Unions were taken up; social geographer Samantha Shave has pointed out that the early twentieth-century economists Sidney and Beatrice Webb, whose retrospectives and reports on workhouses contributed to a reform of the system in the 1930s, argued that the Unions were primarily rural, while historian Peter Mandler (1987, 133) has conversely argued that the Unions were taken up primarily in urban areas. This confusion among historians makes it difficult to pin down a historiographical consensus on the issue.

Regardless of its de facto success, Gilbert's Act succeeded in establishing the idea of the Union as a means of reforming the whole system, and in 1834 the Poor Law Amendment Act (known henceforth as the New Poor Law) made the establishment of dedicated Unions compulsory. One of the aims of the new system, as built around the workhouses, was to tackle the number of able-bodied men and women who applied for relief. The workhouses would be able to address the needs of the destitute elderly, children without parents and the infirm, while the able-bodied could seek help from charities and friendly societies (Boyer 2019, 38). The small rural workhouses and other smaller institutions such as almshouses were superseded by new, dedicated institutions – large, purpose-built workhouses – into which the ideas of the New Poor Law were to be codified. The architecture of the new workhouses, unlike their predecessors, was centrally imposed by the New Poor Law Commission, a body based in Somerset House in London whose Inspectors and Assistant Inspectors witnessed first-hand (and in some cases, contributed to) the turmoil of establishing the new system, until their replacement by the more centralised Poor Law Board in 1847.

The architecture of the New Poor Law workhouse marked a significant material departure from Poor Law workhouses of old. The new workhouses constructed after the 1834 Act conformed to plans and ideas set out by reformers such as Sampson Kempthorne, whose radial-plan institutions bore closer resemblance to prisons and asylums of the early nineteenth century than to the almshouses and Houses of Industry that they were replacing or supplementing. The New Poor Law stipulated that 'no Parish, Township, Hamlet, or Place ... shall be situated more than Ten Miles from any Poorhouse or Workhouse' (Poor Law Amendment Act 1834, chapter 31). Within the workhouses themselves, the experience of being a dependant of the institution changed fundamentally, as the industrialised means of processing increasing numbers of pauper admissions led to a level of uniformity of practice that had no precedent in workhouses of old. The inmates' bodies themselves were subject to the mortification of poverty, as their clothes were removed on entry and stored until their discharge, their bodies washed and hair shorn (Longmate 2003, 93) to prevent the spread of lice and disease.

Conditions in workhouses varied by institution. Urban workhouses, workhouses just outside of urban centres and rural workhouses were very different, though their architectural forms were similar (as discussed later in this chapter). Workhouses under the New Poor Law were intended to support *deserving* poor, those for whom poverty was an unfortunate circumstance about which they could do nothing. This included the sick, the elderly, children, widows and the mentally ill. The workhouses were also designed to deter able-bodied, *undeserving* poor from taking advantage of the system. The 'workhouse test' was one of the underpinning ideas behind the new system, that paupers entered a workhouse as a last resort, and that the institution was a deterrent to poverty and not an incentive (Fowler 2007, 17). As such, conditions were not supposed to be comfortable for the general inmate population (with a few exceptions, discussed later in this book). In the 1840s, a scandal of particular note brought conditions within workhouses to the attention of the public. Andover Union Workhouse in Hampshire, regarded early in the New Poor Law era as a well-run institution, was the subject of an inquiry under the New Poor Law Commission due to a report of inmates there resorting to gnawing old bones to extract marrow and gristle (Brundage 2002, 88). This reportedly took place while the paupers were engaged in bone-crushing, a common activity in workhouses in which animal bones were crushed for fertiliser. The management of the workhouse came under scrutiny, as inmates were found to have insufficient food according to government guidelines. For opponents of the New Poor Law, scandals like Andover only proved that the system did not work. Even so, the system still proliferated and workhouses were constructed across the country.

The English landscape was to be materially changed to accommodate a new network of workhouses. In practice, the process of constructing workhouses was much more gradual. Out of a number of idealised designs for workhouses, several variations on plan emerged in the 1830s and 1840s that proliferated across England and Wales. The designs of the architect Sampson Kempthorne are frequently held up as a paragon of the New Poor Law workhouse model, so vaunted were they in the reports of the Commissioners of Lunacy. '[They] appear to us, from a cursory inspection', they said, 'excellently arranged; it is most gratifying to see the attention that has been paid by the architect to the principles of separation and classification, to cleanliness, to ventilation, and to general convenience' (Annual Report of the Poor Law Commissioners for England 1835). This kind of praise evidences the priorities of the Commissioners: maximum classification and separation, cleanliness and utility. Though Kempthorne himself emigrated to New Zealand in 1840 after constructing just a few workhouses, his much-lauded designs were applied as a base model by many architects who followed in the construction of workhouses throughout England (Markus 1993, 142). So, what did Kempthorne's designs look like? According to the Poor Law Commissioners' First Annual Report (1835), there were to be accommodations for seven classes of inmate in a workhouse, and each was to have indoor and outdoor space. These classes were aged or infirm men, able-bodied men and youths (over 13), boys aged 7–13, aged or infirm women, able-bodied women and girls (over 16), girls aged 7–16 and children under 7 years. In practice, these classes were frequently mixed and another class – the mad – was soon added to this; gender was the only consistent separation criteria. Kempthorne's Hexagonal Plan, which proved an ideologically popular choice, if not as readily adopted as his more practical cruciform plan, provided for six separate inmate classes within the workhouse and in yards without, as well as cross-ventilation of wards to promote fresh air (an increasing concern), and the situation of officers at the centre of the structure to allow for maximum supervision. Twenty-six of these hexagonal workhouses were constructed in the 1830s (Morrison 1999, 74).

After Kempthorne, his one-time apprentice George Gilbert Scott is the other architect whose name is associated with workhouse architecture. Gilbert Scott and his partner William Bonython Moffatt designed a workhouse that departed from the single-structure plan, dividing the workhouse into three: an entrance block, a main building and an infirmary, surrounded by a wall within which separate yards were drawn to maintain inmate separation outdoors (Morrison 1999, 71). Each section of the building was connected, but it departed from an earlier model of institutional construction that had seen its height during the grand designs of prison architects like William Blackburn at the end of the eighteenth century and the first of the big public lunatic asylums in the 1810s. By the 1830s, the problems with these monolithic structures were becoming apparent, as more and more inmate classes and an increasing demand on services exposed the limitations of an institution that radiated from a central spoke (Evans 2010, 309). Though Kempthorne and his fellow architect Francis Head's hexagonal plans were visually pleasing on paper, the expense and inconvenience of expanding a site that was already built to its limitations would soon become known. Scott and Moffatt's more loosely arranged collection of connected structures proved more practical. However, these plans and the ideal designs that informed them are just starting points, and do not reflect the reality of how workhouses operated day-to-day, or the sometimes highly regional challenges that informed their expansion over time.

An archaeology of these kinds of institutions requires an interdisciplinary approach, an engagement with both the documentary and the material (Piddock 2007, 17) to understand how the architecture was understood and engaged with. This book employs an interdisciplinary toolkit to explore historic workhouses from both a material and archival perspective. Workhouse buildings after 1834 were constructed to an ideal plan of how a workhouse *should* look. As such, it is tempting to consider them as homogeneous institutions, whose distinguishing or individualising factors were the activities that took place within their walls. However, there is a danger in this approach of assuming that workhouse buildings *worked*, and that the use of space was not influenced by human agency and the architecture not also influenced by regionality. Administration reform in England in the middle of the nineteenth century meant that pro forma overtook more nuanced means of reporting to central government (Fennelly 2019, 113). As such, regional differences, factors and influences are harder to discern from the historical record. With the exception of instances of scandal at Andover in the 1840s, or political unrest, as in the North of England in the late 1830s, significant regional differences are only accounted for in scholarship through micro-studies of individual geographic areas. L.A. Botelho's (2004) excellent work on the elderly and the Old Poor Law in Suffolk, from which Chapter 3 of this book will draw, and Frank Crompton's (1997) detailed exploration of children in workhouses in Worcestershire, discussed in Chapter 4, are examples of this kind of scholarship. As such, English workhouses are on one hand treated as both highly regional and fragmented, while on the other, discussions on architecture are necessarily general due to the scale of the workhouse system after the 1830s. This book is subject to the same limitations of scale and is not an exception to the published scholarship, taking as examples of regional practice the workhouses of Yorkshire, Nottinghamshire and Derbyshire, and aiming to demonstrate regional difference through the case studies presented. England is a highly regional country, however, both now and in the nineteenth century. While central government and national legislation dominated welfare provision throughout the island, local identity and regional pressures still impacted individual institutions. The benefit of a materially focused approach to workhouses is in the potential for empirical comparison of building features and architecture, and aids in the identification of features that are distinctive to individual institutions.

Building on the work of historians such as Brundage (2002) to set workhouses within their wider social and legislative context, this work also contributes to archaeological approaches to institutions. Building surveys and architectural analysis are employed to identify areas of activity and discuss the division of space in workhouse buildings. This builds on both academic and commercial approaches to institutional buildings. Significant research has been carried out on institutional buildings in the context of development-led (sometimes commercial; cultural resource management in North America) archaeology. The previously mentioned special issue of the *International Journal for Historical Archaeology* showcased the potential of cultural resource management projects to inform interesting avenues of research with regards to institutional buildings (Spencer-Wood and Baugher 2001, 15). We have previously shown how development-led archaeology contributes to the study of institutional buildings in the United Kingdom (Fennelly and Newman 2017), and recent scholarship (such as Shapland 2020) has further explored the potential for non-invasive, archaeologically informed examinations of buildings that are still standing but are inaccessible or are now demolished and survive only in their plans and records. Archaeologists are well situated to inform on both the material and historical facets of a historical institution. In her work on lunatic asylums in Australia and Britain, Australian archaeologist Susan Piddock (2007, 5) has argued that buildings and spaces reflect ideas that are not always explicitly written about in documentary evidence. As such, an interdisciplinary archaeological approach to the study of workhouses, incorporating archival research, standing building surveys, comparison with grey (unpublished, commercially focused) literature, and spatial analysis, can identify issues and narratives that lie between disciplinary boundaries.

Overview

Traditional archaeological approaches to institutional buildings in the United Kingdom are not always possible. While building surveys are sometimes feasible where the buildings survive and are open to be investigated, many former workhouses have been demolished or redeveloped, or continue to operate as general medical facilities. As such, this book begins with a short methodological overview of the ways in which we approach workhouse buildings here. This chapter outlines the methods employed in this study for examining workhouse architecture from a distinctively archaeological perspective. The application of a broad disciplinary toolkit is described in detail, with a note on how these methods could be applied in the study of problematic buildings beyond workhouses and other institutions.

Most workhouses that continued to operate as institutions in England after the abolition of the Poor Laws in the mid-twentieth century became hospitals. As such, the first discussion chapter focuses on sick inmates, as a significant and increasing portion of the workhouse population. Workhouses of the New Poor Law were part of a wider institutional drive towards the confinement of those elements of society that could not contribute meaningfully to the industrial economy, which included criminals, the sick and the insane. Even as lunatic asylums were constructed en masse following the Lunacy Acts of 1808 and 1845, workhouses still housed lunatics throughout the nineteenth century in dedicated spaces or separate buildings. The nature of this provision and the extent to which each workhouse related to nearby lunatic asylums were regionally dependent and often closely connected. The needs of specific local populations and regions were reflected in the material construction and built environment of the workhouse.

The old and infirm were traditionally the largest user groups before the New Poor Laws, and a significant proportion of the population after. Chapter 3 will focus on the elderly as a specific classification of inmate in the nineteenth-century workhouse. Taking Michel Foucault's idea of the institution for confinement as a solution to the problem of unproductive populations, this chapter will broadly explore the idea of what it means to be 'elderly' in the nineteenth century, and how the New Poor Law supported that idea. The workhouse as a site for housing and managing the elderly and infirm will be explored through spatial analysis, using architectural plans, material interiors and cartographic evidence. This chapter will focus on the concerns of workhouse Guardians as reflected in minute books for specific workhouses. Employing census data and workhouse records for admission, the idea of 'old age' will be addressed. The elderly will be examined through architectural provision for their management, the permeability of the institution (ostensibly an institution for confinement) for this class of inmate, and the activities they engaged in, such as leisure activities and social interactions within and outside the workhouse.

Children formed a marginal and contentious group in the New Poor Law workhouse, though they were ubiquitous. Their care contrasts significantly with that of other inmates, and could include education, industrial training and sometimes even forced migration. Leisure activities often formed part of their management. Unlike the elderly or the infirm, emphasis in the management of children was on moving them on from the institution as soon as they were fit to contribute meaningfully to society. Chapter 4 will explore the dedicated spaces for children in individual workhouses, as part of the landscape or the workhouse buildings proper. How this provision altered over time in response to changes in national legislation such as the Elementary Education Act of 1870 will be examined in relation to education provision and apprenticing before and after 1870. This chapter will link to the previous chapters on the sick and the elderly by exploring dedicated spaces for inmate provision (in this case, the schoolhouse, dormitory or infirmary), which was also changed in response to public health concerns and social issues. Significantly, the divisions between these more *deserving* inmate classes were more permeable than the division between able-bodied adults and the rest of the workhouse population. This chapter contributes to the expanding published literature on the history of childhood, and more recently, archaeological approaches to children and childhood in the past. Chapter 5 examines specialised provision for lunatics in the regional workhouse, comparing the landscapes and material fabric of spaces for lunatics in the workhouse with those of local lunatic asylums. The mentally ill was a broad category in these non-specialised institutions, so we will use the phrase 'lunatic inmate' to refer to any inmate who was not explicitly categorised otherwise. This language reflects the language of the sources of the period. This term, used throughout the primary source material, further reflects the lack of classification on anything but the broadest of terms in most workhouses in this period, which were very adamant for the most part that their mission was not the care of the mentally ill or disabled. Even so, paying to accommodate a pauper at an asylum or other specialised institution at the expense of the Union was sometimes more expensive than housing them in the workhouse, such that there are often very broad classifications of patients that fall under the category of 'mad', 'lunatic' and 'insane'. From a terminological perspective, this makes it difficult to account for what exactly each inmate under these categories would have been categorised as in a more specialised facility. To reflect this ambiguity, this class of inmate is referred to in this book as 'lunatic' or 'insane' as per the terminology of the records (unless specified as otherwise). This chapter will refer to published scholarship on the history and archaeology of medicine and lunatic asylums and contribute to literature on the archaeology of institutions.

Although primarily an architectural form designed for the institutionalisation of the poor, the workhouse became a home for employees supporting the workhouse system. Over the course of the New Poor Law, the number of workhouse employees increased and diversified. Chapter 6 will explore the varied roles and professions that developed to support the workhouse system and how they manifested themselves within the workhouse architecture, as well as the role of the workhouse as a dwelling space or home. The built form developed alongside staff specialism and training as one informed the other, resulting in a hierarchical system that prompted staff institutionalisation. This chapter examines how regional needs directly impacted the development of staff roles in rural workhouses where employment was limited and varied. Each workhouse provided for their staff in different ways, and in many cases accommodated them. As a kind of hidden class of inmate, mid-level workhouse staff occupied an interesting position in the workhouse spatial hierarchy. Their movements were managed and dictated by the manager at the top and other actors like the porter, while inmates worked alongside staff to manage the sick and the infirm. This final chapter will spatialise their experience.

The book will conclude with a summary of workhouse provision for the sick, infirm or otherwise unemployable. This chapter builds on the idea of the workhouse as a varied and highly regional institution, as evidenced by the examinations of medical provision as a single aspect of their remit in the preceding four chapters. Regionality will be put forward as a natural consequence of the expansion of urban centres and the development of the English landscape in light of the agricultural and industrial revolutions. As such, local workhouses became embedded in the state-sponsored provision of welfare and healthcare at a regional level. Following the different uses to which workhouses were put during the First World War and in the interwar period (as hospitals, prisoner of war camps or schools), workhouses underwent a significant transformation in the mid-twentieth century, with many ending up as hospitals.

Chapter 1

Poverty Archaeology

This book represents the collaborative and individual efforts of the two authors over the last decade and a half to navigate the complexities of carrying out archaeologically based research on a variety of site types in the British Isles. Before embarking on our detailed study of workhouse architecture and built heritage, it is necessary therefore to account for the methods applied here. As an exercise in the archaeology of poverty in the nineteenth century, this study draws on multidisciplinary methods to adequately account for all aspects of the material world of the Poor Law workhouse, traditional archaeological approaches to sites above and below ground and desk-based methods of research that are drawn from development-led archaeology and professional practice in the United Kingdom.

Carrying out archaeological research and fieldwork on institutional sites in the United Kingdom and Ireland requires a multidisciplinary methodology, foregrounded in standing building surveys and later historical archaeology, and encompassing historical archival research, historical geography and cartographic study, and spatial analysis. The archives for these institutions are spread between local authority archives and historic environment records, national archives and sometimes private enterprises. The buildings themselves vary in their states of repair. Some are still standing while others have fallen into dilapidation or have disappeared entirely (Figures 1.1 and 1.2). Most workhouse sites studied in this book and more broadly have been transformed beyond recognition from how they were

Poverty Archaeology • 15

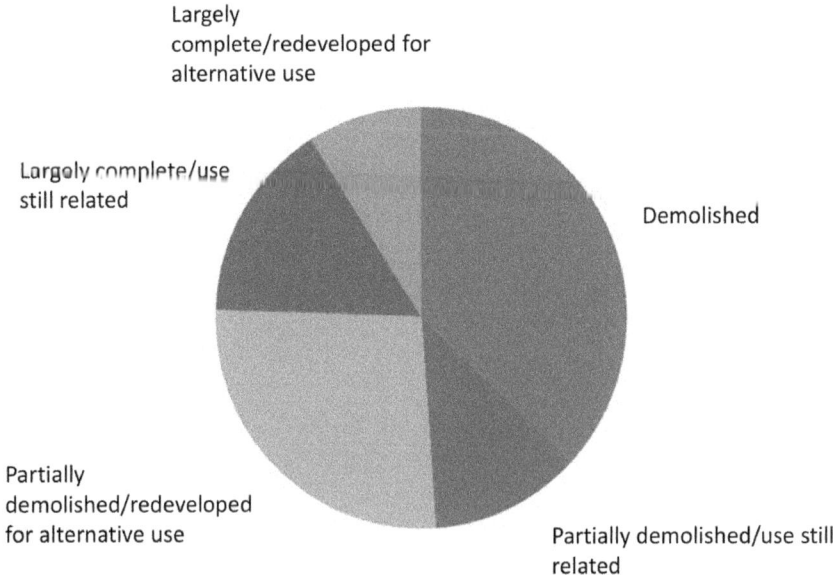

Figure 1.1. Pie chart illustrating condition of workhouses in the north of England in 2007. Demolished 33%; partial demolished/use still related 12%; partial demolished/redeveloped for alternative use 28%; largely complete/use still related 19%; largely complete/redeveloped for alternative use 8% (drawn by Charlotte Newman).

constructed. Many former workhouses became hospitals after the abolition of the Poor Laws in 1930, and in England and Wales this meant that former workhouses became part of the sprawling National Health Service in 1948. Before this, workhouses-cum-hospitals were part of a tripartite structure of healthcare provision in England, comprising the Poor Law institution infirmaries, local council provision usually for infectious diseases, and the voluntary sector (Doyle 2010, 379). Becoming part of the wider infrastructure of health provision from the late 1940s meant that many former workhouses were adapted, their built fabric expanded beyond the original confines of the workhouse or workhouse infirmary buildings as they were designed. Their use changed significantly, and many were demolished when their upkeep proved more expensive than investment in purpose-built hospitals in the late twentieth century. Functional, civic architecture like hospitals and other institutions falls curiously outside of the dual and sometimes contradictory late twentieth-century practice in the British landscape of intensive modernisation and the preservation in situ of the remains of the past (Holtorf 2008, 130). It makes for unique archaeological sites in light of this ambivalence towards their value as built heritage (at least until relatively recently). As such, carrying out fieldwork

16 · Poverty Archaeology

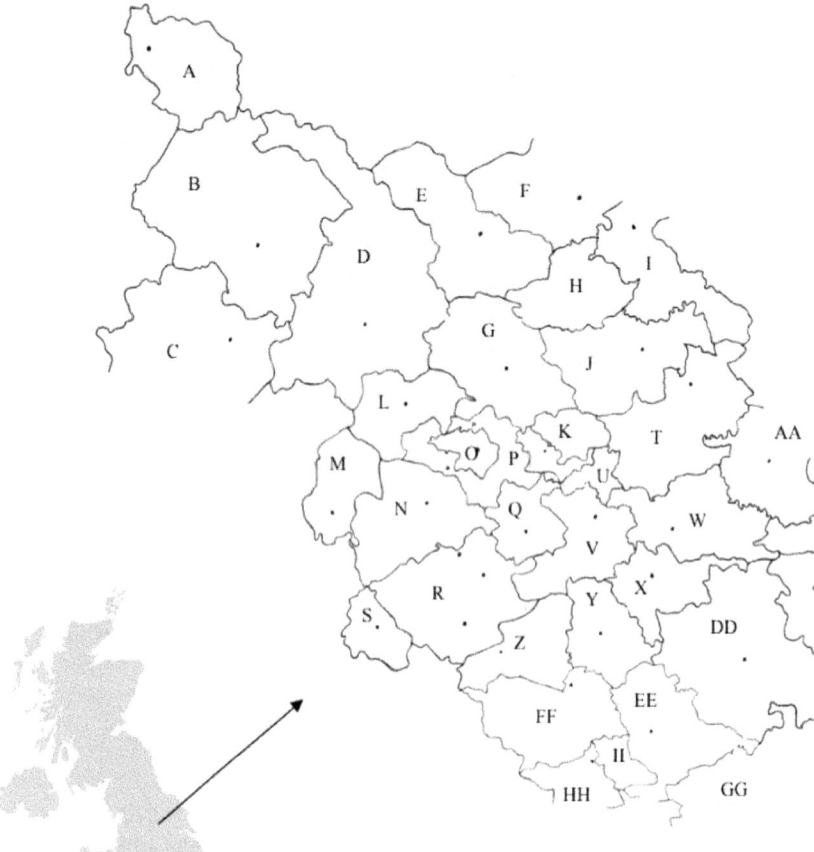

Figure 1.2. Plan of West Yorkshire workhouse locations (drawn by Charlotte Newman).

and architectural analysis on these buildings has proved to be difficult, and a case-by-case approach is required.

There are significant mitigations impacting the study of the built heritage of historic institutions in England. As Susan Piddock (2007, 14) pointed out in her archaeological study of lunatic asylums in Britain and Australia, 'institutions are not always amenable to excavation'. Building on Piddock's work and our own on workhouses and lunatic asylums (Newman 2013, 2014, 2015; Fennelly 2018, 2019, 2020), we offer an alternative to a more traditional excavation-led approach to archaeological sites. As such, we have had to think about how we interpret 'archaeology' for this study. 'A wide range of theoretical perspectives and research questions have been applied to the archaeological study of institutional sites over the past century' (Baugher 2009, 12). Not all of these approaches require a shovel in the ground. Indeed, even an archaeological 'excavation' of the kind applied by Victor Buchli and Gavin Lucas (2006) in their study of recently abandoned social housing – in which the remains of contemporary practice were recorded and planned as if in a trench or on a site – was not always possible, due to the inaccessibility of some of the former workhouse sites, or their complete demolition. In this study, we applied archaeological questions to the material and documentary record, seeking to understand the workhouses as buildings and artefacts, and as sites situated within a broader landscape. We understand the Poor Law landscape as a composite of long-term narratives and historical processes (Fairclough 2008, 409). Rather than proposing a framework for the study of these buildings more broadly, we outline here our method for approaching these highly regional and idiosyncratic buildings to demonstrate the importance of a case-by-case approach in considering institutions for social improvement and confinement. Though most of these buildings were constructed to an ideal form initially, their operation on the ground and their subsequent histories evidence the significant differences between them, as outlined in this book.

West Yorkshire as a Case Study

A detailed regional case study of architectural responses to the poor has provided a framework for research in other regions and highlights the importance of micro-histories in understanding the complexity of workhouse provision in the development of social welfare. Political, social and economic contexts had a significant impact on the scale and nature of poverty, while fashioning attitudes towards those on the margins of society, such as the poor, orphaned and mentally ill. West Yorkshire was selected as the principal focus because the region witnessed particularly rapid growth as a result of industrialisation throughout the nineteenth century. Circumstances in the north of England also meant that there was a much higher degree of local autonomy, creating significant local variance in this area. The 'peculiar circumstances' of the north led to some of the more stringent requirements of the New Poor Law being relaxed or deployed in variation (Driver 1993, 49). The New Poor Law met particular resistance in the industrial north, and was bound up locally in political movements. As such, it makes for a narrow geographical case study in which many different interpretations of the Poor Laws can be seen in effect. Lack of intense centralised control means that northern workhouses like Leeds could put new approaches to poverty management into effect, for instance in the education of children. Workhouses became proving grounds for ideas of social and moral improvement, with varying degrees of success.

There were important differences in the economic experiences of individual towns and villages that were reflected in the diverse architectural responses to the poor. Different Unions in West Yorkshire responded to New Poor Law legislation in a number of different ways, so the region provides a useful, though complex, microcosm for national histories and a clear demonstration of the myriad ways in which the Poor Laws were applied. The selected case studies in this book are representative of the different architectural plans and styles, and the numerous alterations and additions that were made to each complex. Despite the survival of architectural features and documentary evidence, the workhouses of the north of England remain largely neglected in New Poor Law scholarship, thus warranting more detailed investigation.

A detailed study of the New Poor Law workhouse reveals its development to be far more complex than any typological architectural study of workhouse buildings would suggest. Diverse economic, political and social development during the nineteenth century led to variations in architectural design, which in turn led to dramatic differences in the experiences of paupers. The New Poor Law workhouses of rural West Yorkshire provide a revealingly varied sample. In some cases, they conform to national trends in design and construction. Skipton, for example, followed closely the Poor Law Commission's guidelines. After the passing of the New Poor Laws in 1834, Skipton unionised promptly as the act intended, and built a model-plan workhouse conforming to the Commission's design ideals. Elsewhere, however, Unions failed to implement the New Poor Law immediately or in the ways that the government envisaged. Some Unions that formed later, for example, such as Pateley Bridge Union, built workhouses to outdated standards or failed to adopt national ideals at all. Such varied implementation of the New Poor Law among the rural workhouses of West Yorkshire reflects significant differences in historical, political, economic and social conditions in the region. Growth and development during the nineteenth century differed substantially from one settlement to the next. Rural and agricultural areas, such as Great Ouseburn and Pateley Bridge, experienced little development during this period. Their populations remained steady, and their expansion was limited. Socially, they retained a village identity, with community-orientated values typical of settlements of their size. Skipton and Otley, conversely, industrialised rapidly. Although they began the nineteenth century as small villages with agriculture-dominated economies, they transformed dramatically. The expansion of the factory system and improved transportation in the region turned these villages into industrial market towns. Increased wealth and greater social mobility cultivated a middle-class society that constructed buildings such as assembly rooms, market halls and town halls to reflect its newfound civic pride.

Other Unions experienced industrialisation rather differently. Ripon, for example, had already developed the civic values and institutional propensities that were elsewhere associated with sudden industrial growth. Although Ripon did expand throughout the nineteenth century, its growth was not as sharp as that of Skipton or Otley. No single industry dominated, although there were many trades associated with hospitality. Owing, again, to its long history of settlement, Ripon had long established fifty-seven relief systems for the poor, and private charity was firmly embedded within its culture. The development of Wetherby tells yet another story. Surrounded by an agricultural landscape, Wetherby served as a coaching stop between London and Edinburgh. Landownership restricted its development, and industry did not flourish as it did in Skipton and Otley. However, trades associated with the coaching industry and a regular market distinguished Wetherby from surrounding rural villages. Due to the differing cultural and economic conditions in these areas, the level of poverty varied substantially, as did the way in which each area perceived its poor.

West Yorkshire's rural Unions had very different values and priorities when it came to treatment of the poor. In some areas, charitable giving continued to relieve many paupers throughout the nineteenth century, which ultimately stopped these paupers from ever entering the workhouse at all. Relief may have been provided by the church, neighbours, the local gentry or in some cases philanthropic industrialists. Charitable giving – part of the *economy of makeshifts* – as exhibited in Ripon, provided clothing, medicine and ale to those most in need, but many did not benefit from charitable gifts, which were reserved only for those categories of paupers deemed more deserving. Another regional practice that undermined adherence to the New Poor Law in the region was the provision of out-relief by the Union. Many paupers in rural areas were able to avoid the workhouse because they received out-relief from the New Poor Law Union. Archival evidence suggests that the practice of out-relief in many regions continued long after the passing of the New Poor Law. Regions in which paupers received out-relief tended to have more understanding attitudes towards poverty. The giving of out-relief reflects a reluctance to institutionalise the paupers in receipt of it, which may relate to a desire to preserve the family unit and echoes traditionally paternalistic attitudes towards the rural poor. Only certain categories of pauper were entitled to out-relief, however. Like the selective charity described above, variable entitlement to out-relief affirms that some paupers were always considered more deserving than others.

Able-bodied paupers who were ultimately sent to the workhouse were considered in need of character reformation and moral guidance out of poverty, a policy often reflected in the built form of the workhouse. In some areas, their situation may have been considered infectious. Pauperism was believed to cause disorder, so the removal of paupers from society was essential for the protection of its citizens and the maintenance of order. Certain classes of pauper were seen as a contaminating threat even to order within the workhouse. Examples of this attitude in practice can be seen in the case of vagrants at Pateley Bridge, who were treated as potentially contagious and accordingly were isolated even from mainstream workhouse society as thoroughly as possible. Elsewhere, such as in Great Ouseburn, vagrants were regarded somewhat less harshly, and the location and style of the vagrants' wards there reflect this nuanced difference in attitude. As both of these examples indicate, differing attitudes and values towards different classes of pauper created dramatic variation in the way in which the New Poor Law was implemented through the built form.

In Yorkshire, workhouse locations, styles and plans varied enormously. The majority of workhouses were located on the outskirts of the settlement; however, this was not always the case. In the case of Ripon Union Workhouse, for instance, the workhouse was incorporated into the town. The styles workhouses adopted also varied. Workhouses such as Skipton, Wetherby and Great Ouseburn adopted more classical styles whereas Ripon's style is Elizabethan (Figure 1.3), and Wharfedale's verges on Gothic (Figure 1.4). West Yorkshire workhouses were designed based on a variety of plans, including the Kempthorne model plan, T-plan, corridor plan and pavilion plan. Finer details revealed during investigation of these buildings, concerning segregation, surveillance and the provision of heat, light and other such facilities, also differed between workhouses, as will be described below. Changes in workhouse facilities over time reveal changes in attitudes towards poverty. Some paupers in certain regions saw significant improvements in the facilities in which they were housed and in the care they received, whereas for others elsewhere (or even within a given Union) the experience of life as a pauper changed little throughout the nineteenth century. The case studies applied here will illustrate how regional values influenced the built form of rural West Yorkshire workhouses and how these in turn impacted the lives and identities of the region's poor.

The diversity of West Yorkshire's urban workhouses further undermines the explanatory power of general, national approaches to the study of workhouse buildings, emphasising the wide variety of ways in which the New Poor Law was implemented within this one region. The New Poor Law urged the immediate formation of Unions and the prompt construction of workhouses to relieve the able-bodied poor. Among Yorkshire's

Figure 1.3. Ripon Workhouse, north-west elevation (photographed by Charlotte Newman).

urban areas, however, these guidelines were not adopted uniformly. Leeds and Bradford Unions were established shortly after the passing of the New Poor Law, in contrast to rural townships, which often resisted forming Unions for decades. Because Leeds and Bradford were urban centres, the Poor Law Commission likely placed particular pressure on them to Unionise and thus to set an example for surrounding areas. In contrast, Bramley and North Bierley developed on the edges of urban centres in the latter half of the nineteenth century, as Leeds and Bradford expanded into their surroundings. Although Leeds, Bradford and North Bierley Unions were established at different times, their workhouses were constructed within a comparatively short span of time, between 1850 and 1858, in response to a number of shared contextual factors. Firstly, industrial centres were more financially secure during the 1850s than in previous decades due to national economic stability, and they could thus afford to construct new institutions. Secondly, like rural workhouses, urban workhouses were used to promote civic order and the status of the Unions in which they were built. It was not until the 1850s that Leeds and Bradford were in a position (socially or economically) to promote their national standing through the construction of a workhouse, but in subsequent decades, Leeds and

Figure 1.4. Wharfedale Workhouse, principal north-east elevation (photographed by Charlotte Newman).

Bradford continually promoted their modernisation and national status, to a much greater extent than rural examples. Finally, despite anti-New Poor Law sentiments in West Yorkshire and Unions' general nonconformity to New Poor Law guidelines, the New Poor Law and the construction of a workhouse provided urban areas a much-needed mechanism through which to offer social welfare for the vulnerable poor. Beyond such broad similarities, however, urban Unions also experienced different economic, social and political contexts. Bramley Union was not formed until it was required to support the expanding city of Leeds in 1862, and it did not choose to construct a workhouse until 1872, again responding to regional need and West Yorkshire's continued resistance towards indoor relief. Urban Unions industrialised at different speeds, featured working-class populations of varying size, experienced differing levels of mass migration of workers and witnessed large-scale employment or unemployment depending on unique economic conditions. For example, at the beginning of the New Poor Law, Leeds was already an established town, whereas Bradford initially grew slowly and then sped up due to mass industrialisation during the nineteenth century. Because of the size of urban centres, they all required a more organised social welfare system than their rural counterparts. The nature of the relief offered by Unions was decided in part by the local industrialists and entrepreneurs who acted as Guardians and had different agendas and perceptions of poverty. For example, the Guardians in Leeds opted to construct Leeds Moral and Industrial Training School whereas Bradford's Guardians initially adopted a more laissez-faire attitude towards poverty.

Whereas in rural Unions a history of relief through Gilbert Unions and a long-standing tradition of charitable giving were balanced against limited economic resources in the implementation of the New Poor Law, in urban areas, it was more the pace of progress, the growth of capitalism and lingering paternalism that determined attitudes towards poverty. The high populations of urban Unions rendered the accommodation of able-bodied paupers advocated by the New Poor Law even less practical than in rural areas, so out-relief remained high. In urban Unions, indoor relief increasingly focused on the sick over the course of the New Poor Law era. Rural areas, such as Wetherby, also increasingly focused on the sick, but in urban areas workhouse infirmaries developed on a greater scale. The Unions' desire to promote civic order and modernisation led to the provision of increasingly specialised care and facilities. Like rural paupers, urban paupers were primarily classed by degree of able-bodied-ness, gender and age. Urban pauper classes were treated differently from one another and from their rural counterparts based on their perceived 'deservingness', which as in rural Unions was determined by perceived vulnerability and responsibility for poverty. For example, children in Leeds were offered a separate school from the beginning of the New Poor Law, the Leeds Moral and Industrial Training School, whereas the children in Bradford were provided with a school within the main workhouse building.

The possibility of contamination between pauper classes is a prevailing theme in all the urban case studies. Like rural workhouses, urban workhouses were in some ways architecturally similar to one another and in some ways different. Locations and plans were by and large in keeping with national recommendations of the time. For example, urban workhouses were initially located in isolated areas distanced from population centres. Workhouses in urban areas were influenced by local architectural trends and values towards poverty and consequently adopted more elaborate styles than those in rural areas. Style also differed between urban workhouses. For example, Leeds was more paternalistic in its approach to poor relief and adopted an Elizabethan style. Bradford, on the other hand, was more severe on its poor and adopted a classical, industrialised style accordingly. Although all of the urban Unions discussed in this book conformed to national trends in terms of broad architectural styles, these workhouses operated and evolved very differently. Such differences in operation among workhouses featuring the same or similar types of architectural plan reveal the need for a more complex classification within the urban workhouse category.

Workhouses on the outskirts of urban centres demonstrate common attributes that clearly differentiate them from workhouses in urban centres. Unlike rural workhouses, urban workhouses did not prioritise surveillance. Instead, control was maintained through architectural planning, segregation and specialisation. Workhouses aspired to segregate all classes, but segregation was enforced at different levels at different times, depending on inmate and staff numbers, both of which were determined by economy. Leeds provided specialised facilities from the outset and in many ways set the precedent for other urban Unions in the region. Bradford and the outer-urban workhouses of Bramley and North Bierley initially provided specialised facilities only for the sick. It was not until the stabilisation of economic conditions around the turn of the century that Bradford, Bramley and North Bierley began to develop separate, specialised facilities. No urban workhouse in West Yorkshire focused its indoor relief on the able-bodied, as the New Poor Law advised. Like that of rural workhouses, urban workhouse architecture reveals an interclass pauper hierarchy. However, the complexity of urban workhouses led to instances of a further, intraclass hierarchy, a phenomenon less apparent among rural examples. All paupers in urban Unions initially experienced a general, mixed workhouse (apart from children in Leeds, who were the exception). At various stages of the New Poor Law, however, urban workhouses developed separate, specialised facilities that resulted in dramatically varied experiences among paupers, dependent on their classification. In contrast, for those in outer-urban workhouses, experience of the workhouse altered very little during the New Poor Law era. Focusing on Yorkshire, the broad variety of interpretations and applications of the New Poor Law is illustrated here.

Methodology

The methods employed in this study were standing building surveys involving photographic surveys of standing building remains, desk-based assessment of plans and historic photographs, and archival research. A necessarily multidisciplinary approach was adopted here in order to account for all aspects of the historic buildings in question, analysing the location, style, plan form, access routes, decoration and development of workhouse buildings to shed light on the ways in which paupers were categorised and controlled. As far as reasonably possible, available sources relating to the architecture and material development of the buildings were consulted in order to paint a holistic picture of the ways in which workhouses developed over time. A broad interdisciplinary toolkit was applied here in order to build and illustrate multiple narratives and experiences in these diverse institutions.

The standing building survey is an archaeological survey method, part of the toolkit of the historical archaeologist. As in archaeological excavation, a building survey reimagines the 'site' (the building) according to phases of construction and development. Understanding how the building changes materially over time helps the archaeologist to determine why these changes take place. Initial phases of construction of a building, for which plans will frequently exist, will be easier to understand than subsequent phases (Morriss 2000, 155). As Morriss suggests in *The Archaeology of Buildings*, where a building has been 'adapted to cope' with change over time, the extant structure will retain its earlier phases even as newer phases overtake them (ibid.). For a building type like a former workhouse, standing building surveys are limited by access issues and current use, and the safety concerns associated with buildings that have long fallen out of use. Each building poses its own challenges to survey, and as such a single methodological approach is not possible or appropriate. The toolkit for standing building surveys is varied; for the surveys carried out here, a measuring tape and sketchpad were employed to record notes on the buildings, and a camera used for recording. The surveys were carried out by Charlotte Newman from 2007 to 2009, employing Barbara Hutton's (1986) method for standing building surveys as a guide. Photographic surveys were carried out in cases where buildings were still standing, and surveys of the interiors were conducted where permissions could be gained. In all cases, the exterior of the buildings was photographed extensively, and a photographic record of each example compiled where possible and practicable. This photographic survey formed the basis of much of the architectural description and analysis presented here. Finally, the photographic survey results were compared with historical photographs and architectural plans to situate them within the wider site.

The region-based approach applied here makes use of Guardians' Minutes, newspapers, contemporary accounts, as well as architectural plans and maps to demonstrate the broad interpretations at local level of national policies and discourses. The differing experiences or circumstances of different classes in workhouses are more apparent from the documentary evidence than from the architecture alone, and a collaborative use of the two can build a more substantial picture of experience. Surveillance, for example, was both a mechanism of control and a means of care and management. For the elderly, the young and the sick, workhouses could be a refuge, though the paupers themselves may not have considered it so on admission.

Local archive offices held the bulk of archival source material for the individual institutions, as well as Ordnance Survey maps, which were supplemented by digitised County Series maps. The West Yorkshire Archive Service holds much of the archival material consulted here, at offices in Leeds, Bradford, Northallerton and Keighley. County record offices in the United Kingdom are not consistent in their institutional archive holdings. Though local archives are searchable via the National Archives of the United Kingdom database, each local authority manages their own record offices and archives, and as such records can vary considerably from place to place. The disparity is linked to how the buildings evolved or were used after the Poor Law era. The larger urban Unions that were co-opted into the National Health Service after the Second World War had more surviving records by virtue of their records forming part of a wider bureaucratic framework (the National Health Service, colloquially known by the abbreviation NHS). The smaller workhouses in rural areas had more patchy record survival rates. In all of the examples used here, Guardians' minute books – the minutes of meetings of the Union Guardians who governed the Poor Law institution – were examined. Local press and national publications like *The Builder* and *The Lancet* were also studied, alongside building plans compared with first- and second-edition Ordnance Survey maps from the 1850s to the 1930s. This desk-based research underpinned the fieldwork that was possible on the sites and informed the surveys of the buildings.

This study makes heavy use of documentary sources, not to supplement or to fill in gaps in the material record but to collaboratively build a holistic picture of the sites. Plans do not always reflect how buildings were used, but they do give an indication of how the buildings were intended to be used, offering insight into the intentions and conversations around their construction. The material remains, alterations and changes to the buildings inform on how the buildings or the rooms therein were adapted to reflect use. This is an archaeological approach to the documentary record, a human-centric reading of the material remains alongside the paper record. The 'site' (described in the following section) is a composite of both the material remains, where they exist and are accessible, and the documents – the plans, minute books, accounts ledgers, correspondence and press.

The Archaeological Site

Workhouses, in the form in which they were constructed in the New Poor Law era, were the outcome of conversations regarding state management of poverty since the sixteenth century. As outlined in the previous chapter, workhouses were constructed widely across the British Isles in stages, usually following major legislation on poverty, and as the government 'increasingly codified and refined specific types of activities requiring confinement' (Casella 2007, 9). Workhouses were institutions for civic improvement in themselves, part of a wider network of institutional solutions to the 'imperative of labour' (Foucault 1989, 43) – the increasing centrality of the working body in economic life. As Foucault (1977, 235) says of the prison, that it should not be considered inert but a constantly transforming space and an active field for improvements and experimentation, the workhouse was constantly in flux, even as the 1834 Poor Laws sought to centralise and standardise practice. However, the workhouse building itself is only part of the story. The historic workhouse existed and operated within a legal and social framework that was concerned not with the institution itself but with the improvement of the British landscape in general. The workhouse was but the means by which the government could remove unsavoury or undesirable elements (Tarlow 2007, 138) – the unsupported elderly, the pauper sick, unmanaged children, even under-skilled workers – from the land and streetscape.

The main workhouse site is comprised of the buildings that make up the physical workhouse itself. There are common buildings or architectural elements to workhouse buildings that include exercise yards, infirmary blocks or wards, lunatic blocks or wards, a central administration space and the main workhouse wards for able-bodied paupers. The uniformity in physical form throughout the workhouse system – especially in the first decade of the Poor Law era – was due to architects using as their models the workhouse plans issued by the Poor Law Commission, notably the plans of Sampson Kempthorne and Francis Head (Morrison 1999, 54). Even so, a high degree of diversity in built form by the end of the nineteenth century was the consequence of each individual workhouse responding to the demands placed on them by their own Unions. A secondary element of the workhouse 'site' are the architectural plans on which the workhouse buildings were based. These plans, not all of which were fully or faithfully realised in the built workhouse, inform on the intentions behind the buildings and the motivations of the architects, the governors and other interested parties. The archaeological site is a composite of both the remains of the built workhouses themselves and the plans that preceded their construction. The operation of the buildings is bound up in both intention and reality, and thus both aspects of the 'site' need to be considered.

This book makes use of a number of case studies around which to organise discussion of broader themes of relevance to the nineteenth-century archaeology of poverty throughout the British Isles. The workhouse case studies considered here are the rural Unions of Pateley Bridge and Great Ouseburn, the outer-urban or town-based workhouses of Wharfedale, Skipton, Ripon and Bramley and the urban workhouses of Leeds and Bradford. Each workhouse was constructed after the 1834 Poor Laws, and development on the sites continued throughout the nineteenth and early twentieth centuries, until the end of the Poor Law era. They are all in Yorkshire and faced similar challenges to their construction; the north of England, by virtue of the fact that the poor there were comparatively better off materially than those in the south (Fowler 2007, 20), was one of the more intense areas of anti-Poor Law sentiment in the 1830s. As such, the sites and the wider landscape are comparable yet different enough to support individual analysis and provide a sense of the breadth of practice between different institutions.

In an archaeology of poverty and pauperism, the site is not singular, but as big as necessary to support a reading of the material. In her study on the Maze or Long Kesh prison site in Northern Ireland, archaeologist Laura McAtackney considered multiple sources, the material culture and built heritage as well as the portable material assemblages available. McAtackney contended that this multiplicity of sources available to the contemporary (to which we add also the later historical) archaeologist offers us an opportunity to access multiple narratives on a site and not just a single dominant narrative, a 'definitive account of how the site "was"' (McAtackney 2014, 39).

In this book, we argue that looking at workhouses singularly and together, at elements of the institution distinctive from the main building and at workhouses both within and on the margins of their communities, we can identify multiple workhouse narratives and experiences beyond the gender-neutral, region-less, classless norm of 'pauper'. The lot of the pauper was to be both a singular exception to the norms of society and part of a wider class of people who shared common ailments, so the archaeological site should be treated with such multiplicity too.

Chapter 2

The Sick

Finally, in 1864–5, we have an outburst of public indignation at the condition into which the sick wards of the workhouses had been allowed to drift. The death of a pauper in Holborn workhouse, and of another in St Giles workhouse, under conditions which seemed to point to inhumanity and neglect, led to an enquiry by three doctors (Anstie, Carr, and Ernest Hart), commissioned by the *Lancet* newspaper, the formation of an 'Association for improving the condition of the sick poor', and a deputation to the Poor Law Board. The publication of various reports on the workhouse infirmaries, in which terrible deficiencies were revealed, led to public discussion and Parliamentary debates. The Central Authority at once accepted the new standpoint. It made no attempt to resist the provision of the necessarily costly institutional treatment for the sick poor, whether or not their ailments were infectious or otherwise dangerous to the public.
—Sidney and Beatrice Webb, *English Poor Law Policy*

This summary by social economists Sidney and Beatrice Webb of the circumstances and public outcry that led to an increasing focus on just one element of the workhouse population – the sick and the infirm – evidences the way in which the role of the workhouse became increasingly specialised towards the care of the ill as early as the middle of the nineteenth century. This summary focuses on London, however, as did many of the conversations surrounding Poor Law provision in press discussions of workhouses. By the late 1850s, outside of London, many regional workhouses had already begun to address their accommodations for the sick and infirm, though practice was far from consistent across the country. It is this inconsistency that is reflected in the material record of the buildings, as each individual workhouse managed its sick and infirm differently. By this time, the sick and infirm were a significant demographic in their diverse populations. The haphazard scramble to accommodate the sick in appropriate accommodation in an already-stretched system for poverty management is evident in a number of enquiries and scandals in the 1850s and 1860s. The rapid and inconsistent provision of dedicated, specialised facilities for the accommodation of the sick in workhouses in the second half of the nineteenth century, and the form that these facilities took, reflects the piecemeal way in which concerns for the sick poor were managed throughout England.

This chapter will look at one specific aspect of Poor Law provision for a discrete demographic in the workhouse population, the inmate category whose status within the workhouse rose exponentially over the course of the New Poor Law era: the sick. From their early years of operation, the workhouses constructed after and in response to the 1834 Poor Laws came under criticism from the public, from politicians and from their own centralised authorities, first the Poor Law Commission and then the Poor Law Board, as well as Local Government Boards, and later from advocates for a more refined welfare system centred around healthcare. Economists like Sidney and Beatrice Webb (1910, 1929) called for a departure from the Poor Laws altogether. As workhouses gradually expanded in the face of increasing demand on their services in both rural and urban Poor Law Unions, an increasing concern with the number of pauper sick drove the construction of separate, specialised hospitals, wards or wings for the sick and infirm. These provisions took the form of separate wards, or more commonly, separate infirmaries, some of which grew so large as to overtake their host workhouse entirely. New infirmaries were a mix of architectural styles, some but not all informed by discourse on healthy hospital design, popularised by people like Florence Nightingale during the period. These wards and infirmaries were far from uniform across the country, and differences in provision underscore the high regionality of the Poor Law era. This chapter considers a number of examples of regional workhouses whose provision for the sick and infirm both reflects practice more broadly and demonstrates the different ways in which Poor Law Unions responded to the demand on their services. Materially, workhouses reacted differently to the demands placed upon them by their inmates, their catchment areas and the authorities over them, so that even a small dataset of examples reflects the multiplicity of approaches to the way hospitals specifically and public healthcare more broadly were refined in the wake of the New Poor Law.

Hospitals and the Sick in the Nineteenth Century

The modern idea of the general hospital or general infirmary – a catch-all institution to which all members of the public can turn when they need medical help – is relatively new. Though well established in the late modern city as an essential institution, general hospitals were a relatively late addition to the landscape and townscape of industrial England. Institutional provision for the care of the poor and the sick has a longer history, however, and infirmity and illness have long been linked to poverty. From the middle of the sixteenth century, hospitals like St Bartholomew's and St Thomas's in London took in sick paupers of the city for care, while those not of the city returned to their own parishes. The hospitals and general infirmaries built in the eighteenth century were constructed for this purpose: to care for the sick and infirm in rapidly growing urban populations (Thompson and Goldin 1975, 84). Other specialised hospitals proliferated across expanding cities, including lying-in hospitals for pregnant women and private clinics for the well-to-do. Morality still trumped poverty when it came to illness in the case of venereal disease, so specialised hospitals were constructed in urban centres for the reception of these kinds of illnesses. Specialised Lock hospitals were built for the reception of women, separating them from the general sick for reasons of propriety, while some larger infirmaries added specialised wards for venereal disease to keep these types of patients separate (Casella and Fennelly 2022, 627). This chimes with a wider pathologising of poverty in the nineteenth century, in which poverty, morality and sanitation became institutionalised and more closely associated.

The Contagious Diseases Acts of the 1860s were the ultimate expression of the increasing interference of the state in the lives of the poor, providing for the routine inspection of female prostitutes for venereal disease in garrison and port towns (Walkowitz 1992, 22–23). Concurrently, reformers like Florence Nightingale agitated for the construction and management of more appropriate facilities for housing the sick, facilities that could not only treat infectious diseases but also stop their spread. Nightingale had coordinated nursing at military field hospitals during the Crimean War and observed the dangers of fever and environmental conditions at the hospitals at Scutari during that conflict. Returning to England, she wrote on hospital design, advocating for open ventilation and specialised nursing practices in her *Notes on Nursing* (1859) *and Notes on Hospitals* (1863). As such, there was a public discourse around hospital design and the need for specialised institutional spaces by the middle of the nineteenth century. By this time, infirmary design had seen a period of trialling, around a hundred years of architectural experimentation in which different designs were applied with varying degrees of success.

Hospitals for the poor, which began to proliferate in provincial cities from the mid-eighteenth century, borrowed more of their design principles from their charitable and religious predecessors than from contemporaneous institutions. This began to change as architects like Thomas Worthington began to apply the principles of pavilion-plan hospital architecture – wards arranged into rectangular blocks (the pavilions) with large windows, separated by gardens and connected by a central access corridor – to the infirmaries he was commissioned to construct for two Poor Law Unions in Manchester (Butler 2013, 92–93). As the state became increasingly concerned with the intersection of poverty and public health, Poor Law Unions were the proving grounds for these new innovations in hospital architecture. Poverty and public health intersected as the nineteenth century went on, and concerns and discourse surrounding poverty at a national level did not always necessarily reflect what was happening in the provinces. Policies and directives sought to refine and redirect the Poor Laws towards the needs of the 'deserving' poor. The 'deserving' poor were those who were poor through no fault of their own, largely referring to the sick and infirm (but also other categories discussed later in this book). Even so, by the end of the nineteenth century, the poor were the ultimate sufferers in retrenchment when it came to the Poor Law (Hurren 2005, 401–2). The impact of national and centralised policy can be seen at local level, and this chapter builds on other studies of regionality in Poor Law provision in English contexts.

Sickness in the Workhouse

Within a few years of the construction of the workhouses after the 1834 Act, workhouse provision became increasingly focused on managing and accommodating the sick. This mission countered a lot of the initial anti-Poor Law sentiment in parts of the country like Yorkshire, where the New Poor Law was both an outlet for political opposition to the status quo and governance practices more generally, and a particular social fear (Brundage 2002, 82). This fear was fed by writers like Charles Dickens in his popular descriptions of urban institutions, and newspapers like *The Times* in their coverage of scandals at workhouses like Andover. Inconsistency in provision for the sick and infirm at workhouses fed a discourse that workhouses were not sanitary or fit for the purpose of housing these kinds of inmates.

At the rural Pateley Bridge Union workhouse in West Yorkshire, paupers categorised as sick remained in the main workhouse building rather than being removed to a separate infirmary building. Initially, after the 1834 Act, the Guardians at Pateley Bridge were reluctant to construct a new workhouse at all, as the local economy was unable to support the cost. The economic circumstances of the region meant that once a workhouse was commissioned, it was extremely limited by budget constraints. The local population often refused to pay the poor rates, evidencing how unpopular the New Poor Law was in this part of Yorkshire. The Guardians of the Pateley Bridge Union never commissioned additional facilities for the sick beyond the main workhouse building while the institution operated as a workhouse, and few changes at all were made to the accommodations. The workhouse was closed in 1914 due to its state of poor repair. In his survey of county Poor Law institutions, Platt (1930) described the sanitary fittings at Pateley Bridge as especially unsatisfactory and noted that the building was lit by gas. By this time, most other Unions had installed electricity. On the whole, Platt described the Union workhouse as 'very primitive' (ibid., 27; Figure 2.1). Categorising and separating paupers or removing them to specialised institutions or out-relief programmes was, over the course of the New Poor Law, seen as an effective means of maintaining the buildings (as was not done at Pateley Bridge) and maintaining lower numbers in the workhouse. This practice was not actually prescriptive in of the New Poor Law so uptake was regional, as evidenced here.

Figure 2.1. Pateley Bridge Workhouse, principal south-west elevation (photographed by Charlotte Newman).

Despite practice in small Unions like Pateley Bridge, late nineteenth-century advances in medical science and a rapidly growing population inspired many rural workhouses to extend and expand their medical facilities and accommodations. Workhouses can thus provide a lens through which to interpret changing attitudes towards physical healthcare in the nineteenth century. A spate of infirmary-building at Poor Law Unions at the end of the nineteenth century and into the early twentieth century saw the addition of infirmary facilities to many small rural Unions. Ripon, Skipton, Wharfedale, Wetherby and Great Ouseburn all built separate infirmaries during this period. Each Union adopted a different architectural style. For example, the Wharfedale Union constructed a large, pavilion-style hospital in line with leading architectural trends in hospital design. In consequence of its expanding and industrialising locale, Wharfedale required more substantial facilities than surrounding rural Unions and was influenced in its provision by the workhouses at nearby urban centres like Leeds. In contrast, the Unions of Ripon, Skipton and Wetherby built single pavilion blocks that reflected their smaller catchment populations and the need to economise on scale.

Great Ouseburn constructed a small infirmary, almost domestic in appearance, reflecting the traditional architecture associated with almshouses and the Gilbert Unions of the past (Figure 2.2). The workhouse at Great

Figure 2.2. Great Ouseburn Workhouse infirmary, north-west elevation (photographed by Charlotte Newman).

Ouseburn occupied the same site from as early as 1828, predating the New Poor Law. As the area did not form a New Poor Law Union until 1854, a New Poor Law workhouse was not constructed until 1856. Even in the new institution, facilities for sick inmates were incorporated into the main workhouse building (Figure 2.3). It was not until 1891 and the beginning of a third phase of development at the workhouse that construction began of a single-storey infirmary to the south of the site at a cost of £1,500. Although the infirmary was constructed largely using similar materials to the main building, additional red bricks were also used for decorative purposes. The lintels, the corners of the south-facing bay-window projection and the four courses of brick that were placed to run through the southern façade were ornamented using red brick, drawing out these architectural features with this more modern building material. Three large windows were built into a central projecting bay, which was capped with a hipped roof and finial. Four ornamented chimney stacks provided heat to the building, and ventilation was encouraged through triangular vents integrated into the roof. Building ventilation into the infirmary demonstrated an awareness of the discourse on hospital design in England at the time, popularised by figures like Nightingale, that ventilation and airflow were key to maintaining a healthy interior space. This discourse on ventilation underpinned the

Figure 2.3. Great Ouseburn Workhouse, principal south-east elevation (photographed by Charlotte Newman).

popularity of the pavilion-plan infirmary (Cook 2002, 354). The windows facing the wider workhouse complex on the northern façade were significantly smaller than those on the southern façade, and they were situated high within the fenestration, obscuring infirmary inmates' view towards the main workhouse. Such features highlight the separation of this class of inmate from the general population of the workhouse. Public distaste and ingrained cultural fear of the workhouse were mitigated by separating the inmates spatially as well as visually from each other. The infirmary consisted of two six-bed wards and two separate four-bed wards, accommodating twenty patients in total (Platt 1930, 19). The four-bed ward on the female side was reserved for maternity cases. Though lying-in hospitals were common in urban centres from the middle of the eighteenth century as childbirth emerged as a specialist field of medical expertise (Richardson 1998, 105), in rural Unions like Great Ouseburn, pregnant pauper women would have turned to the workhouse for help. Although the workhouse sent lunatic cases to the Yorkshire county asylums at Wakefield and Menston, records indicate that lunatic cases were still accommodated in the workhouse (Great Ouseburn Guardians' Minutes 27/2/1899), likely due to overcrowding at the county asylums. It is possible that this class of inmate, or inmates who required particular attention or isolation, were accommodated in the smaller four-bed wards. A catch-all infirmary housing multiple classifications of inmate would have put immense strain on the single nurse who was charged with staffing the Union infirmary; it is probable that she was aided by the more able-bodied inmates, a reasonably common practice. The nurse was frequently reported in the Guardians' Minutes as being sick, which is not surprising considering the physical and mental strain incurred by managing so many patients.

Infirmaries were continually altered to keep up with modern medical practices. Infirmary buildings in rural areas were always struggling to achieve modern standards and alleviate overcrowding in the main workhouse buildings, so Unions built new sanitary towers and extended ward space in both the workhouse proper and the infirmaries throughout the nineteenth and twentieth centuries. In contrast, Great Ouseburn did not make major alterations to its infirmary buildings from the time they were built. Great Ouseburn Union was constrained by economic limitations, and so could not expand continually. Despite the less-than-perfect provisions of Great Ouseburn infirmary, sick inmates received better treatment in this specialised infirmary than they had in the main workhouse building or in their homes. It also separated sick inmates from the rest of the general workhouse population, a certain concern in areas like Yorkshire where the Poor Law Unions and fear of poverty in general had a long negative historical association. The provision of a separate facility maintained the dignity of inmates who were seeking medical treatment and improved overall hygiene and sanitary conditions in the workhouse by removing this class of inmate from the general population.

By the end of the Poor Law era in 1930, conditions at the Great Ouseburn infirmary were reportedly fair (Platt 1930). The interior of the infirmary was more domestic than institutional in character. There were boarded floors throughout, and the walls were all plastered and painted. The building was heated by open fires, and in addition to natural light from the windows, electric light lit the rooms. The limitation on space indicates that the majority of patients in the infirmary spent most of their time in the wards. In 1925, a wireless and a loudspeaker were gifted to the infirmary by Mr Ripley of Great Ouseburn, which provided some entertainment and added comfort for the patients (Great Ouseburn Guardians' Minutes 29/05/1925). Although Platt considered the infirmary to be in a reasonable condition, the facilities within it appear in retrospect to have been far from adequate to the needs of a healthcare institution. In each ward, sanitary facilities consisted of a bath and a toilet, finished with a tiled floor and plastered walls. By 1930, the baths were reportedly badly worn, and no lavatory basin was provided for the patients (Platt 1930, 19). The infirmary first came under criticism from the Local Government Board for not providing day rooms for the use of the inmates. In response, the Great Ouseburn Guardians ordered that the bathrooms be converted into two day rooms. However, this only served to reduce the sanitary facilities while providing less-than-adequate day rooms. As such, although Great Ouseburn constructed an infirmary, it was not comparable to the purpose-built infirmaries of urban Unions or the general infirmaries by then in operation. However, for the residents of Great Ouseburn, this facility was a substantial improvement on having no facility at all.

In larger Unions in towns such as Skipton, facilities for the sick were initially incorporated into the main workhouse building (Figure 2.4). Skipton Workhouse's courtyard plan facilitated the separation of this class of inmate into the rear block, the furthest from the initial site entrance. This remained the case until the last phases of construction at the site, in the early twentieth century. There were some earlier attempts at separating these inmates (Figure 2.5). However, the beginning of the second phase of construction at the Skipton workhouse in 1870 was marked by the creation of a separate fever hospital for the workhouse, undoubtedly intended to prevent the spread of contagious disease. At some point after the construction of a new infirmary in 1901, this 1870s building became the Nurses' Home. The five-bay, T-shaped-plan stone building with a slate roof was of a similar style to the main workhouse complex. The entrance was marked by an ashlar-framed doorway located in a central

38 • Poverty Archaeology

Figure 2.4. Skipton Workhouse, north-east elevation (photographed by Charlotte Newman).

projection. There was a round-arched stair window above the entrance, with a moulded stone surround and pediment. Cast-iron grilles set within stone square blocks in the front and rear elevations allowed for ventilation. Though functional, these iron grilles also evoked a kind of institutional architectural visual culture and emphasised the functional over the aesthetic. By 1909, a two-storey sanitary annexe had been added to the north-east corner of the building. The front entrance led to a hall with a stone staircase, which rose to a half-landing. Originally, each floor had a tall, two-bay ward on either side of the central staircase. These were heated by stacks at either end of the building. These spaces were divided after the Poor Laws were abolished. The rear wing featured paired, narrow windows, suggesting that it housed sanitary facilities. The passage between the two rooms likely led to a kitchen and scullery on the ground floor and staff accommodation and a sitting-room on the first floor. Throughout the building, the floors were boarded, and the walls were painted (Platt 1930).

The new infirmary for Skipton Workhouse was authorised in 1899 at a cost of £4,000 (*The Builder* 26/1/1901, 93). It was designed by architect James Hartley and completed in 1901. The Chairman of the Skipton Union Board of Guardians, Mr J.A. Slingsby, reportedly said that the new

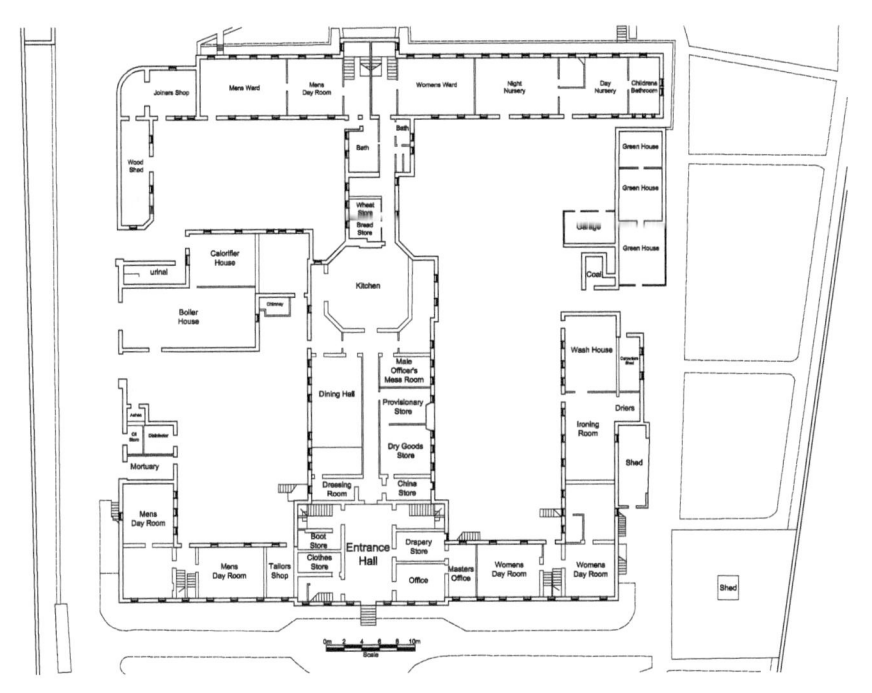

Figure 2.5. Skipton Workhouse plan (1930), part 2 (after National Monuments Record, reference unknown, digitised by Charlotte Newman).

infirmary was located in a 'splendidly elevated' position above the original workhouse; the elevation of the infirmary symbolically separated the building from the Poor Law Union workhouse and all ideas of poverty associated with it, as well as encouraging ventilation. Although it was considered 'nothing elaborate in design and had few luxury's, there was everything necessary to make a patients stay comfortable [*sic*]' (*Telegraph and Argus* 18/1/1901). Such comments on the building's siting and design clearly illustrate how proud the Guardians were of this development, and how keen they were to promote a new facility. The philanthropic image of the Union and of themselves that the Guardians were keen to project was promoted through the building's design. The two-storey infirmary adopted a style sympathetic to earlier workhouse buildings. It centred on a five-bay projection flanked by three-bay wings, each featuring a centrally placed sanitary annexe. The central, round-headed entrance was surmounted by a pediment and featured a keystone dated 1900. The date-stone reiterates the Guardians' pride in the new, modern facilities. The new infirmary building clearly reflected advances in contemporary hospital planning mentioned earlier in this chapter, which emphasised the importance of fresh air and ventilation in preventing disease and hastening recovery (Taylor 1991). The front of the central block boasted a veranda supported by cast-iron columns, an aesthetic feature that, while materially similar to the workhouse building, was stylistically reflective of a more respectable, civic architecture than the institutional styles of workhouses built in the previous century. The entire infirmary featured sash windows for light and ventilation and was further aired by means of two circular ridge ventilators. An isolation block was also constructed to accommodate the most contagious sick and to separate them from the rest of the infirmary patients and prevent disease from spreading. The block (now demolished) was located in the far north-east corner of the site.

It appears that the infirmary was always trying to catch up with improving standards of medical care and technology. In its original plans, the Skipton Union underestimated its needs in terms of space and resources, and allocated inadequate funds for the infirmary, too low to cover costs. This short-sightedness resulted in the need for an extension just six years after original completion (Skipton Guardians' Minutes 18/5/1907; 26/6/1907). This was not uncommon in public institutions, where unprecedented demand led to a continuous cycle of expansion and admission. Indeed, the potential to expand was written into many early lunatic asylum plans in the nineteenth century (Fennelly 2019, 55). Due to an increase in cases of tuberculosis at the start of the twentieth century, the Local Government Board granted £3,150 in 1908 to the Union, almost the cost of the original infirmary, to make necessary improvements and extensions (Local Government Board 1908 XXVIII 753). The infirmary architect James Hartley initially designed an extension to the west wing to accommodate the increasing number of patients. This extension to the building meant the demolition of the original sanitary annexe of the infirmary to incorporate a five-bay extension, which adopted the same style as the original building. A two-storey sanitary tower was added to the west wing to serve the new extension (Royal Commission of Historical Monuments of England 1993, 5). Even so, these extensions to the form of the building were not an ultimate solution to the problem of overcrowding. Additional works continued and improvements were made over the following decades, including the addition of service lifts (Skipton Guardians' Minutes 2/6/1927). The entrance provided access to a central corridor, from which the wards were reached. The central block housed the nurses' quarters, bathrooms and day rooms (Platt 1930, 16). Inmates were accommodated in the wings. During Phases 4 and 5 of the building's construction history, men were accommodated on the ground floor and women and children on the first floor. Each floor held two wards, featuring partly wooden-block and partly stone floors, plastered and painted walls, and hot-water-pipe heating throughout. The male ward could accommodate twenty-four patients and included a duty room for the nurse, a service kitchen and a bathroom. The first floor accommodated thirty-nine female patients. It also featured a labour ward and space for thirteen cots, an operating theatre and a day room. These facilities were considered far from satisfactory in relation to 1930s standards (Platt 1930, 16). Despite government reports calling out the inadequacy of the building, the Guardians frequently received letters of thanks from local residents. On one occasion, for example, the minutes record: '[R]ead letter of Mr Knowles, Gargrave, expressing grateful thanks to the Boards officers for their kindness towards Clara Knowles whilst a patient in the infirmary' (Skipton Guardians' Minutes 23/3/1929). Such sentiments imply that facilities were seen as a benefit by the people who made use of the institution and their relatives. The date of the Knowles letter, 1929, suggests that by the end of the New Poor Law era, Skipton Union Workhouse had become entirely a hospital for the poor. Workhouses were used increasingly to serve the needs of the sick throughout the nineteenth and early twentieth centuries; in this respect, Skipton Workhouse evolved in a typical fashion.

Outer city workhouses like the one at Bramley Union already included an infirmary building in the initial design of the workhouse site, which indicates that from the outset the Guardians regarded caring for the sick as a crucial role of the workhouse in the community. This chimed with general feeling nationwide in the 1860s and 1870s, where the nature of the workhouse was increasingly geared towards caring for the sick (Brundage 2002, 121). However, the original Bramley infirmary was not entirely completed during the initial phase of construction. Only part of the plan was constructed. This may have been because the Guardians were debating the necessity of an extensive extraneous facility for separate accommodation of individual pauper classes, considering the need to be economical. Such hesitancies illustrate that even in the 1870s, thirty years after Anti-Poor Law sentiment was rampant and concerns over economy had stunted the launch of the New Poor Law in the regions, cost was still vital in determining the level of specialised facilities with which inmates were provided. This was felt at local level.

The infirmary at Bramley Union was characteristic of the kinds of infirmaries constructed in the 1860s. It was sited behind the main workhouse building and separate from it, which gave the sick a level of privacy denied to other pauper classes within the workhouse. The original infirmary building was constructed in a similar style to other buildings on the site, maintaining an institutional aesthetic. The orientation of the infirmary to the west of the main workhouse, facing out of the complex, supports the idea that it was considered to be separate from the workhouse, materially and institutionally, from the beginning. The two-storey, twenty-one-bay building featured a plain, central projection in the north-west elevation, which housed the staff and administrative area of the infirmary. Either side of the central projection was a sanitary tower. Usually, sanitary towers were located behind the building, as they were a utility feature, but at Bramley Union they were more ornamental, incorporated into the style of the building itself. The sanitary towers were set oblique to the building, with pyramid roofs. There were two taller windows per floor in the outward-facing elevations. To the rear of the building, external space was provided for patients' exercise. This was also the direction from which patients entered the infirmary through Moorhead arched entrances at either end of the southeast elevation. The interior of the building divided paupers according to gender and the nature of their illness. Staircases at the far end of each ward provided access between floors and allowed movement through the building without the need to cross through the central administration building and risk mixing genders. The infirmary accommodated twenty-two male patients and sixteen female patients, with a lying-in ward for five patients in the female wing. Separate wards were provided for six female and six male 'imbeciles' (*The Builder* 25/5/1872). Like other Unions at this time, Bramley Union provided facilities to house disabled and lunatic paupers in order to relieve overcrowding at local asylums. The presence of lunatic paupers in the workhouse infirmary reflects their ambiguous status within the New Poor Law workhouses, and the variable provision of specialised facilities. This will be discussed in more detail in a later chapter.

One permanent nurse was appointed to oversee the management of the infirmary's fifty-five patients. At nearby Leeds Union Workhouse, inmates capable of working supported the nurses who cared for the sick. The lack of more appointed staff at the infirmary suggests that Bramley did the same. The nurse's role and responsibilities were extremely demanding, but in contrast to the many Unions that had a high turnover of nursing staff, Bramley Union retained its nurses for long periods. Nurse Ann Greaves, for example, appears on two consecutive census records, serving the workhouse for at least eleven years. Despite the constraints the Union's finances placed on facilities, space and treatment, the inertia of the Union's staff turnover suggests that morale remained high among the staff.

At nearby Leeds Union, separate, specialised accommodation for sick paupers became a priority in the late nineteenth century. Bramley Union followed Leeds's example. At the end of the nineteenth century, extra sanitary facilities were added to both ends of the existing infirmary block, reflecting the Guardians' understanding of the importance of sanitary conditions in improved medical practices. Such additions drastically improved cleanliness within the wards and provided additional privacy for patients. At the same time, the infirmary was finally extended to completion according to the original 1871 plans. The Guardians' decision to complete the original plan indicates that there was a strain on existing facilities and an acknowledgement that the workhouse required more extensive facilities than it had when it opened. The new infirmary wing and administrative block comprised the site's largest addition. The Guardians prioritised improvements for the sick, as new facilities were not added to the main workhouse block. The emphasis on facilities for the sick reflects increasing numbers of sick paupers turning to the workhouse for treatment and aid in the last quarter of the nineteenth century, compared to other pauper classes at the same time. Once again, this was reflected nationally; workhouses during this period were increasing their medical facilities in line with refinements in interpretation of the Poor Laws, advances in medical practice and improvements and innovations in hospital planning (Morrison 1999; Richardson 1998).

The infirmary facilities at Bramley Union assumed a pavilion H-plan, centred on the administrative block from which covered walkways provided access into the existing and new infirmary buildings. Constructed in 1895, the second infirmary building was similar in style to the original 1871 building, but with some architectural elaborations (Figure 2.6). The

Figure 2.6. Bramley Workhouse second infirmary, south-east elevation (photographed by Charlotte Newman).

two-storey brick building featured stone detailing and focused on a five-bay central block that projected to the front and rear of the building, with nine-bay wings on either side. The main entrance was set into a gabled projection, with a pointed arch of alternating brick and stone blocks and a date-stone ornament above the window above the entrance. The only building on the site to include a date-stone, this infirmary building reflects a material departure from the initial aims of the workhouse and a new focus on treatment of the sick. The Guardians' shifting attitude towards prioritising the sick was reflected through the stylised buildings and architectural harmony of the site. In the nine-bay wings, all windows feature stone sills and lintels, while one bay featured a pyramid-roofed bay window, which would have provided additional light to the day rooms. The south-west elevation featured three sanitary annexes, offset from the building, and styled identically to those in the first infirmary.

In many ways, Bramley Union infirmary conformed to national trends in hospital planning, including inmate segregation. The plan conformed to that of a traditional pavilion hospital and the principles espoused by reformers like Nightingale who emphasised the importance of light and ventilation. The separation of the infirmary from the rest of the workhouse materially underscored the separation of inmates. With its own utilities, the infirmary was effectively a separate institution, even though it was within the broader workhouse complex. The central block contained separate kitchens, offices, general rooms for staff and likely a labour ward mentioned in the Guardians' Minutes (Bramley Guardians' Minutes 26/8/1901). A central staircase provided access between floors for staff. Each wing housed general wards and featured a stone staircase at its gable-end. The north wing had two sanitary annexes, each featuring a bathroom, toilet and sluice room; the south wing had only one sanitary annexe. The discrepancy in facilities between the two wings reflects how the wards were used during the New Poor Law period. That there were two sanitary towers for the north ward suggests it was subdivided to provide private accommodation or to separate patients by type of illness (or both). The south ward, with only one sanitary tower, was probably a traditional long 'Nightingale' ward. The two-storey administration block, centrally sited between the two infirmary wards, also assumed a style that was similar to that of the original workhouse and infirmary buildings. Predominantly constructed of brick, with some stone detailing and moulded decorative bricks around the roofline, the administrative block featured three bays and a central entrance. The main entrance, set within an arched, stone surround, led into the central hallway from which the rest of the institution could be accessed. The administrative block also provided accommodation for nurses and other medical staff. Covered walkways between buildings improved access within the complex for staff. Timber posts set within a low wall supported the pitched roof of the covered walkway. Although these walkways were originally open, they have since been glazed.

Around the same time that the much bigger Leeds Union workhouse significantly expanded its infirmary, Bramley Union also expanded its medical facilities, but it did so on a much smaller scale. Ordnance Survey maps of Bramley indicate that two new infirmary buildings were constructed between 1906 and 1915. One infirmary was located east of the main building, the other to the west. Typical of contemporaneous infirmary buildings, the two-storey infirmary east of the workhouse featured a five-bay projecting central block similar in style to those of the two previous infirmaries. The main entrance was flanked by window-lights in the central block of the principal façade. Stairs within this area provided access between the wards and space for small offices and storage rooms. Six-bay wings either side of the entrance block provided ward space for patients. Two entrances per wing provided access to the grounds behind the infirmary. The grounds were completely secluded from the workhouse, disassociating the patients from the workhouse inmates, indeed reinforcing their separation. The infirmary included covered areas like those at Skipton Union Workhouse, which enabled patients to benefit from fresh air. A tower provided each ward with sanitary facilities. The irregular fenestration of the towers suggests they were extended at some point. In comparison to the east infirmary, the west infirmary was much smaller and plainer in design. The eight-bay, red-brick building featured stone sills and a slate roof. The entrance was located at the end bay of the south elevation, and the north elevation featured a central sanitary tower. The extremely simple design of this building reflects the Union's limited funds and is typical of late Poor Law-era buildings in its focus on function.

Despite investment from the Bramley Union in new infirmary buildings for sick paupers in the early twentieth century, conditions were inferior to those in nearby Union infirmaries like Leeds. For example, in the male infirmary at Bramley, there was no flushing water in the toilets, and joints in the heating system were leaking. Furthermore, the supply of water in the female hospital was described (vaguely) as 'needing attention' (Bramley Guardians' Minutes 7/7/1924; 1/9/1924). Other instances of inadequate or questionable facilities include a lack of running water in the female wing, into which water had to be carried from the outside yard. The roof also collapsed in places in the 1920s due to escaping steam (Bramley Guardians' Minutes 28/4/1924). Such inefficiencies were continually reported in the Guardians' Minutes throughout the year, which suggests that the Guardians did not have the funds or inclination to fix problems as they arose, or to maintain the workhouse with any degree of regularity.

Although the Guardians' Minutes acknowledged the need to refurbish the entire workhouse complex in the 1920s, the 'comfort' of the inmates was always reported as 'satisfactory' (Bramley Guardians' Minutes 12/5/1924; 21/7/1924). This seeming contradiction may indicate that the Guardians deemed a low degree of comfort appropriate to the needs of paupers. It is likely that the Guardians regarded the provision of basic essentials, such as a qualified staff and superficial luxuries, including a piano in the day room and hired entertainers 'for the pleasure of all patients', as compensatory for the building's poor condition (Bramley Guardians' Minutes 6/8/1924; 1/9/1924).

This neglect had an impact on the lives of the patients in material ways, however. For some patients, infirmary conditions were unbearable. In 1924, the police rescued a workhouse infirmary patient from the canal. The patient had attempted to kill himself because he was so 'fed up' with his experience at the Bramley Union workhouse (Bramley Guardians' Minutes 29/9/1924). Dissatisfaction was likely exacerbated by the proximity and consequent knowledge of the newly developed and seemingly superior Leeds infirmary (discussed below), which gave cause for paupers at nearby Unions to particularly resent their treatment. The obvious contrast between the experience of paupers in Leeds and that of paupers in Bramley illustrates the inconsistencies in Poor Law provision nationally. Although Bramley's Guardians and the Guardians of other outer-urban Unions were inspired by the modern, specialised facilities provided by urban Unions, they were limited financially in situations more akin to rural workhouses than their urban neighbours. As such, the provision of separate facilities for all pauper classes was unfeasible given the scale of the sites. Other than extensions to the infirmary, no specialised facilities were ever constructed on the site of Bramley Union or elsewhere for its use. Unlike the majority of workhouses in West Yorkshire, Bramley never entirely removed any pauper class from the workhouse to a separate facility or to other forms of relief. In Ripon, for example, the able-bodied were not accommodated in the workhouse by 1930. At Bramley, the lack of specialised or separate facilities even at the end of the New Poor Law era is unusual, even when compared to rural areas, and resulted in substandard relief compared to that provided by neighbouring Leeds, which offered highly specialised care, or that in rural workhouses, which offered more out-relief. In contrast to the complicated pauper hierarchies in urban workhouses, to be discussed shortly, Bramley Union's lack of specialised or separate facilities resulted in only a very basic class hierarchy within the institution overall. The Guardians prioritised care for the sick by the end of the nineteenth century, but all the rest of the inmates were treated very similarly. As in all West Yorkshire workhouses in the period, the transient nature of vagrants as an inmate class placed them firmly at the bottom of the pauper hierarchy in Bramley Union. Neither the architectural evidence nor the documentary evidence suggests that there were any very complex class hierarchies beyond this. The impact of such a basic social hierarchy on an individual pauper depended on where they would have fallen within a more refined hierarchy within the region. Economic considerations largely determined conditions at Bramley Workhouse. As a result, conditions generally remained poor. The Guardians' Minutes feature numerous entries relating to poor facilities. Sick paupers in outer-urban workhouses like Bramley Union had, overall, a worse experience of the New Poor Law workhouse than those in urban or even rural workhouses.

The development of infirmary facilities at urban workhouses such as those at nearby Leeds and Bradford was far more complex and driven by economic, political and social considerations. At Leeds Union Workhouse, numerous infirmary buildings were constructed on the workhouse site during the New Poor Law era, evidencing the Leeds Guardians' aim to improve pauper health by modernising methods of care (Figure 2.7). The

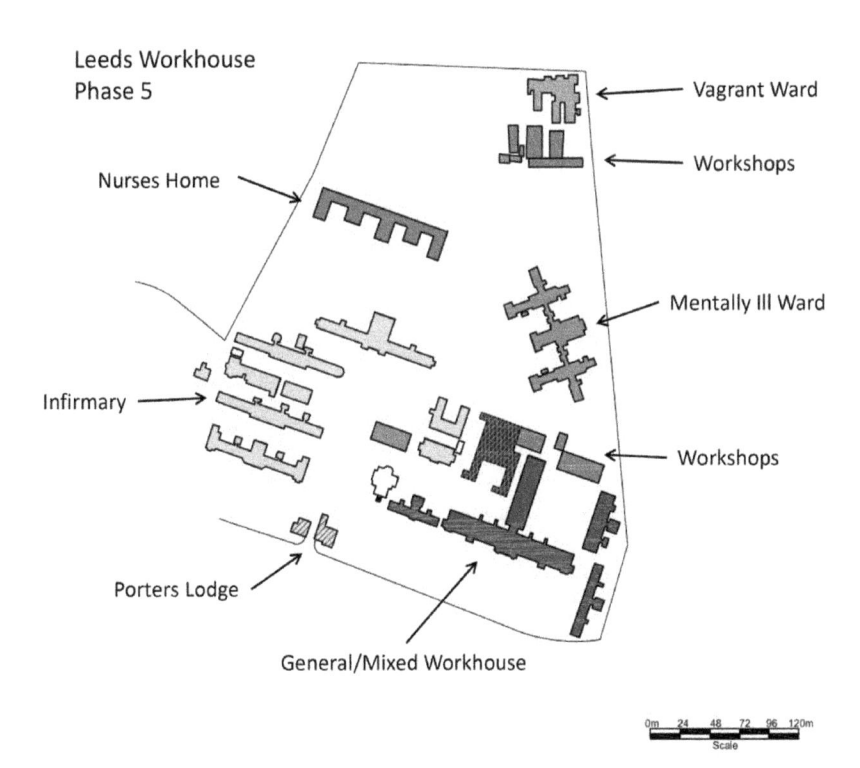

Figure 2.7. Plan of Phase 5 development of Leeds Workhouse (drawn by Charlotte Newman).

first infirmary building was constructed during the second phase of construction on the site, as part of the wider workhouse complex. The original infirmary building was constructed in a similar style to the main workhouse building. The three-bay central block, with a central entrance and Italianate windows surmounted by a Dutch gable, was flanked by four-bay wings. The east and west elevations also featured Dutch gables, and a decorative parapet ornamented the roofline. These architectural features speak to an interest in making the buildings aesthetically pleasing. Chimneys either side of the central block indicate that each ward was heated by a single fireplace, which would have provided scarce heating to the long wards. Nonetheless, this was still superior to heating provision in the larger wards in the main workhouse building. Smaller windows within the fenestration suggest that each ward featured separate sanitary facilities, each used by fewer inmates than those in the main workhouse. As such, conditions within were more favourable than those in the main workhouse. Segregation by gender was maintained as in the main workhouse, with women in one wing and men in the other. As was typical of workhouse infirmaries of this period, inmates were cared for by a few nurses (whose training was, before the 1890s, very minimal) and able-bodied inmates. The role of the nurses included bathing the inmates on Tuesdays and Thursdays. The infirmary's small size, limited accommodation and the basic sanitary routine of bathing inmates only twice a week suggests that care within the infirmary was limited compared to contemporaneous medical facilities outside of workhouses. Yet the Leeds Workhouse facilities were superior to other Poor Law Unions. Many workhouses built at this time did not have separate infirmaries at all. The inclusion of a separate infirmary in the initial workhouse phase at Leeds indicates the Guardians' desire to separate the sick from the healthy workhouse inmates from very early in its operation.

As the number of inmates in the workhouse increased due to unprecedented demand on Poor Law services, so did the number of sick seeking relief from the Union. Within ten years of the construction of the initial infirmary, plans for a new infirmary were in place. Original plans devised by the Guardians included separate pavilions, external sanitary annexes and numerous sun lights to provide light to the building (Leeds Guardians' Minutes 18/5/1870; *The Builder* 28/5/1870, 432). By 1870, pavilion hospitals were widely advocated in hospital planning and landmark examples were constructed for Poor Law Unions in nearby Manchester, so the Leeds Guardians' desire to build an infirmary based on these designs highlights their forward thinking and planning. However, advisers to the Poor Law Board rejected the plans because such extensive facilities were not deemed necessary. It is difficult not to see the rejection of plans for improved facilities as part of a much wider, national cost-cutting exercise, part of the 'new business ethos' that the Poor Law Board increasingly encouraged regional Guardians to apply (Hurren 2005, 403). While aimed specifically at the reduction of outdoor relief in regional Unions, these cost-cutting initiatives also impacted spending elsewhere in the workhouse. The Guardians abandoned their original ambitious ideas and opted for a single infirmary building (*The Builder* 13/4/1872, 289). The outdated thinking of the central Poor Law Board hindered the advance of some New Poor Law workhouses; attitudes towards pauperism had not evolved nationally beyond the narratives around ideas like the workhouse test from before the 1834 Act.

Adopting the Poor Law Board's recommendation of just a single infirmary building, the Leeds Guardians constructed the new infirmary in 1872 (it was demolished in 1972). Photographic records show a three-storey building centred on a gabled, four-bay central block with ten-bay wings either side, each featuring three chimney stacks. Adopting a Gothic style, the infirmary was constructed from brick with sandstone dressings and was surrounded by a small, landscaped garden. Entry was gained through the central block, above which stood a statue of Queen Victoria. The Guardians still aspired to display Leeds's civic pride through the architecture. Doorways in each wing provided separate access for male and female patients and thus maintained segregation by gender. Within the infirmary, the central block housed accommodation for the nurses, chaplain and dispenser; ward sculleries; a hoist; and separate staircases to the wards (*The Builder* 13/4/1872, 289). The kitchen was located in a separate block with a courtyard behind the building. The kitchen was connected to the main infirmary via a corridor. Such facilities completely separated the infirmary from the workhouse. In all, the complex comprised three materially separate institutional entities: the school, the workhouse and the infirmary.

The internal plan of the infirmary building indicates that the Guardians in their selection of an architectural plan for the Leeds infirmary attempted to follow the principles of the pavilion hospitals as much as the Poor Law Board and the limitations of economy permitted. The patients' accommodation separated men and women into two wings, as was standard practice in all public institutions. Each wing was divided into nine sections, each of which was divided into three suites on each floor. Polished birch bedsteads were placed in pairs between the windows, accommodating a total of 216 inmates (Leeds Guardians' Minutes 4/2/1874). Dividing patients into separate suites rather than providing long wards like other workhouse infirmaries implies that the Guardians aimed to achieve the isolation and privacy provided by pavilion buildings as much as possible within a single building. The suites were all interconnected by large double doors, and there were day rooms at the end of every ward. The walls were to be painted dark from the floor to the window (Leeds Guardians' Minutes 2/9/1874). This was intended to be practical, but to the patients, the colour scheme may have affirmed the institutional nature of the building.

Facilities within the wards suggest that the moral and physical well-being of inmates was of particular concern to the Guardians. 'Framed texts of scriptures' were placed on the ward walls, emphasising the importance of religion and moral instruction within the institution, even for inmates who could not attend services (Leeds Guardians' Minutes 15/10/1873). Other comforts, such as chairs, blankets and rugs, were issued to the infirmary, providing comfort beyond that offered in the workhouse (Leeds Guardians' Minutes 4/2/1874). At some point speakers and a wireless were installed in the infirmary, which, as noted by a Leeds newspaper, 'might have been regarded in the days of [Mr] Bumble as a serious breach of discipline' (Bedford and Howard 1985, 8). The newspaper's remarks draw upon Dickens's minor antagonist and stereotypical portrayal of earlier Victorian workhouses to provide a contrast to the comparatively comfortable conditions in Leeds Union infirmary. Separate sanitary facilities were provided for each ward, and each suite also had a double stove and ventilation. Clearly attitudes towards this pauper class quickly progressed after the passing of the New Poor Law, reflected in the level of comfort permitted within workhouse sub-institutions like the infirmary.

The Guardians' interest in the treatment of the sick led to the provision of a permanent residence for the Union's medical officer in the 1870s. Commissioned in 1875, the medical officer's house was located south-west of the industrial school on the workhouse site. Constructed from brick with a small amount of stone detailing, the double-fronted house (now demolished) assumed an L-shaped plan. The role of the medical officer was certainly central to the successful treatment of sick inmates, and the house provided a visual representation of his importance within the hierarchy of the Union. The medical officer was responsible for the sick in the school and the workhouse. Initially, he had just eight unqualified staff carrying out duties under his oversight, which hampered the effectiveness of his work. However, his position within the workhouse expanded as the infirmary facilities and nursing staff improved.

The rapid expansion of the workhouse at Leeds and the increasing number of poor seeking relief from the state led to several extensions of the New Poor Law workhouse buildings in quick succession. Census records indicate that the infirmary was constantly overcrowded, and facilities were stretched. Extensions to the 1872 infirmary were planned as early as 1877 (*The Builder* 9/3/1877, 256). Designed by architect C.R. Chorley, the additional infirmary accommodation provided 139 new beds to be arranged in a U-shape building located behind the original infirmary (now demolished). The sick in the institution then outnumbered the able-bodied inmates. Administration of the two institutions must have caused complications, as in 1878 the infirmary was separated from the workhouse, creating the first separate Poor Law Infirmary outside of London. When they were moved to the infirmary, sick inmates were disassociated from the workhouse, which dramatically reduced the stigma attached to sick paupers and the infirmary buildings. It was popularly believed that sickness was a significant cause of poverty, so the Guardians' improvement of the general health of Leeds's paupers may have been intended to reduce poverty in the long term, like the Leeds Moral and Industrial Training School was. The establishment of Leeds Union Infirmary highlights the morality-driven thinking of the Leeds Guardians. By 1914, still only 10 per cent of Unions had created separated Poor Law infirmaries (Local Government Board, *43rd Annual Report*, 1914). As in their establishment of the Moral and Industrial Training School, discussed in a later chapter, in creating a separate infirmary, the Leeds Union Guardians demonstrated their ability to break with tradition to improve the lives of paupers in Leeds beyond those in comparable urban Unions.

In the 1880s, the focus of the Leeds workhouse site moved increasingly towards the treatment of sick paupers, and facilities designated for sick inmates continued to expand. A visitor to the infirmary at this time commented, 'I would remind the Guardians of the ever-growing need of beds for the sick. Last night there was not a single bed to spare on the male side, and on the female side there were two spare beds, both of them in the Lying-in Ward, at the same time about nine or ten infirmary patients were being accommodated in the dormitory at the main building (women's side)' (Leeds Guardians' Minutes 11/1/1983). This report indicates that the main building was still accommodating sick paupers, even though separate infirmary buildings had been provided. The average stay for inmates in 1884 was one hundred days, which would obviously have strained facilities (Bedford and Howard 1989, 8). In 1883, the infants' section of the industrial school was adapted to be used as lying-in wards for the infirmary. The infants were moved to the main school building. Further sections of the school were converted for infirmary use in 1887. The Guardians' Minutes from this period record that sick paupers were given treats similar to those given to the children, affirming the dissociation of the sick from the main workhouse population (Leeds Guardians' Minutes 25/7/1888). Developments in the treatment of the sick echoed developments in the treatment of children. Initially, children and Leeds Moral and Industrial Training School were the focus of the site, but children were increasingly moved away from the workhouse to specialised facilities as ideas about the education and management of children in an institutional setting evolved.

Likewise, as improvements and advances in medical treatment developed, the infirm became the Guardians' focus and were increasingly removed to specialised facilities, albeit on the same site as the workhouse. Activities at Leeds were considered exemplary in the region, and Hunslett Union deemed Leeds infirmary so successful that it transferred its sick inmates to Leeds in 1890 (Leeds Guardians' Minutes 14/10/1890).

In the early twentieth century, the continuous rise in the infirm population in the workhouse resulted in the massive expansion of facilities. Prior to expansion, three infirmary buildings, the rear block of Leeds Moral and Industrial Training School and other makeshift facilities in the main workhouse block accommodated 707 inmates. Although the infirmary was administratively separated from the workhouse in 1878, sick paupers continued to reside in other workhouse buildings. By 1904, the Leeds Moral and Industrial Training School children had been removed to specialised facilities, so the rear block of the former Moral and Industrial Training School was demolished, and three new infirmary buildings were built in its place. Designed by Thomas Winn and Sons, the new buildings accommodated 505 paupers. The new buildings combined with the three existing infirmary buildings enabled all sick and infirm paupers to be removed from the workhouse and the school to specialised facilities. Rather than simply increasing the number of beds, the Guardians chose to improve care for sick paupers.

A date-stone, that is a stone on which the date of erection is carved, set into the main front elevation of the former Leeds Moral and Industrial Training School building indicates that the expansion of Leeds Union Workhouse began with the demolition of the rear block of the former school. Externally, the most significant change to the main building was the addition of balconies, which were removed at some point later in the twentieth century. French windows and bay windows were added to the central projection. The main block was converted for its new administrative purpose through the addition of an entrance hall, committee room, matron's quarters, quarters for the assistant medical officer and servants' bedrooms on the upper floors (*The Builder* 19/5/1900, 497). The wings were used as wards. Receiving wards were on the ground floor, and general wards were located upstairs. Proper sanitary blocks were added at the rear of each wing (ibid.). Two new, three-storey blocks were constructed behind the school. *The Builder* reports that the blocks included receiving and serving rooms, male sick wards (186 beds), sick and venereal wards (183 beds), male venereal wards (20 beds), maternity wards (26 beds), an infectious diseases ward for ten males and twenty females, children's wards (60 beds) and an operating theatre. Other blocks included a kitchen, stores and a mortuary, which were all located between the infirmary buildings (*The Builder*

22/10/1904, 423). In 1922, an additional dining room was approved by the Local Government Board, subject to the inclusion of central heating (Leeds Guardians' Minutes 11/10/1922). The building was lit throughout with electricity, which provision set the Leeds infirmary apart from infirmaries elsewhere (Bedford and Howard 1985, 8). By recommending and executing the inclusion of electricity, the Local Government Board encouraged the Union to improve material comforts and general standards, reflecting evolving national ideals about pauperism or, at the very least, a more sympathetic attitude towards the sick regardless of class. In 1906, when the final Poor Law infirmary opened at Leeds Union Workhouse, the Leeds infirmary was the largest workhouse infirmary facility outside of London, with accommodation for over a thousand patients managed by eighty-four qualified staff. Due to post-Poor Law developments, few of these buildings survive, and those that do are obscured by later extensions.

A progressive and innovative streak in the way the Leeds Guardians managed the workhouse prevailed during the New Poor Law era. The Guardians were hailed as 'having provided for the sick and infirm under their charge in a manner so thorough and up to date that few like Authorities will be able to challenge comparison' (*Yorkshire Daily Observer* 30/3/1906). The opening of the final Poor Law infirmary was celebrated with a dinner in the workhouse dining room for two hundred guests from all of Leeds's public institutions (Bedford and Howard 1985, 11). The Guardians' celebration of their achievements in the workhouse reflects their genuine pride in the facilities they provided for Leeds's poor. However, not everyone agreed with the Guardians' perceived generosity. In his toast at the dinner, the Lord Mayor warned the Guardians against 'extravagance' (ibid.), reflecting the wider national drive towards retrenchment in spending on the poor that had been part of poverty discourse since the 1870s. The mayor's concern indicates that the Leeds Guardians were somewhat exceptional in their modern and novel attitudes towards provision for the poor and the sick in particular, attitudes that were firmly materialised in the buildings they commissioned.

The gradual disassembly and eventual abolition of the Poor Laws led to further developments in medical facilities on the site of Leeds Union even after the Poor Law period. In 1925, Leeds Workhouse Infirmary became St James's Hospital. The site continued to develop under the National Health Service after its establishment in 1948 and was incorporated into the University of Leeds teaching hospital in 1970. Each of these phases of management entailed redevelopment, construction and demolition of buildings. The evolution of the site during these phases reflects advances in medical technology and the continuing innovation of the Leeds Guardians and their successors.

The nearby Bradford Union workhouse followed a similar path to Leeds by the turn of the century. However, inspired by a national fervour for progress and modernisation, wider change occurred throughout the workhouse site. The Bradford Guardians removed children, the able-bodied and elderly paupers from the workhouse proper to separate facilities on different sites, and designated the workhouse a pauper hospital, marking the beginning of a fourth phase of development and management at Bradford Union. Four new pavilions were added to the site during this phase: one to the east, in 1904; two to the west, in 1905 (now demolished); and one to the rear, in 1906. The new hospital blocks reinforced the site's new function as a hospital and disassociated it from the stigma of its workhouse past. The style of the new workhouse buildings suggests a desire to emulate the modern Leeds Union Infirmary. The first pavilion building, to the east of the site, launched the transformation of the site from a workhouse to a pauper hospital. A date-stone on the building's gable-ends proclaimed the site's new function. In its large size and modern style, the T-shaped-plan, three-storey stone building renounced the early New Poor Law perception of the workhouse as punitive, disassociating the new hospital from the older, negative attitudes towards workhouses. The most significant architectural difference between the different infirmary buildings on the site is the use of Dutch gabling, a decorative feature popular in vernacular architecture at the time. The 1904 infirmary features decorative Dutch gables similar to those used at Leeds Union Workhouse. Facing west, the building featured a five-bay central projection with single, double and triplet windows and a large, embellished stone entrance. The fifteen-bay wings either side of the central entrance are more ornate than the earlier infirmary elevations, featuring archivolt windows on the first and second floors and decorative cast-iron fire escapes.

The Bradford Guardians' efforts to modernise the site are further illustrated through the improvement of conditions within the infirmary. The east elevation of the 1904 pavilion features large sanitary towers offset from the building, which were reached by short corridors similar to those at Bramley Union infirmary. The size and position of the sanitary towers drastically improved hygiene within the wards. Conditions were further improved by the inclusion of ventilation shafts in every fourth bay and the large window-lights in the gable-ends. The Guardians continued to transform the site through the construction of three additional hospital blocks between 1905 and 1906 (Figure 2.8). Segregation was always a high priority of the Bradford Guardians, and the creation of new hospital blocks continued this trend. Specialised blocks for men, children and maternity cases reflect a contemporary understanding of medical practice elsewhere. Although the surviving pavilion behind the workhouse conforms to the plan and style of earlier pavilions, featuring a four-bay central projection

Figure 2.8. Bradford Workhouse infirmary (1906), principal eastern elevation and sanitary towers, East (photographed by Charlotte Newman).

with eight-bay wards on either side and rear sanitary towers, the two hospital blocks at the front of the site (both now demolished) assumed an entirely different style. Three photographs survive to give an impression of these buildings. Their foregrounded location made them highly visible to the passing public. Interestingly, unlike the first pavilion building, they emulated the style of neighbouring Leeds Union Workhouse, where attitudes towards deserving pauper classes appear to have been more charitable and paternalistic than those at most other Unions. The building featured Dutch gables, which gave it an Elizabethan style and improved decorative aesthetic. The two-storey stone buildings also featured a stone that read 'B.U.H.', for Bradford Union Hospital, as mentioned above. Their style and location demonstrate the Guardians' intention to destigmatise the workhouse site and remodel it as a hospital.

Discussion

Unlike the experience of the able-bodied, the workhouse experience of the sick and infirm transformed and improved significantly during the New Poor Law era. In rural areas, the year in which a rural workhouse was constructed and the discourse surrounding workhouse management and the poor at that time largely determined the separateness of the facilities it offered the sick. For instance, Wharfedale Union included an infirmary in its first phase of construction, but this was not until the 1870s, when the Poor Law Board were encouraging care for the sick, at a similar time to the construction of other infirmaries in West Yorkshire. Separate facilities for the sick proliferated throughout the region, beginning in the middle of the century and gaining momentum as discourse on poverty turned towards discourse on healthcare in the 1870s. Wharfedale, Ripon and Skipton all constructed separate infirmary blocks at their workhouses within a decade. These rural Unions were relatively large compared to other rural Unions, and their populations demanded more extensive, specialised facilities like those developing in urban centres. The extent of separate facilities depended very much on the size and location of the Union. Pateley Bridge Union, for example, being remote in its location, did not build a separate infirmary. Although Pateley Bridge provided a designated nurse, sick inmates continued to be housed in the workhouse throughout the Poor Law era. The diversity of provisions for the infirm in rural Unions attests to the inadequacy of even regional generalisations regarding the treatment of a given pauper class.

In contrast to the rural Unions, the urban Unions all included a separate infirmary in their initial workhouse designs. As they served much larger populations from the very beginning, classification was always built into the urban Unions. The urban examples discussed here evidence the fact that in some Unions the Guardians immediately recognised the importance of medical facilities and prioritised separate, somewhat specialised facilities for the sick accordingly. At both outer-city and urban workhouses, the infirmary was usually located behind the general workhouse, away from other pauper classes. Physically separating the sick from the other pauper classes afforded them a level of privacy not granted to other workhouse inmates. The workhouse attended to the physical comfort of the sick through the provision of items such as rugs, blankets and books. Evidence from the Guardians' Minutes at Leeds indicates that the sick inmates' moral well-being was promoted through the hanging of scriptures on the infirmary ward walls. Despite the provision of separate facilities for the sick in urban and outer-city workhouses, infirmaries encountered problematic issues similar to those of general workhouse buildings. For example, staff shortages and inadequacies continually compromised inmates' treatment. At Leeds, the infirmary adopted an identical paint scheme to the general workhouse, which still very much associated the sick with the main workhouse and reminded patients of their institutionalisation and pauperism. Challenges faced at both Leeds and Bradford suggest that infirmary facilities at urban workhouses were overcrowded from the outset. Even so, workhouses cooperated with each other to ease each other's burdens. Bradford suffered from overcrowding, so it transferred patients to Leeds Workhouse. Such actions may reflect the region's traditional relief methods of cooperation between institutions, as well as maintaining the sick on out-relief and sourcing medical facilities outside of the workhouse. At Bramley Union, despite plans for an extensive workhouse infirmary, the full plan was never fully realised, arguably for economic reasons but also due to debates over the necessity of separate facilities in less populated areas.

Late nineteenth-century advances in medical science and a rapidly growing population inspired rural workhouses to extend their medical facilities out of necessity if nothing else by the end of the century. Workhouses thus provide a lens through which to interpret changing attitudes towards civic responsibility for public healthcare. A second regionwide spate of infirmary-building towards the end of the nineteenth century and the beginning of the twentieth century saw the addition of infirmary facilities in some of the small, rural Unions. Ripon, Skipton, Wharfedale, Wetherby and Great Ouseburn all built infirmaries during this period, but the architectural styles and hospital plans they each adopted reflected the high regionality inherent in workhouse architecture. For example, Wharfedale constructed a large, modern, pavilion-style hospital. Because of its expanding, industrialising nature, Wharfedale needed more substantial facilities than smaller areas and was influenced in its provision by nearby urban centres, such as Leeds. In contrast, Ripon, Skipton and Wetherby built single pavilion blocks reflecting their smaller population sizes and need to retain economy. Great Ouseburn chose to build a small infirmary, almost domestic in its appearance, reflecting the traditional architecture associated with almshouses and past Gilbert Union architectural styles.

Infirmaries were continually altered to keep up with developments and discourse in medical practice. Infirmary buildings in rural areas were always struggling to achieve modern standards and alleviate overcrowding, so Unions built new sanitary towers and extended ward space. The rear of Wharfedale infirmary demonstrates this point particularly well, with its additional sanitary towers, balconies and connecting corridors. In contrast, Great Ouseburn did not make major alterations to its infirmary buildings. Great Ouseburn needed to retain strict economy and could not commission extensive facilities from the start. Despite the primitive provisions of Great Ouseburn infirmary, sick and infirm inmates received better treatment in this specialised facility than they had in the main workhouse building or in their homes. The provision of a separate facility maintained their dignity and improved overall hygiene and sanitary conditions in the workhouse. In urban and outer-city workhouses, the second phase of workhouse development increased existing provisions to an even greater degree. The workhouses discussed here all increased facilities for the sick more than for any other pauper class. As previously mentioned, facilities for the sick were constantly severely overcrowded. Although nationally facilities for the sick were increasingly prioritised in Poor Law Unions, in urban and outer-city areas in the region under study here, the demand for facilities made new infirmaries a necessary addition to the workhouse plan, rather than solely a reflection of the Guardians' or the Poor Law Board's desire to improve provision for sick inmates and turn the workhouses increasingly towards healthcare provision. Despite national trends in infirmary building from 1870, infirmary provisions at Leeds were still hindered by the desire of the Poor Law Board to prevent facilities outclassing those available to the working poor. The Leeds Union's more innovative pavilion design for a new infirmary was firmly vetoed by the Poor Law Board, which resulted in the construction of another infirmary that was quickly outdated. However, institutional growth at Leeds resulted in the administrative division of the infirmary and workhouse in 1878, which created the first pauper infirmary of this scale outside of London. Infirmary developments at Leeds were unique within the case study area and provide a further example of Leeds breaking from wider Poor Law practices despite the efforts of the Poor Law Board to standardise provision from the centre.

Urban workhouse infirmaries constructed in the latter half of the nineteenth century were larger than their predecessors. They practised improved cleanliness, hygiene and patient treatment, and they continued to be stylised in keeping with original workhouse architecture. In urban Bradford, medical officers petitioned for improved surroundings, comfort and diet, as well as the need for individualised treatment. Bradford's medical officer also campaigned for the admittance of a wider admission demographic, so as to prevent long-term pauperism and improve the city's health. Although not on the same scale, infirmary facilities at outer-city workhouses expanded at a similar time to those in urban centres. While facilities for the sick paupers in outer-city workhouses improved to include more sanitary provisions, better heat, increased light and better ventilation, facilities for other pauper classes altered very little. Throughout this period, workhouses, particularly in outer-city areas, increasingly focused on the sick, assuming the role of workhouse infirmaries. Guardians at Leeds and Bradford had to balance improved facilities with maintaining a gap between provisions for paupers and those for the employed poor. Therefore, overcrowding persisted, and the Leeds Union Guardians recorded instances of the sick still being housed in the general workhouse. The sick poor resisted Poor Law medical facilities in the workhouse despite the fact that in Bradford, for instance, they were more likely to recover in the workhouse than in other available facilities. Paupers' reluctance to embrace workhouse infirmaries likely fuelled the disillusionment of the Union's medical officers, reflected in the high turnover of medical staff at Bradford.

The development of infirmary facilities at workhouses more generally indicates a move away from Poor Law values and punitive approaches to poverty, towards a focus on providing medical facilities for the poor. A result of this change in focus and the medicalisation of workhouse facilities, however, was that by the early twentieth century large numbers of institutionalised paupers were sick, and in extreme cases, such as in Wetherby, all indoor relief was reserved for the sick. Changing the emphasis of workhouse facilities from accommodating several pauper classes with varying needs to focusing on the sick and modernising medical care altered the dynamic of the workhouse. The extent of medicalisation varied, but advanced facilities like those at Wharfedale even included an operating theatre. Over the course of the Poor Law era, paupers' expectations of and demands on workhouse medical facilities increased as industrialisation and population growth led to new kinds of health problems and work-related injuries (Hey 2005). In some cases, paupers were appreciative of workhouse facilities. Skipton's Guardians recorded letters of thanks from inmates after their treatment in the infirmary. The inclusion of new medical facilities meant that for the first time, the workhouse was opened up to the poor seeking curative care, not just to those seeking general relief. As a result, new demographics began to seek care in the workhouse, beyond just the pauper class. Facilities were continually overcrowded, staff were overstretched and, subsequently, patient care suffered, especially in Unions such as Ripon, where severe overcrowding completely discouraged staff from working for the Union.

Although outer-city Unions expanded medical facilities throughout the nineteenth and early twentieth centuries (albeit on a smaller scale), economic constraints hampered attempts to parallel the radical improvements achieved in urban Unions. As a result, infirmary buildings at Bramley adopted plain, functional styles reflective of the Union's primary needs. Attempts were made to provide patients with comforts, such as books and music. At North Bierley, improvements were made to the infirmary's decorative schemes, which this research suggests aspired to the new image of modernisation that was adopted by infirmaries in urban centres. However, these provisions cannot have compensated for the infirmary's many inadequacies. Archival evidence from both North Bierley and Bramley Unions records instances of leaking roofs, insufficient water supplies and overcrowding. North Bierley's Guardians even recorded an occasion on which a section of the infirmary was demolished because it was unsafe. It is likely that inmates resented the treatment they received in these workhouses, especially when they could easily compare it to the far superior facilities at nearby Bradford and Leeds. The extent of inmate dissatisfaction is clearly evident in an instance of inmate suicide at Bramley and of inmate complaints to the Local Government Board at North Bierley. These instances highlight inmates' increasing expectation of Poor Law medical provisions by the early twentieth century. The initial mission of the 1834 Poor Law to provide uniform relief across the country was clearly not achieved.

In urban Unions, the twentieth century sparked an extensive and innovative building program of medical facilities, which sought to alleviate the severe overcrowding that had thwarted the effectiveness of workhouse infirmaries throughout the nineteenth century. Leeds continued to construct infirmary buildings on the original workhouse site, which soon boasted the largest infirmary outside of London. Bradford also continued to develop facilities on the original workhouse site, but due to the removal of all other pauper classes to separate institutions elsewhere in Bradford, the site came to be used solely as an infirmary. The adoption of a neo-Elizabethan style, similar to Leeds's, including inscribing the letters B.U.H. (Bradford Union Hospital) in the façade, arguably indicates Bradford's desire to remove the stigmas associated with the workhouse and reinvent the site as a medical facility. The infirmary illustrated the city's modernisation and progress to the passing public and the city's poor. The archival evidence indicates that several neighbouring workhouses transferred sick inmates to Leeds's and Bradford's infirmaries, suggesting, unsurprisingly, that their own facilities could not match those in urban centres. Unsurprisingly, not all civic leaders supported the rapid expansion of medical facilities in urban workhouses. Many still saw the investment in Poor Law facilities as an incentive for pauperism, even towards the end of the century. The Malthusian influence on perceptions of the poor did not wane even as the country rapidly industrialised. The Mayor of Leeds warned against 'extravagance' and urged caution. Evidently, tension was emerging yet again among the middle and upper classes regarding relief measures for the poor and the causes of poverty. Tension among the governing classes fuelled and informed the debates later published in the Minority and Majority reports on welfare reform. In general, a lack of uniformity and high regionality are clearly seen in this examination of one pauper class – the sick poor – in just one region of England.

Chapter 3

The Elderly

In a letter to *The Times* in 1837, London-based surgeon Henry Rugg sought to draw public attention to the plight of a woman belonging to Lambeth parish who was at that time residing in the Clothworkers' Company almshouses at Sutton Valence in Kent. Elizabeth Buckhurst was 77 years of age, and infirm. Rugg had tried to organise a campaign among the respectable inhabitants of the parish to memorialise the Guardians of Lambeth Union to grant her outdoor relief to supplement her meagre income. These requests were denied under new workhouse rules. In 1837, Lambeth Union was no longer offering out-relief. Despite the explicit provision for out-relief in cases of age and infirmity in the New Poor Law itself, Rugg blames the Law for the suffering of Mrs Buckhurst. Rugg's letter, later included in the anti-Poor Law collection *The Book of the Bastiles* (Baxter 1841, 269), illustrates the ways in which the ageing poor who relied on the 'economy of makeshifts', those 'patchy, desperate and sometimes failing strategies of the poor for material survival' (King and Tomkins 2003, 1), represented here by the charity of many different bodies and people, found themselves at odds with the new system of institutionalised poverty management.

This chapter will explore the varying means of material provision for the elderly poor in the New Poor Law workhouses after 1834. Much of this provision was institutional in character, involving sometimes-crowded dormitories where elderly inmates resided either by themselves or with others. The elderly and children sometimes shared spaces in these institutions, too. Despite comprising a 'shrinking portion of the population', older people accounted for an increasing percentage of the institutionalised population of England in the eighteenth century (Ottaway 2013, 42). As a class of 'deserving' poor, the elderly were in some cases treated with several degrees more kindness by overseers than the able-bodied poor in the same institutions. Indeed, despite Rugg's anger towards the Lambeth Union and the 'Whig Poor-Law' (Baxter 1841, 269), many institutions did offer outdoor relief to elderly inmates particularly. Accounting for rural, outer-urban and urban examples of workhouse provision, this chapter will address how the elderly managed and were managed in the New Poor Law workhouse.

Old Age in the Later Historical Period

Old age in the nineteenth century was a far-removed experience from old age in preceding or succeeding centuries. By the end of the eighteenth century, poor harvests contributed to a surge in applications for poor relief from the state. The adult children of the poor, themselves looking to the state for relief, were no longer in a position to care for their ailing parents (Ottaway 2004, 11–12). In England, massive urban migration separated individuals from family and community networks that had managed care or support in old age in previous centuries. As workers in the new industrial economy aged, they no longer contributed meaningfully to the workforce. The anonymity of the town and the city meant that the elderly poor – these aged former workers and widows – became a problem for the state. What actually constituted *old* or *elderly* is a matter of some ambiguity, however. Somebody who was *old* was classed as such due to their capability to work and level of infirmity (Looser 2008, 9). There is some consensus among scholars that the age of 60 was significant as the year in which both sexes might be considered 'old'. The designation of elderly changed from the early to late modern period. L.A. Botelho (2004, 13) has argued that the arduous nature of rural labour meant that visually, people became recognisably 'old' by age 50. Devoney Looser (2008, 9) understands old age in this period as 'having reached the age of 60', and in her study on ageing in the eighteenth century, *The Decline of Life* (2004), Susannah Ottaway states that the marker of old age at the end of the eighteenth century was 60. Elizabeth Buckhurst of Sutton Valence, at 77, was very advanced indeed by this calculation. 'Over 60' was a classification category in New Poor Law workhouses, one of three main classifications that included 'aged' (meaning 60 and older; sometimes called 'infirm'), 'able-bodied' and children under 7. The age of 60 was the point at which industrial labour became physically challenging, or when people began to lose their spouses, the point at which poor women became widows without a means of financial support, and poor men became widowers unable to care for themselves. Without a means to support themselves, older men and women at the lowest levels of society turned to the state for aid. There was a growing awareness throughout the Industrial period of age and ageing. In her analysis of the journals of biographer and historian Mary Berry, who died in 1852 in her late eighties, Amy Culley (2019) illustrates the awareness of ageing and social obsolescence among the elderly in the mid-nineteenth century.

Given their visibility in the material record of historic workhouses, relatively little attention has been granted to the 'aged' and 'infirm' of the New Poor Law workhouse system in England and Wales compared to other classes of inmate. Most institutional studies of poverty focus on an ungendered norm – primarily able-bodied, usually adult. Interestingly, while studies on children in workhouses and institutional childhoods grow in number, the aged and infirm are still relatively anonymous in archaeological approaches to the institutional built environment. The bioarchaeology of elderly inmates has been a subject of considerable study in Ireland, including interesting comparative analysis of the demographics of workhouses and the ages of individuals in graveyards (see, for examples, Geber 2015; Lynch 2014). Historical scholarship has fared better, notably with the publication of *Old Age and the Poor Law, 1500–1700* (Botelho 2004), which focuses on the Old Poor Law records of two villages in Suffolk. Susannah Ottaway's (2013, 41) study of elderly inmates in the eighteenth century states that while older people in England often partook of welfare provision in the form of outdoor relief, most lived in their own homes. This may have made them more difficult to study, as they were not in residence in workhouses like other inmate classes. This goes some way towards explaining why elderly people as a discrete group do not make up a greater portion of the historiography on Old Poor Law institutions. The elderly in the New Poor Law have most frequently been written about in terms of the history of pensions and economic policy regarding welfare (for instance Boyer 2019). The spatial separation and classification, as well as the material experience, of the elderly have not been the subject of much study, however. This is surprising given that the New Poor Law was geared specifically towards the improvement of institutional provision for the aged and infirm, as *deserving* poor. Given that much of the commentary on the New Poor Law in the nineteenth century centred around the exposure of bad practice and the sensationalisation of workhouse experiences (an interesting cultural by-product of the rhetoric behind the workhouse test), can we view the inattention to the elderly in scholarly discourse since as an acceptance of their better treatment?

An awareness of the 'problem' of old age in society is a facet of modernity, an issue facing an industrialising society that turned away from the communal and familial in terms of support, towards the civic collective as a productive force. An increased awareness of the limitations of age more generally in the nineteenth century, and very material demands on the workhouse system to accommodate as many deserving poor as possible, meant that the elderly were specifically provided for, on paper at least. The text of the New Poor Law specifically accounted for the relief of those suffering from 'old Age or Infirmity of Body' who could neither contribute to work within the workhouse, nor gain a living outside of it. The Law stated that

> Relief shall be given to any adult Person who shall from old Age or Infirmity of Body be wholly unable to work, without requiring that such Person shall reside in any Workhouse: Provided always, that One of such Justices shall certify in such Order of his own Knowledge, that such Person is wholly unable to work. (Poor Law [Amendment] Act 1834, 295)

This provision would, in theory, mitigate the uncomfortable prospect of housing married couples. Segregation by gender was one of the primary classificatory divisions in workhouses, and an easy architectural principle to execute at scale. In the first report of the Poor Law Commissioners for England and Wales, the reception of married couples into workhouses is expected to be 'extremely rare' and probably relating to cases of paupers receiving outdoor relief (*Annual Report of the Poor Law Commissioners for England and Wales* 1835), such as the elderly. Despite this, by 1840 married couples over the age of 60 were allowed a room of their own in many workhouses, but space was an issue in most cases. Though workhouses allowed elderly married couples a room of their own, there may not have been the space to accommodate this in all cases, especially in rural workhouses. Despite the ability to share a room with a spouse, exemptions from work and small treats such as tea and sugar, people over 60 were not induced to enter workhouses long-term, due to a provision in the 1832 Anatomy Act that if older people were to die in the workhouse, their bodies would be given to medical schools (Brundage 2002, 80–81). Yet even despite this deterrent, and the best intentions of the authors of the New Poor Law to separate the deserving aged and infirm from the idle and able-bodied through outdoor relief, many elderly inmates resided in workhouses throughout the nineteenth century.

The Elderly in the Workhouse

As fringe elements of the 'productive' workhouse workforce, children and the elderly were often housed together. The benefits to children of learning from the elderly was a tenet of Christian doctrine and teaching in the modern period (Botelho 2004, 8), so their association in the workhouse aligns with contemporaneous thinking. This was the case at the rural Skipton Union workhouse in Yorkshire. Until the elderly inmates at Skipton were moved into the old infirmary building in the 1920s, they resided with the children in the north range of the workhouse proper. The north range was divided into two wings, with the elderly men in the east wing and the elderly women and children in the west, which mirrored the division of gender in the rest of the workhouse – men to the east and women to the west. Such divisions illustrate the extent to which the Union conformed to Poor Law Commission guidelines concerning segregation. Skipton Union Workhouse was constructed in 1837, very soon after the New Poor Law was passed. Adopting the square workhouse model of architect and workhouse specialist Sampson Kempthorne, the building was thus typical of its type. The actions of the Skipton Union are in direct contrast to the Unions of Oldham and Huddersfield immediately to the south, whose objections to the New Poor Law meant that new workhouses there were delayed. Nearby political rallies such as the Hartshead Moor meeting in 1837, for instance, spurred on the anti-Poor Law movement in the north of England (Driver 2004, 120–21), headed by political leaders such as the radical Richard Oastler. As such, it is interesting to note that Skipton not only constructed a workhouse so quickly after the passing of the Act, but that it used as its model one of the ideal workhouse designs of Kempthorne. Allowing the children to mix with the elderly women suggests that elderly inmates were perceived as more worthy inmates – *deserving poor* – whose influence would not damage the children's characters. In fact, in workhouses more generally, it was not uncommon for elderly women to help with the care of the children as a form of required work (Crompton 1997; Longmate 2003).

On the ground floor, the men's accommodation at Skipton consisted of a twelve-bed dormitory, a day room and a bathroom. A *terrazzo* double staircase per wing allowed independent access to each wing, further enforcing segregation. Accommodation on the first floor included another day room, a twelve-bed dormitory, a two-bed dormitory, a bathroom and twelve toilets. For the women, there was a day room and a twelve-bed ward, which contained four cots and a bathroom (Platt 1930). The provision of new, separate sanitary facilities suggests that treatment of the elderly changed substantially in the years after the construction of the workhouse and throughout the nineteenth century. Documentary records indicate that after 1907, the Guardians offered outdoor relief to the elderly, who were also receiving state pensions at that time (Skipton Guardians' Minutes 9/2/1907). By 1925, the Guardians' Minutes for the workhouse record that treats were provided for the inmates, but especially for the elderly. This relief would have helped keep this category of pauper out of the workhouse and supports the idea that elderly inmates were seen throughout the nineteenth century, but especially going into the twentieth century, as more worthy of public relief and state support.

As mentioned above, workhouse buildings were designed to separate inmates on the basis of gender. The further segregation of inmates according to their age and their health or infirmity, however, was relatively limited initially in some workhouses, such as Great Ouseburn in North Yorkshire. Documentary evidence sheds some light on this oversight or disregard of the Poor Law Commission recommendations, and indeed the Poor Law Amendment Act, in this workhouse. The majority of inmates in the workhouse at Great Ouseburn towards the end of the nineteenth century were elderly or children. Despite the dissolution of the earlier Gilbert Union to which Great Ouseburn had previously belonged, the workhouse and its overseers continued their established methods of poor relief, reserving the workhouse for those who could not care for themselves (Great Ouseburn Guardians' Minutes 28/8/1899), to the exclusion of able-bodied poor. This shows that adherence to the New Poor Law varied from place to place. In 1899, the Guardians of the Union of Great Ouseburn resolved to remove any elderly pauper to the workhouse who could not care for themselves. Rural sympathy towards the elderly echoes the concerns of Old Poor Law institutions such as almshouses, and contrasts significantly with the aims of the New Poor Law. Outdoor relief continued to be granted to the able-bodied in contravention of the Poor Law Amendment Act, illustrating the value placed on the family unit by the rural Union, and the established belief that the able-bodied should not be in the workhouse. It would appear from the census records of the area that the workhouse at Great Ouseburn was never actually full to capacity, and the Guardians' Minutes indicate that outdoor relief was often offered in place of housing the petitioning poor in the workhouse. As such, segregating the pauper classes further than by gender was not necessary in this case, as children and elderly were allowed to mix. A simpler workhouse design in this case, the T-plan, was therefore adequate to the needs of the Great Ouseburn Union (Figure 3.1). This seems to have been a relatively common occurrence in rural workhouses. The majority of paupers at Pateley Bridge in the West Riding of Yorkshire, for example, were also relieved outside of the workhouse. In the case of Pateley Bridge, inmates who required specialised care were sent to specialised institutions – children to schools or orphanages, and lunatic inmates to the asylum at Leeds – while the workhouse was preserved for paupers who had nowhere else to go. Keeping inmate numbers down was a priority for the Guardians of Pateley Bridge, for although the New Poor

The Elderly • 67

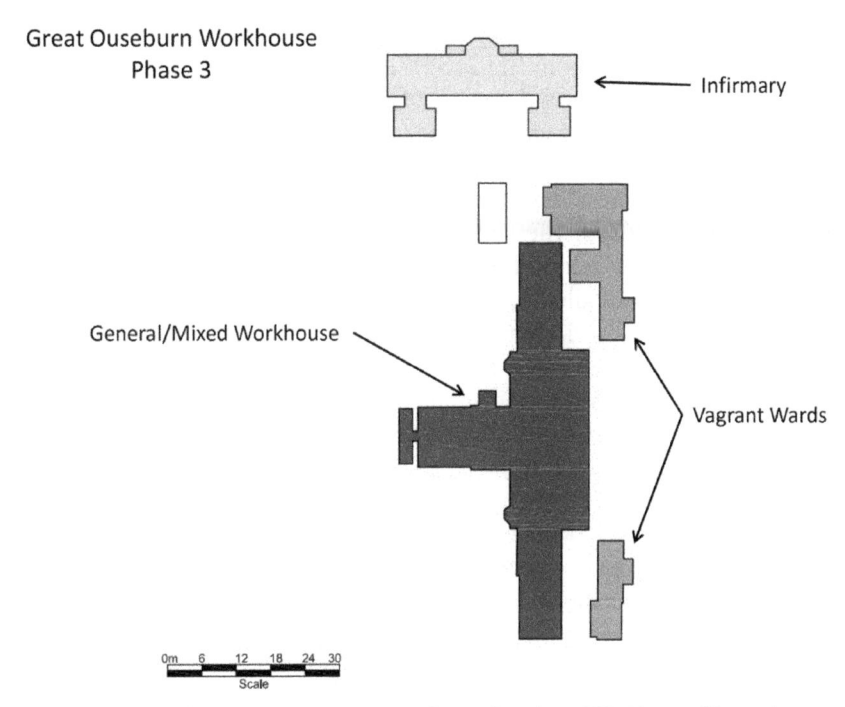

Figure 3.1. Plan of Phase 3 development at Great Ouseburn Workhouse (drawn by Charlotte Newman).

Law workhouse was the administrative centre of the Union, the Guardians clearly did not consider it central or singular to how they distributed relief.

Not all rural workhouses operated without specialised, spatialised practices for management of inmates, however. The workhouse at Wharfedale in the West Riding carefully divided workhouse space for classes of inmate, including the elderly. For example, the ground floor of the workhouse featured a four-bed ward, a lavatory and a day room for men, all of which had boarded floors, painted walls and central heating. These domestic-style furnishings and features set this area of the workhouse apart from other areas for able-bodied inmates. Indeed, the elderly inmates at Wharfedale occupied a part of the workhouse more closely associated with the running of the institution than the other inmates. By the start of the twentieth century, the ground floor of the other wing not used for elderly inmates was occupied by an engineer. He attended to the block and was provided with a sitting room and kitchen. His whole family lived there, and his child apparently slept in a screened-off section of the first-floor female ward (Platt 1930, 38). Accommodation on the first floor consisted of a six-bed male ward and a ten-bed female ward. The old infirmary in

68 • Poverty Archaeology

the workhouse was supervised by both the engineer and a night nurse, who had her own separate room (ibid., 39). The designation of a discrete block for the elderly and the employment of specialised staff for their care and management indicates that their needs were recognised as a priority for the Union. However, the census records for Wharfedale Union indicate that there were more elderly housed in the workhouse than could have been accommodated in the specialised block, which suggests that some elderly inmates were relieved in the main workhouse building, with all of the privations that entailed. Clearly the substantial amount of indoor relief available to workhouse inmates and the poor in Wharfedale was focused on the elderly, indicating that the Guardians of this Union prioritised institutional care for those they deemed most in need and unable to care for themselves. Indoor relief at Wharfedale for the able-bodied was very limited. The Guardians' preferential treatment of the most vulnerable paupers reflects the priorities of the earlier Gilbert Union period, which influenced Wharfedale's interpretation and implementation of the New Poor Law.

Bramley Union near Leeds opted for a mixed workhouse building, in which children, the elderly and the able-bodied were separated into different areas of the same building (Figure 3.2). Segregation according to gender was also enforced. The wings of the workhouse accommodated 144 inmates with female paupers in the west wing and male paupers in the east

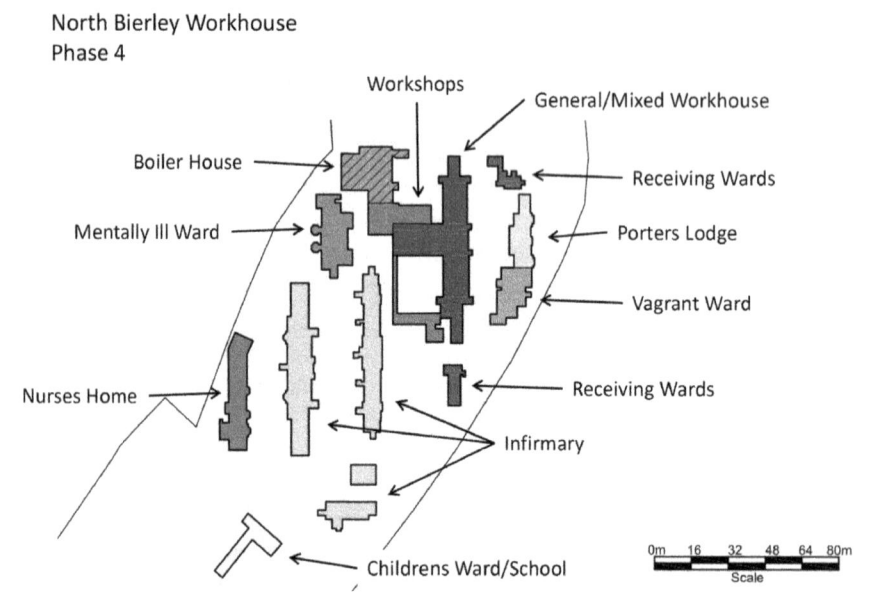

Figure 3.2. The Phase 3 and Phase 4 development of Bramley Workhouse (drawn by Charlotte Newman).

wing (*The Builder* 25/5/1872). A central corridor ran through the building, operating as a primary arterial route through the centre of each floor. Day rooms and dormitories could be accessed from this corridor. The ground floor accommodated elderly inmates and children together. These two classes of deserving poor were separated from the able-bodied and married couples' accommodation, which was on the first floor, from which separate access stairs led to the external exercise yards and dining room (ibid.). The separation of inmate accommodation in this manner spatialised the idea that there were fundamental differences between different classes of inmate. By keeping the elderly separate from the able-bodied, the workhouse designers and authorities were reinforcing the difference between deserving and undeserving poor. Rooms in the workhouse were heated by open fireplaces, while hot-water pipes later supplemented fireplaces, and gas lighting provided artificial light by the end of the nineteenth century (Platt 1930). Interestingly, like the nearby Leeds workhouse (discussed below), Bramley offered accommodation for elderly married couples, reflecting similarly sympathetic attitudes towards this class of pauper. The Bramley and Leeds Guardians shared the opinion that the elderly were not always responsible for their pauperism, and consequently disregarded the need for a stricter segregation. The privilege of shared accommodation for married couples made the experience of the workhouse less isolating, and the experience of an elderly pauper in Bramley was very different from that of an able-bodied pauper in the same institution. By the end of the New Poor Law era in the 1920s, many West Yorkshire workhouses had developed substantial specialised facilities for certain pauper classes. In the case of the elderly, management practices varied considerably. Indeed, in some areas, by the 1920s attendants were employed to care for some elderly paupers in their homes, though the majority of support services remained in the workhouse and contingent upon institutionalisation (Bramley Guardians' Minutes 28/4/1924).

From its opening in 1855, the new North Bierley Union workhouse prioritised care for the elderly over that of other inmates. Elderly paupers were housed within the main workhouse building, but the Guardians' Minutes for the workhouse indicate that they received more attention and better treatment than other inmates. As in the majority of West Yorkshire workhouses under the New Poor Law, the elderly inmates were separated into wards away from the able-bodied (North Bierley Guardians' Minutes 28/5/1868). Like the Guardians of the nearby Leeds Union, the North Bierley Guardians provided elderly married couples with private accommodation (North Bierley Guardians' Minutes 29/9/1897). These wards for married couples had special fixtures such as wooden handrails to enable mobility and ease access around the ward (North Bierley Guardians' Minutes 28/5/1863). Rocking chairs were provided for the comfort of elderly women in the day rooms (North Bierley Guardians' Minutes 3/8/1865). In contrast to the facilities for the able-bodied, the elderly regularly received entertainments, reflecting their perceived deservingness. In one instance, the elderly inmates were even permitted to leave the workhouse to be entertained at the houses of local residents (North Bierley Guardians' Minutes 24/7/1895). The Guardians' attitudes towards the elderly changed over the course of the nineteenth century. In 1908, workhouse regulations were changed to allow the elderly more privileges, and the workhouse increasingly assumed the role of an old people's home. The new regulations allowed the elderly to leave the workhouse to spend a day or weekend with friends or for daily walks, so long as they returned in time for meals (North Bierley Guardians' Minutes 14/1/1908). The elderly inmates were no longer required to wear the workhouse uniform, and their meals were served in the day rooms instead of the general dining room. Further entertainments were provided in the form of daily newspapers, draughts, dominoes and tobacco for the smokers. Provisions for this pauper class far exceeded those for the able-bodied class. The Guardians ultimately sought to remove the elderly permanently from the workhouse. As early as 1900, the Guardians' Minutes record debates regarding the provision of a separate facility for the elderly (North Bierley Guardians' Minutes 9/5/1900). No action was taken at that time, but the Guardians reviewed the elderly paupers' accommodation again in 1911. They visited Bradford Union's Daisy Hill Cottage Homes for the elderly, which they considered to be an inspirational best-practice example of modernised care for the elderly class of pauper (North Bierley Guardians' Minutes 29/3/1911). However, despite the Guardians' inquiries into separate facilities for the elderly, North Bierley Union could not ultimately finance or justify the construction of such dedicated, discrete facilities. A substantial number of elderly paupers remained in the workhouse until the end of the New Poor Law in 1930.

The urban workhouse at Leeds was subject to different pressures, demographics and social concerns than its rural counterparts, catering for the urban poor on a much larger scale. The Leeds workhouse was carefully segregated into strict classifications in order to manage these pressures. Over time, completely separate buildings were constructed at Leeds for different inmate categories, creating an extensive institutional landscape (Figures 2.7 and 3.3). The exception to strict segregation and classification of inmates was in the accommodation for married elderly couples, which was shared. The accommodation was located in the two-storey block to the rear of the workhouse, away from the main area of operations and, crucially, the busier areas where able-bodied inmates were put to work. Nationally, the separation of married elderly couples into their own discrete accommoda-

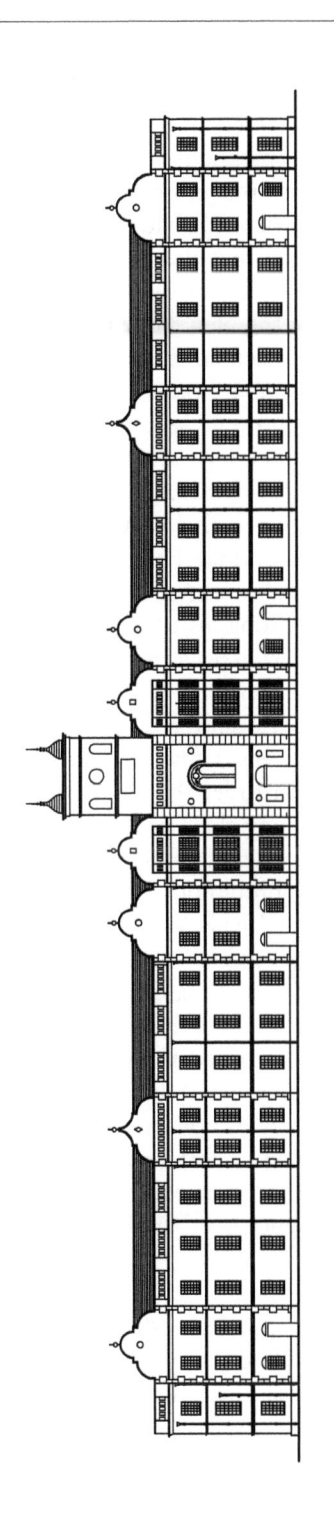

Figure 3.3. Leeds Workhouse, principal elevation (digitised by Charlotte Newman).

tion was not uncommon. However, in this part of Yorkshire, there are no known examples of separate, dedicated accommodation for married couples. The Guardians of the Leeds workhouse clearly privileged this inmate class, deemed more deserving and thus more entitled to comfortable, less stringent facilities. That the Guardians provided couples' accommodation for the elderly specifically suggests that the workhouse also assumed the role of a home for the elderly early on in its life as an institution, which went beyond the requirements of the New Poor Law on workhouses.

At Leeds, inmates who were deemed more deserving received privileges that were not granted to the able-bodied, the less deserving. The infirm and elderly inmates, of which there were a significant number at the Leeds workhouse, had their own separate day rooms, wards and washing facilities, distinct from other pauper classes. By the 1880s, these deserving poor who lived in the workhouse were also allowed to leave it once a fortnight to visit Roundhay Park. Roundhay Park was a public park opened by Leeds City Council in the 1870s, part of a wider urban movement in the British Isles addressing the problems of disease and moral concerns with urban living. Public parks provided a space for the circulation of fresh air and a place for walking and exercise (Tarlow 2007, 111). When elderly and infirm patients visited Roundhay Park, the workhouse master provided them with refreshments: buns, tea and coffee (Leeds Guardians' Minutes 19/8/1885). The decision to let the elderly leave the workhouse was not uncontroversial even among the Leeds Guardians, however, and the Guardians frequently debated whether or not the elderly should be allowed out of the workhouse. Throughout the 1880s and 1890s, however, the majority of Guardians at Leeds Workhouse agreed to allow the elderly to leave. The privilege granted to the elderly reinforced the idea that they were uncomplicit and unfortunate victims of poverty, and not responsible for their circumstance. The elderly inmates also occasionally enjoyed entertainments and accompanied the workhouse children to the theatre (Leeds Guardians' Minutes 24/2/1886; 12/11/1890; 3/2/1892). At Leeds as in rural and outer-urban workhouses, the activities of the elderly were frequently associated or joined by children. These pauper classes were frequently considered in conjunction with each other, and the elderly were not considered an immoral influence over vulnerable children (unlike the able-bodied inmates).

Similarly to the elderly inmates, able-bodied inmates were separated from other pauper classes. Their experience differed from that of the elderly, whose experience of the workhouse may be glimpsed in comparison. On entering the Leeds workhouse, the able-bodied were numbered and dressed in a workhouse uniform (Leeds Guardians' Minutes 19/5/1858; 28/8/1863). Instances of the Leeds Guardians purchasing second-hand clothes for the inmates reflects on the one hand the degradation of this pauper class (Leeds Guardians' Minutes 24/11/1897), but also the lack of *uniformity* in the workhouse uniform. The personal identity of the inmate was stripped along with their own clothes, however, institutionalising them through induction into the physical embodiment of an inmate. Sociologist Erving Goffman (1961, 16) has argued that this practice of submission, this mortification of the human body through cleansing and hygiene practices (such as giving up one's clothing for a uniform), was part of the inmate-making admission process in institutions. The individual was all but lost in the machine of poverty management. In contrast to smaller, rural workhouses, the vast workhouse of the city of Leeds rarely recorded individual inmate cases. The lowly status of the able-bodied was further defined in instances such as the conversion of the labour yard at Leeds for temporary sleeping accommodation for able-bodied men (Leeds Guardians' Minutes 7/12/1898). These conditions were particularly harsh given the climate of the north of England, and contrasted greatly with the conditions of the elderly and infirm.

By the 1890s, the main workhouse building at Leeds was ostensibly given over to the accommodation of the able-bodied, the elderly and vagrants. This was how the space was officially divided. In practice, the workhouse building accommodated mostly elderly inmates and those too infirm or mentally ill to be accommodated with the able-bodied. Designated specialised facilities for these classes of inmate were perpetually overcrowded. As such, the workhouse was adapted to accommodate this overflow. In 1895, the married couples' accommodation at Leeds was modified into wards for the infirm (Leeds Guardians' Minutes 20/11/1896). As in previous phases of building and spatial allocation, the Leeds Guardians underestimated the need for specialised facilities, failing to anticipate Leeds's rapid population growth at the end of the nineteenth century. Between 1831, on the eve of the New Poor Law, and 1901, the population of the borough of Leeds rose from 123,548 to 428,969 (Beresford 1980, 48). This was due to several factors, not least mass rural-to-urban migration and emigration to the growing industrial centre. As such, planning for an increase in inmates was almost impossible, as the population quadrupled over the century.

The rapid and massive expansion of facilities across the Leeds workhouse site from the end of the nineteenth century included the addition of three new residential workhouse blocks. Late nineteenth-century workhouse additions in West Yorkshire were generally less ornate and more functional than earlier constructions. At Leeds, though not as ornate as the original workhouse building, the new blocks were constructed to a similar style, suggesting that the retention of a consistent architectural style and the reinforcing of the centrality of the original workhouse were still priorities for the Guardians, despite the additional cost of less utilitarian features. The two three-storey red-brick buildings constructed in 1908, one to the east of the main building and one to the west, were almost identical in design and plan. The entrance, set within a stone surround with small window lights and a dated stone pediment, was in the projected central bay of each building. The first- and second-floor windows above the entrance also featured stone surrounds in the classical style. A brick parapet with stone detailing ornamented the roofline. Either side of the central bay were the wings, which differed in that the north block featured eight-bay wings and the south block six-bay wings. The large windows within stone surrounds provided substantial natural light into the wards, concurrent with contemporaneous thinking on institutional design. Similar to the previously discussed 'Nightingale' layout, applied widely in pavilion-plan hospitals across Britain and at the nearby Leeds General Infirmary, constructed four years after the main workhouse building (Historic England 2017), the projecting wings with their large windows were designed to maximise light and minimise the risk of infectious disease. By the early twentieth century, the type and quality of glass, which determined the amount of natural light that penetrated the building, was crucial to the mission of the workhouse. Light was a precious commodity in the city of Leeds due to the high levels of industrial pollution (Leeds Guardians' Minutes 23/1/1929). Every other bay in the workhouse featured an external chimney stack, with ornamental stone brackets. One gable-end of each building featured a three-storey bay window. The north-facing ornate Dutch gable faced outward from the complex. Evidently, in the parts of the building that were visible to the passing public, the Guardians communicated their reforming values through the building's ornamentation and style. Adopting a similar design to blocks one and two, with stone detailing and Dutch gables, the third block, constructed in 1909, featured four storeys and a basement. The building was connected to the northern block via a three-storey extension.

Although the internal plans of these buildings were basic, heat, light and ventilation facilities evidence development in institutional architectural design in the early twentieth century, which ultimately was aimed towards improving inmate experience in workhouses. The internal design of the buildings included basic open wards either side of the central staircase. The wards were well ventilated and electric lighting was installed, and heat was provided through fireplaces and probably additional hot-water pipes (Leeds Guardians' Minutes 8/3/1905). Sanitary facilities were in towers, separate blocks attached to the rear of the buildings. The sanitary tower at Leeds, constructed in 1909, also housed numerous workshops. Maintenance of the rapidly expanding site demanded the employment of on-site workmen. Given the daily demands for active site management, it was more economical for the Guardians to employ full-time, knowledgeable employees than to outsource the required labour as needed.

The construction of new wards at Leeds and the development of attitudes towards accommodating specialist classes of pauper such as the elderly and infirm meant that inmate conditions were generally improved over the course of the nineteenth century. The number of able-bodied in the workhouse in the 1890s was relatively low, so it is likely that most of the new buildings constructed housed the elderly and infirm. Treats and entertainments were increasingly offered to all inmates, and not just the elderly or children. This indicates that the inmates of the workhouse were all considered to be deserving of relief by the early twentieth century. In one instance in 1929, the inmates of Leeds Workhouse were taken to the former stately home of Temple Newsam outside the city, then under the ownership of the Leeds Corporation. They were given tea at the house and, on returning to the workhouse, were given tea and chocolate (Leeds Guardians' Minutes 26/6/1929). Increasingly, the Guardians discussed inmates in general, however, rather than distinguishing between different pauper classes. This makes the task of researching distinctive classes more difficult.

By the twentieth century, the unprecedented popularity of the fever hospitals and infirmaries at workhouses meant that many Guardians began to turn towards reframing the purpose of the workhouse as a medical or care-focused facility (as discussed in the previous chapter). At Bradford, the Guardians of the Bradford Union Workhouse designated the workhouse an infirmary in the early twentieth century, and all able-bodied inmates were relocated to a new workhouse in 1913 (Bradford Guardians' Minutes 1/5/1901; 22/1/1913). Bradford's old workhouse was modified for the reception of the elderly, though there was little in the way of segregation. Although some alterations were made to the second floor in the early twentieth century, there is no evidence to suggest that the floor was ever divided into male and female inmates. Rather, it was divided into a series of dormitories, and though two staircases provided access to the floor, there is no other evidence of gender segregation among the inmates.

Bradford (Figure 3.4) was somewhat behind its nearby contemporaries in some ways. Whereas Leeds and Bramley workhouses constructed numerous sanitary towers for their institutions in response to modernising hygiene standards, Bradford Workhouse did not. Indeed, Bradford's workhouse was a legacy of the old Poor Laws, and predated the New Poor Law of 1834; thus, much of the architecture and spatial layout of Bradford was reminiscent of a less systematic architectural approach to poor relief. An article in *The Builder* from 1851 indicates that sanitary facilities at Brad-

Figure 3.4. Bradford Union Workhouse, principal elevation of New Poor Law workhouse (photographed by Charlotte Newman).

ford were located throughout the building, a report supported by the extant fabric of the buildings. Integrating sanitary facilities into the main body of the workhouse would indicate that the Guardians were not influenced by improving architectural knowledge concerning health and hygiene, which recommended the removal of sanitary facilities to separate towers, away from the main buildings. The lack of additional sanitary towers also indicates that improvements to the main workhouse building in the wake of the New Poor Law were minimal. This reflects the Guardians' desire for economy, which is also suggestive of the influence of public opinion in Bradford. Lancashire and the West Riding of Yorkshire were among the most vocal anti-Poor Law counties in the 1830s and 1840s. Massive gatherings such as the above-mentioned Hartshead Moor demonstration less than 10 km south of Bradford in 1837 attracted huge numbers and energised the public in the local area against the recommendations of the New Poor Law (Driver 2004, 121). Resistance to the New Poor Laws was not against the system in general, but rather in favour of the maintenance of the Old Poor Laws' more piecemeal and highly regional relief arrangements that had built up in places like the West Riding. The New Poor Law was, eventually, applied throughout England, and the innovations in architecture and technology that came alongside the new workhouses even made their way to Bradford, where the existing workhouse building was adapted. The sanitary facilities built at Bradford reflect a somewhat punitive and control-centred approach to inmate management. Some toilets were located in the exercise yards, and *The Builder* describes the use of a mechanical device in the external toilets that prevented two paupers from entering the toilet at any one time (*The Builder* 9/6/1851, 379). This device restricted pauper freedom of movement, but also freedom of association in spaces that were not observable by the institution. This reflects the Guardians' general mistrust of inmates, and an active move against any kind of pauper community or economy outside of institutional surveillance and control. Indeed, the measures against these kinds of illicit associations and clandestine uses of spaces suggests that they were happening.

The workhouse building at Bradford that was eventually converted into an infirmary was divided into a main range and two cross-wings. Access to the workhouse from the outside was possible from the front and rear. Doorways in the front and rear of the workhouse provided access into the cross-wings. Within the main range, a cross-plan corridor with an octagonal centre divided the area into several rooms. Three rooms and a stone staircase opened off the central octagon. The size of the rooms off the octagon suggests that they were used for storage. The internal decoration of the workhouse was scant, but the brickwork was painted. Like the main range, the cross-wings were partitioned to maintain gender segregation; these cross-wings underwent significant and complicated alterations between their use in the nineteenth century and the survey for this book in the 2010s. The remaining fabric suggests that the areas on the north side of the building, facing out of the workhouse complex, were initially divided into three or four spacious rooms, which were all heated by open fireplaces and benefited from the light and heat provided (in summer) by large triplet windows. These conditions were superior to those in the main range, which suggests that before their designation in 1901, the cross-wings were reserved for inmates considered more deserving of relief and less responsible for their poverty. These inmate classes included the elderly and children.

While the elderly at Bradford were segregated from other pauper classes and accommodated in a more comfortable area of the workhouse, one of the other distinctions between them and the able-bodied was entertainments. Both inside and outside of the workhouse, the elderly were provided with special entertainments while the able-bodied were not. Outside the walls of the workhouse, the elderly inmates were invited by local societies to attend exhibitions or take part in excursions to view Christmas decorations (Bradford Guardians' Minutes 9/11/1870; 2/2/1876; 30/5/1900). One such society was the parish committee of Great Horton, a nearby village. The inclusion of elderly inmates in the life and society of the local area evidences a difference in attitude towards this pauper class when compared to the able-bodied. Local populations were generally more understanding and compassionate towards the elderly. Given that, this class of pauper was central to the variety of poverty-management apparatuses that made up the Old Poor Law. Indeed, Thomas Gilbert's reforms of the Poor Law system in the 1780s mandated that institutional provision be only available to the elderly, the infirm or the very young (Brundage 2002, 21), such that the *real* poor to be cared for *should* be the elderly, in the eyes of many. As such, it is not surprising that this class continued to enjoy privileged treatment.

By 1901, plans were drawn up by the Bradford Guardians to construct a series of cottage homes for Bradford's elderly paupers (Bradford Guardians' Minutes 20/2/1901). These cottage homes would remove the elderly entirely from the workhouse and provide them with more dignified accommodation. Interestingly, this approach was more in line with the almshouse approach to poverty that predated the New Poor Law than with the post-1834 institutional solution. Rather than being punitive, the new approach of the Guardians towards the elderly was compassionate. Bradford was one of the first Unions in England to establish a system of cottage homes for the elderly apart from the main workhouse building. In contrast to nearby Leeds, where the Guardians largely developed facilities on the original workhouse site, Bradford Union constructed several specialised facilities on new sites, away from the original workhouse site, so long associated with poverty. The disassociation of the elderly from the institutional workhouse also served to distance this class of pauper from the stigma attached to early New Poor Law buildings.

Discussion

Although the New Poor Law workhouses were intended primarily to deter the able-bodied from institutional provision through a stringent system, the so-called 'workhouse test', this was never codified in law (Brundage 2002, 76), and therefore many workhouses became overcrowded with able-bodied poor. Even so, inmate demographics varied across the system, and most workhouse inmates in the West Riding of Yorkshire were elderly. Most of the Unions discussed in this chapter were evolutions of pre-existing systems rather than brand new, post-1834 Unions. In the Gilbert Unions, care was focused predominantly on the most vulnerable inmates, usually the elderly. This was sometimes out of necessity and driven by the limitations of the system. The urban Unions discussed catered to such large population centres and numbers of poor that housing all able-bodied paupers was impractical, and as such workhouse accommodation was reserved for, or more often allocated to, the elderly or other vulnerable pauper classes. In the Poor Law rhetoric of the modern period, from the first Poor Laws in the early seventeenth century to the twentieth century, the elderly were deemed less culpable in their own poverty than the able-bodied. As part of the latent and ever-present impotent poor of society who could not help themselves (Slack 1995, 6), they were historically considered a group for whom assistance would always be required. Like children, the elderly frequently received favourable treatment from workhouses in the form of gifts, treats and entertainments, and were provided with comfortable accommodation.

As discussed above, in rural regions the tradition of caring for the elderly was so deeply embedded in poor relief that the practice continued under the New Poor Laws. At Great Ouseburn, the elderly were removed to the workhouse if they were found unable to look after themselves and the Union generally accommodated large numbers of elderly paupers. The workhouses at Ripon and Wetherby ceased housing the able-bodied by the 1920s, and facilities by then were largely used by the elderly. Indeed, accommodating fewer classes of pauper meant that small, rural workhouses were able to provide a more specialised service for the elderly within the original workhouse buildings. For elderly paupers who had worked all of their lives and had grown up in the New Poor Law era, entering the workhouse due to old age or infirmity may have seemed unjust. However, as previously suggested, the elderly paupers often had the opportunity to develop communities within the workhouse as segregation of classes and genders became more relaxed.

Over the course of the New Poor Law, facilities for the elderly not only improved but also became increasingly specialised and separated from the rest of the workhouse. In larger workhouses in industrial towns like Wharfedale and Skipton, separate blocks away from the workhouse proper were provided for the elderly, who received privileged treatment similar to that offered in smaller, rural institutions. At Skipton, a block was converted for the exclusive use of the elderly in 1928, and in Wharfedale the infirmary building was designed specifically for the accommodation of the elderly. The number of elderly paupers recorded in the region increased throughout the nineteenth century, which likely reflects the availability of improved medical treatment, which meant that more accommodation was required for their specific use. There was also a growing sense of social responsibility for this vulnerable pauper class in discourse surrounding institutions in the period, which prompted the construction of specialised accommodation. Separating the elderly from the main workhouse buildings and goings on afforded the elderly paupers a level of dignity in their institutionalisation, and a sense of independence that was not granted to the general workhouse population. These measures evidence a continuation of the social responsibility for the elderly that predated the New Poor Law.

Like their rural counterparts, urban Unions demonstrated greater compassion towards the elderly than for other pauper classes throughout the New Poor Law. The Guardians' Minutes of the urban case studies discussed above mention elderly inmates more frequently than, for example, the able-bodied. Uniquely among the case studies, Leeds, Bramley and North Bierley provided separate accommodation specifically for elderly married couples. The privacy granted to married couples in separate accommodations allowed for a higher level of dignity among this pauper class and elevated their status within the workhouse population. Although Bradford did not provide separate accommodation for married couples (as far as the evidence indicates), they did provide a superior quality of ward for the elderly than for the able-bodied. Architectural evidence from the elderly wards at Bradford indicates that the elderly accommodation was significantly lighter, more spacious and better heated than other areas of the workhouse. The Guardians' Minutes mention fixtures and furniture in the wards that indicate that greater attention was paid to the needs of the elderly paupers. At North Bierley, for example, rocking chairs were provided for inmates' comfort, and at Bramley, low-level railings were employed instead of high walls in the exercise yards for the elderly inmates, a superior aesthetic to that provided to able-bodied inmates. The provision of separate accommodation for elderly married couples reflects a middle-class view of their status as deserving of relief and privilege. As with the allocation of domestic work to female paupers, the workhouse thus offers a lens through which to view and examine class-based societal norms in nineteenth-century England.

Despite the concurrent efforts of their urban neighbours towards specialisation of facilities for the elderly, many workhouses outside cities did not evolve to the same extent. Neither Bramley nor North Bierley specialised or separated facilities for their elderly inmates, who continued to be accommodated in the general workhouse buildings until the end of the New Poor Law. The workhouse at North Bierley did effect some improvements to their existing facilities for the elderly, though not to the same extent as nearby urban examples. Low-level handrails were installed to ease access and passage around the workhouse, and elderly inmates were no longer made to wear the workhouse uniform. The elderly at North Bierley eventually stopped taking meals with the other workhouse inmates and were allowed to eat in their designated day rooms instead. However, there were significant inadequacies in the accommodation for elderly inmates, and increasing overcrowding throughout the nineteenth century resulted in worsening conditions and poor hygiene. Demands on space meant that at workhouses like North Bierley, some day rooms were converted into wards in order to cope with the number of inmates. The Guardians' Minutes at both North Bierley and Bramley suggest that the Guardians were powerless to improve conditions due to significant economic constraints. Although the North Bierley Guardians visited the new cottage homes constructed by the Bradford Union at Daisy Hill in 1907, and aspired to similar facilities on paper, the same efforts were not, for them, economically viable. Ultimately, the workhouse experience for many elderly inmates at outer-city workhouses was significantly inferior to that of the elderly inmates at urban Unions.

Unlike other inmate classes, the elderly in urban workhouses were permitted to leave the workhouses, which diminished their sense of institutionalisation. At Leeds and North Bierley, elderly inmates were permitted to leave the workhouse to visit friends, usually for a day, provided they returned for dinner. Occasionally, inmates were allowed to leave for an entire weekend (North Bierley Guardians' Minutes 14/1/1908). Elderly inmates were also allowed to attend events outside the workhouse, such as accompanying children on theatre visits. At Bradford, elderly inmates were recorded as having attended local events and associations with the wider community. At North Bierley, for instance, elderly inmates were sometimes invited to the homes of local people for tea. By integrating the elderly into wider society, urban Unions sought to reduce the impact of institutionalisation on this pauper class. Conditions for the elderly improved throughout the New Poor Law. At Leeds, the architectural development of the workhouse site indicates that several new blocks were constructed at the beginning of the twentieth century. Archival and census data suggests that they were used primarily for the elderly. The new spaces featured improved lighting, heating and ventilation, as well as sanitary facilities and separate day rooms for the use of the elderly inmates. Overall, the workhouse at Leeds increasingly assumed the role of a home for the elderly from the start of the twentieth century until 1930. At Bradford, an endeavour to modernise and specialise facilities for the elderly resulted in the construction of Daisy Hill, a collection of cottage homes specifically constructed for the elderly poor. Comprising cottage-style bungalows set around a rectangular patch of grass (see photograph by Peter Higginbotham, 2006, available from Higginbotham 2021), the Daisy Hill homes looked more like pre-Poor Law almshouses than a New Poor Law institution.

Workhouses, claimed Charles Booth in 1892, created a spatial link between the deserving destitute and the idle who would not work. By association, elderly people who were housed in workhouses in close proximity to the wilfully poor were themselves branded as such. Booth's book serves to demonstrate a concern with the welfare of the elderly in workhouses as the nineteenth century drew to a close.

> The common and popular view is reflected in our present law and its administration. Out-relief is granted to a certain extent to respectable but destitute aged people, and exceptional indulgence within the workhouse is dealt out to the infirm; but neither plan is altogether satisfactory. A workhouse is at best a dreary residence. Decent old people who find refuge there cannot but be associated with very questionable companions. Whilst even if actual tyranny is avoided, it is difficult to prevent harsh callous treatment. (Booth 1892, 116)

By the 1890s, attitudes towards the aged and infirm in workhouses began to shift, and a Royal Commission enquiry into provision for the elderly was launched. The Commission recommended the separation of elderly and infirm inmates from the rest of the workhouse population (Morrison 1999, 117).

The increasing specialisation of accommodation and the separation from the workhouse of accommodation for the elderly from the end of the nineteenth century reflect a shift in the mission of the workhouse. The status of the elderly, always somewhat elevated above that of the able-bodied in the New Poor Law workhouses, was confirmed in the construction of dedicated facilities and increasing space given over to their care. Thus, the cultural function of the workhouse subtly shifted from an institution of confinement for the undeserving poor to a facility for the care of the infirm and elderly in many cases. As such, the early twentieth-century workhouse finally came to resemble the institutions envisaged by reformers like Thomas Gilbert, who was responsible for a slew of Poor Law reforms in the late eighteenth century, and paternalistic icons of industrialisation such as Sir Titus Salt, who built almshouses for ex-workers (Reynolds 1983).

Chapter 4

The Young

> The bowls never wanted washing – the boys polished them with their spoons till they shone again; and when they had performed this operation, (which never took very long, the spoons being nearly as large as the bowls,) they would sit staring at the copper with such eager eyes as if they could devour the very bricks of which it was composed.
> —Charles Dickens, *Oliver Twist*

Charles Dickens's (1838) description of the privations under which children suffered in an urban workhouse, narratively situated immediately before the oft-quoted appeal for an extra serving by the titular character Oliver Twist, is now infamous. Dickens's atmospheric description of the workhouse as a cold, unwelcoming space, and the community of children therein as a half-feral gang under the subjugation of the largest boy whose cannibalistic tendencies led Oliver to seek more food, have become cultural shorthands for workhouse life. That children, or any inmate for that matter, did not receive enough food in a workhouse to do more than keep them alive, and that the conditions under which children suffered were cruel and unusual even by workhouse standards, was part of popular (albeit anti-Poor Law) discourse in the 1830s and 1840s. Indeed, the 'enduring and poignant imagery' of *Oliver Twist* has significantly influenced the perception of children's experiences in the workhouse into the present day (Hulonce 2016). This chapter will address the material construction of workhouse buildings in the north of England and the arrangement of space therein to identify what spaces, if any, were set apart for children and young inmates. We will explore the conditions of those spaces and consider the impact of the material environment on experience.

In the last chapter, we explored the place of the elderly in the workhouse. In many cases, particularly in the period immediately following the implementation of the New Poor Law in 1834, the elderly inmates were housed or managed alongside children. In the popular memory of the English workhouse, children were a constant feature of workhouse life. Indeed, children in the workhouse have a storied history that varies from place to place, and many of the most notorious scandals involving workhouses relate to the treatment of children. As a particularly vulnerable group within the increasingly industrialising landscape and cityscape of nineteenth-century England, children were, like the elderly and mentally ill, *deserving poor*. As a group who could not manage their own poverty and whose destitution was beyond their control, children were of special interest in the mission of the New Poor Law. Conversely, the lot of children whose parents had engaged in immoral acts was very much central to the controversies surrounding the New Poor Law in the first place.

In the early nineteenth century, the years leading up to the New Poor Law Act of 1834, there was an increasing concern with sexual promiscuity. This was linked to the growth of urban centres where anonymity made sexual promiscuousness more likely. The concern over promiscuity was also linked to wider thinking on political economy, and ran concurrent to a concern about dependency on the state. In his essays on population control and political economy, Thomas Malthus (1798) argued against encouraging whole social classes to depend on the state. A proliferation of offspring would, he suggested, result. He discussed the importance of the institution of marriage and the shame of bastardy in maintaining the population. Bastardy was a social concern at the start of the nineteenth century. These children of unwed parents would be necessarily poor due to a lack of provision in law for their share of property or work. Malthus and other moralists linked promiscuity and bastardy to moral collapse and degradation. This kind of moralising, linked to some notion of natural justice, was picked up by the government and implemented in the New Poor Laws, where they placed the integrity of the family unit at the centre of their conception of social order (Henriques 1967, 110). This manner of thinking was not confined to the state. Indeed, many of the orphan societies and foundling refuges founded in this period were intended specifically for the children of widowed parents. Foundling hospitals investigated the circumstances of their charges' conceptions and birth – interrogating their mothers and expecting them to show 'signs of shame' – so as to determine moral character

(Weisbrod 1985, 201), in order to protect the moral character of the other children in their care.

The position on bastardy in English law before 1834 was that children were the financial and moral responsibility of both of their parents (though an unmarried mother could still be imprisoned for 'lewdness'). Fathers were liable to pay for the upkeep of their natural children, but if the burden for payment fell on the parish (i.e. the father could not afford to pay), then they could also be imprisoned – for up to three months from 1809. Pursuing the father for the expenses incurred on the parish became an economic (and, notionally, a moral) imperative (Harvey 2015, 377). This changed after the New Poor Law. In the drafts of the Poor Law Bill, the problem of 'affiliation' – the means by which fatherhood was ascertained – was attacked. The New Poor Law made bastard children the sole responsibility of their mothers in order to sidestep this problem of affiliation. The reasons for this change in attitude towards bastardy were both moral and economic. The burden of support could not be seen to fall on the parish or the Union if a man escaped his responsibilities, while the plots of 'lewd women' to lie and blackmail their way to compensation could, it was argued, be avoided. Though several compromises were proposed so that these harsh changes could be softened in the New Poor Law – such as making affiliation proceedings more difficult to apply for or ceasing payments after a child turned a certain age – the Bill passed without a compromise being reached. Even so, workhouses did frequently end up with children whose parents could not or would not support them, in light of the lack of standardised state-run facilities for their care.

Approaches to Childhood and Poverty

Children as a discrete class of inmate in the workhouse were the subject of significant concern and discussions from the start of the New Poor Law era. Even so, scholarship on children has only recently addressed the topic in critical detail. Lesley Hulonce's (2016) comprehensive overview of children and childhood in Poor Law institutions in England and Wales represents the first complete overview of the topic. Hulonce points out that children represented 30–40 per cent of recipients of Poor Law relief. Poor relief accounts for out-relief too, so these numbers were not always reflected in actual workhouse admissions. Even so, this statistic is staggering, given that the focus of scholarship on Poor Law institutional buildings and on poor relief in general has largely focused on workhouse provision for the able-bodied, the adult, a genderless and ageless norm, while historiography more frequently represents children as part of the wider class of deserving poor, alongside the elderly and the sick and, less frequently, women. In common with these other pauper classes, however, the treatment and accommodation of children was not consistent across the country. Differences in treatment are stark when we consider how punishment was meted out at different institutions, a cause of concern for the Poor Law Commissioners in the 1840s. In consequence of a number of early and high-profile scandals, however, the Poor Law Commissioners did attempt to standardise treatment more than for any other pauper class when they laid down regulations for the extent of punishments that could be meted out in 1841. However, at local level, Unions still struggled to manage their staff and have them keep to the rules (Shave 2018, 351), and from the start there was much correspondence with the Commissioners regarding the rules.

Approaches to historical institutions by archaeologists are, as feminist archaeologist Suzanne Spencer-Wood (2009, 33) has pointed out, ungendered. In consequence of the same generalising and homogenising of institutional spaces, many historical archaeologies of institutions for general confinement (hospitals, asylums, workhouses and prisons) are 'ageless' in their approach to the inmate populations. Except where children appear in the material record, as in Eleanor Casella's (2012) study of children in Female Factories in rural Tasmania, the very young are largely absent in studies of large institutions. Notable exceptions are of course studies of institutions established specifically for the reception of children, such as Paulina Przystupa's (2018) work on resistance in late nineteenth-century boarding schools for Native American children, or the author's own work in the same volume (Fennelly 2018). This latter study on the Bedford Asylum for Industrious Children, an annexe to the North Dublin Union House of Industry, which became the North Dublin Poor Law Union in 1839, focuses on the architectural provision for and spatial separation of children from other inmates in an Old Poor Law institution. This study draws on the work of the authors (Fennelly and Newman 2017) in accounting archaeologically for historical institutions in the absence or inaccessibility of material remains. We build on these approaches in this chapter, accounting where possible for architectural features and built heritage through standing building surveys and employing desk-based methods for material culture study and architectural analysis where the buildings no longer exist. In this manner, this chapter situates children within the workhouse buildings of Yorkshire, demonstrating the disparate approaches to providing for the young in institutional contexts in the Poor Law era.

Children in the Workhouse

In rural workhouses, where space was at more of a premium than in the larger urban Unions, children were frequently housed with the elderly inmates, as inmate classes requiring some particular attention and differential treatment than that of able-bodied or sick inmates. This was certainly the case at a rural Union like Skipton, where children and the elderly were housed together until towards the end of the nineteenth century, when children were moved into the workhouse's original infirmary building, which was extended to accommodate the new inmate class, including the addition of new sanitary and service accommodation (Royal Commission of Historical Monuments of England 1993, 3). This gradual movement of children away from the main workhouse continued at Skipton Union, which had developed a reputation by the early twentieth century for keeping children out of the main workhouse building, housing them instead in cottage homes or boarding-out accommodation until they were 18 (Skipton Guardians' Minutes 12/1/1927). They were also sometimes placed in industrial schools. In 1906, for example, the Skipton Guardians ordered that the children 'David Luiwn and John Luiwn be sent to the Humber Industrial School stationed at Hull and maintained thereon at a cost of 8/- per week each together with the usual outfit for clothing' (Skipton Guardians' Minutes 25/8/1906). It was common for children who were not placed in such institutions to be placed in internships with local businesses or farmers (Skipton Guardians' Minutes 29/8/1925). Union Guardians including those at Skipton also encouraged the emigration of mentally and physically able children to Canada while they were still young 'so they [could] be trained to take their part in the development of the empire' (Skipton Guardians' Minutes 12/1/1929). Emigration removed children physically from the social taint of pauperism and reduced overcrowding in the workhouse, towns and cities while also advancing the nation's colonial and capitalist interests (Crompton 1997; Fowler 2007, 146; Thompson 1989). This does not mean that their experience was necessarily improved.

Within Skipton Workhouse, children also received special treatment differentiating them from other inmate classes. This included the provision of the services of a dentist employed by the workhouse for them, and excursions to seaside resorts such as Morecombe Bay (Skipton Guardians' Minutes 15/8/1925; 14/10/1911). By July 1914, the Skipton Guardians were discussing the permanent removal of children from the workhouse, and by the end of the year they were looking to purchase a house in which to accommodate children separately, away from the workhouse entirely (Skipton Guardians' Minutes 2/12/1914). The removal of children from the workhouse was advocated by the Local Government Board from the 1890s, and it had become law by 1913 that no child over the age of 3 should be kept in the workhouse (Fowler 2007, 148). Such decisions reflect changing attitudes towards children, whom it was believed no longer benefited from the workhouse or deserved to remain there. The Guardians clearly did not want these children to repeat the mistakes of their parents or fall into the same perceived traps of poverty. Education, emigration, apprenticeships and ultimately the permanent removal of children from the workhouse lifted the stigma of the workhouse from this class of inmate. These provisions did not apply to all children in the workhouse, however. The Skipton Guardians' Minutes report that child vagrants were sometimes detained in the vagrants' wards. This was uncommon prior to the First World War, but after the war, many returning veterans and their families turned to vagrancy due to a lack of work. Allowances do appear to have been made for children. Unlike other vagrants, for example, child vagrants were not discharged on Sundays (Skipton Guardians' Minutes 23/3/1929). However, given that the Children's Act of 1908 allowed Guardians to remove children from the care of unsuitable parents, that they were instead kept with parents in the vagrants' wards (even as late as 1929) reflects a desire among the Skipton Guardians to preserve the family unit. However, this kind of accommodation situation also served to prevent these children from mixing with others; this can be read as a means of safeguarding against corruption of the mainstream workhouse population through the negative influence of vagrant children.

At other Unions such as Ripon, children were housed in specialised accommodation, often called children's wards, in the workhouse complex but separate from the workhouse proper. The Ripon Union children's block (demolished in the 1950s) was a two-storey structure located behind the main workhouse building. In 1930, it was considered so unsatisfactory in terms of accommodations that it was designated unfit for any institutional purpose (Platt 1930). There was little by way of domestic-style furnishings even in the early twentieth century when such provisions were normal in institutional interiors. The floors on the ground floor were flagged with stone, and those on the first floor were boarded. Though heat was provided by open fireplaces throughout, flagged and boarded floors would have made for an echoey, draughty space. The children's block also featured bathrooms for able-bodied inmates (ibid., 26), which necessitated the intermingling of the two pauper classes. This is problematic given the stress on the moral education of pauper children in the workhouse emphasised by other Unions like Skipton. The ward also contained a day nursery, a one-bed sick ward and stores. A schoolroom was provided. The floors in the schoolroom were also flagged but mats were purchased to provide more comfort (Ripon Guardians' Minutes 4/9/1856). In the schoolroom, girls were instructed in sewing so as to provide them with a trade (Ripon Union Workhouse Master's Report Book 12/1890). The attempt to educate children in employable occupations illustrates the Ripon Guardians' attempts to eventually integrate this pauper class back into society. Accommodation for staff was also provided in this block, including a sitting room, a living room, two officer's bedrooms and a bathroom (Platt 1930, 26). A sitting room and a bedroom were provided for the schoolmistress, and before the addition of the infirmary, the nurse's bedroom was also located in the children's ward (Ripon Guardians' Minutes 12/10/1858; 3/3/1857). Placing staff in among the children enabled a high level of control over this area. Exercise yards specifically for the children were located around the children's block. By the 1890s, the girls' yard included a swing with a trapeze, whereas a football was provided for the boys (Ripon Union Workhouse Master's Report Book 12/1894).

The separate children's block enabled the complete segregation of children from adult paupers in terms of permanent accommodation (if not in practice), which reflects the Ripon Guardians' commitment to the removal of children from the presence of adults who could negatively impact their moral well-being. In one instance, the Ripon Guardians extended this philosophy even to an older child who was seen to rebel against the system and posed a moral danger to the other children. In 1859, the Ripon Guardians 'Ordered that Mary Ann Potts aged 14 years be placed in the class provided for able-bodied women in order to prevent her conduct and character having an injurious effect upon the inmates of the workhouse of her own class' (Ripon Guardians' Minutes 8/2/1859). This order illustrates how seriously Ripon Union took segregation. By separating children from other pauper classes, the Guardians sought to mould them into suitable citizens, which they hoped would reduce the rate of admissions by keeping them out of the workhouse as adults. From its formation, Ripon Union appears to have provided some extra amenities for the children of the workhouse. It was reported in 1883 that children were frequently taken on trips to the nearby picturesque Fountains Abbey by the local gentry and often received gifts of toys (Ripon Union Workhouse Master's Report Book 1883). In addition to helping poor children, this also provided the local gentry an opportunity to display their wealth and practise charity. Education was a priority for the Ripon Guardians, who appointed a resident schoolmistress for inmate children. The appointment of this schoolmistress was a matter of importance, reflected in the fact that in 1863, the Guardians interviewed twelve candidates for the position. They also took into consideration the advice of the region's School Inspector (Ripon Guardians' Minutes 24/2/1863). The appointment of a new schoolmistress in 1863 also closely followed the

Guardians' dismissal of another schoolmistress for a lack of efficiency and an inability to perform duties satisfactorily a year earlier (Ripon Guardians' Minutes 11/3/1862). Whether her care was deemed overly or insufficiently harsh is unclear, but her dismissal by the Guardians indicates that education and the proper treatment of children were very important to them. However, the Guardians' limited ability to control how staff behaved may be why the workhouse school closed in 1878 (Ripon Guardians' Minutes, cited in Chadwick 2008, 5).

At Ripon, education was even offered to older workhouse residents. William Harrison, for example, a boy of over 16, received instruction at Ripon Workhouse, which affirms the desire of the Union to provide younger inmates with the skills to seek employment (Ripon Guardians' Minutes 20/12/1859). When physically well, children were apprenticed out to local industries (Ripon Union Workhouse Master's Report Book 4/11/1883). A number of children received relief outside the workhouse. The value the Union placed on education was reiterated in the stipulation that out-relief children were required to attend school four days per week if the cost of their education was to be met by the Guardians (Ripon Guardians' Minutes 7/9/1859). The Union was careful, though, not to send children into education or employment unless they were in full health. In 1853, for example, inmate James Binns's half-brother requested that James be allowed to apprentice with him, but the request was denied by the Ripon Guardians due to James's poor health (Ripon Guardians' Minutes 8/3/1853; 5/5/1853). The Relieving Officer frequently ordered clothes for children in receipt of relief outside the workhouse, demonstrating a high level of care and paternalism towards the child paupers of his Union (Ripon Guardians' Minutes 5/5/1853). The Ripon Guardians provided children with out-relief to prevent them from having to enter the workhouse, keeping rates down and relieving the burden on accommodations within the workhouse. They also provided children with trades with the intention of ensuring that these pauper children would not have to rely on relief in their adult lives.

The separation of children from other inmates was just one level of subdivision and classification within the workhouse, though practice was not consistent across workhouses. The workhouse at Great Ouseburn, like other New Poor Law workhouses, was designed to segregate inmates based on gender, and often this was the only segregation that was in place. The further segregation of inmates by age or by health (for example) appears to have been limited. Documentary evidence sheds some light on this seeming disregard for the Poor Law Commission's recommendations for classification. The majority of inmates at Great Ouseburn were elderly or children. Despite the dissolution of the Gilbert Union with the creation of the New Poor Law Union, Great Ouseburn continued its traditional methods of relief, reserving the workhouse for those deemed most vulnerable. Like the elderly, children were afforded extra care and considered vulnerable. Elderly inmates and children were allowed to mix by the simpler workhouse design at rural Great Ouseburn. However, by 1899, the Great Ouseburn Guardians resolved to remove any elderly paupers who could not care for themselves properly to the workhouse (Great Ouseburn Guardians' Minutes 28/8/1899). Out relief continued to be granted to the able-bodied, illustrating the value placed on the family unit and the established belief that the able-bodied should not be in the workhouse. It would appear from the census records that the workhouse was never full, and the Guardians' Minutes indicate that out-relief was often offered.

The rural workhouse at Wetherby spatially separated children into the female sphere of responsibility. Located in the female wing, the children's accommodation at Wetherby Workhouse comprised two three-bed wards, one for girls and the other for boys (Platt 1930, 34). Under the previous Carlton Gilbert Union that administered Wetherby, the children were educated in the workhouse. In the Poor Law era, by the 1860s, there were a number of educational establishments in Wetherby, and the workhouse children attended the Church School (an Anglican establishment) in the town. A very public dispute over pauper children mixing with the children of the Church School highlights the stigma attached to pauperism within the Wetherby Union. The local, nonconformist Wesleyan School offered to educate the workhouse children instead, but its offer was dismissed, suggesting that – to some extent – the Guardians rejected religious nonconformity (Unwin 1987, 131–36). It was decided that the children would remain at the Church School, which illustrates the Poor Law Guardians' desire to integrate the children of the workhouse into society and to distance them socially and spatially from pauperism. The attendance at school by children whose parents were receiving out-relief was never contested, which indicates some social acceptability of relief outside of the workhouse.

In other Unions, however, separation by gender was the only classification within the workhouse, such that children and adults mixed. At Pateley Bridge Union, men and boys were reportedly sharing beds in the 1850s (Pateley Bridge Guardians' Minutes 21/8/1858). Not only did such circumstances reduce institutional control over inmates and leave vulnerable children open to violence and abuse, but the Local Government Board believed that children could be negatively influenced by adult paupers who did not uphold industrious values. This was a wider social discourse surrounding the pathologising of poverty, in which it was suggested that pauper attitudes could spread from idle adults to children like contagion, thus making more idle adults. The separation of children from adults was thus deemed paramount if poverty levels were to be reduced in the future. The Pateley Bridge workhouse was never used to relieve large numbers of children; the highest number to be recorded in a year was seven. Space was an issue, so inmate numbers were necessarily low. At Pateley Bridge, there were no separate exercise yards, a concern dismissed by the Guardians, who argued that in a small rural Union such as Pateley Bridge, 'There is not the same occasion for classification of adults and children of the same sexes as in larger Unions' (Pateley Bridge Guardians' Minutes 7/12/1861). Clearly the Guardians of Pateley Bridge did not see the need to apply the segregation rules outlined in the New Poor Law. Allowing inmates of different ages to mix within the workhouse suggests that, unlike other Unions, Pateley Bridge did not feel that pauperism was 'infectious' or that mixing adults and children would encourage immoral behaviour. The Guardians appear to have believed that such rules were only applicable in larger urban Unions where poverty and pauperism had a different meaning and a different perceived cause. The Guardians reported repeatedly that they did not have the funds to build a more extensive workhouse in order to more effectively segregate inmates and that such a workhouse was, in the first place, an unnecessary expense. Correspondingly, they consistently voted against the construction of a new building. This was not dissimilar to neighbouring Unions, including Ripon, Great Ouseburn and Wetherby, where workhouses were built much later than originally intended by the New Poor Law. However, these areas were more rapid to unionise than Pateley Bridge, building new workhouse buildings just after they had adopted the 1834 Poor Laws. In contrast, it took the Pateley Bridge Guardians twenty-five years after they had adopted the New Poor Law to agree on a new workhouse building. Practices at Pateley Bridge differed significantly from those at other Unions and were far less rigidly adhered to. For example, in 1903, local resident Mr Casmey rented a portion of the building. Casmey occupied two rooms in the basement, one on the ground floor and two on the first. He made a number of alterations to the internal plan, including the conversion of the original dining room to an elementary school for local children (Platt 1930). In other areas of West Yorkshire, these facilities would have been provided by the Poor Law Union. A local charity providing schooling for the children is another example of the Union keeping the rates down by relying on local philanthropy, a tradition long embedded in the region and, before the New Poor Law, part of the Gilbert Union's makeshift and disparate approach to poverty relief. Children were sent to schools, such as the Leeds Moral and Industrial Training School, or orphanages, or they were apprenticed, if possible.

In the outer-urban Union of Bramley, which opted for a mixed workhouse building in which all classifications of inmate were accommodated, children, the elderly and the able-bodied were separated into different areas of the same building. They were also further segregated according to gender. In terms of treatment, there does seem to have been some differential treatment afforded to children, with a few exceptions. On one occasion in the 1920s, children received ice cream sandwiches from the female Guardians (Bramley Guardians' Minutes 29/9/1924), but such gifts were not frequent. In the majority of the West Yorkshire Unions, gifts were presented to the workhouse by the local, affluent middle and upper classes. The comparatively small number of gifts received at Bramley may reflect the working-class demographics of outer Leeds, a sprawling northern industrial city. By the end of the Poor Law era, many West Yorkshire workhouses had developed substantial specialised facilities for certain pauper classes including children. Some workhouses had entirely removed children from the workhouse by the end of the nineteenth century, for instance, but Bramley Union had not. There were some accommodations made with other institutions in the local area, however. At Bramley, local children's homes accommodated some pauper children, but many remained in the workhouse (Bramley Guardians' Minutes 6/8/1924).

Sometimes the difference between workhouses in the management of children was in treatment. At North Bierley Union, like the elderly class of inmate, workhouse children were permitted privileges not granted to the able-bodied. Entertainments that children partook in included trips to Morecambe Bay by rail, attendance of the Royal Yorkshire Jubilee and visits to the pantomime, among others (North Bierley Guardians' Minutes 18/8/1864; 26/10/1887; 2/1/1901). In the workhouse, children were provided with toys (North Bierley Guardians' Minutes 15/8/1888).

Like those in many West Yorkshire workhouses, the children of North Bierley Workhouse were educated to improve their employability, so that they could contribute meaningfully to society and not continue a cycle of poverty. The children at the nearby urban workhouse of Bradford were educated in the workhouse, whereas the children in North Bierley Workhouse were generally sent to the local school (North Bierley Guardians' Minutes 1/3/1850; 29/8/1888; 18/10/1893). The Union also appointed a schoolmistress (North Bierley Guardians' Minutes 9/2/1860) for children unable to attend school for any reason, but Browne, a visiting inspector, regarded this provision as 'amounting to nothing', suggesting that he considered in-house education facilities negligible (Ashworth 1982, 94). Finding the children employment remained the Guardians' priority. Boys were apprenticed at the age of 10 if they passed their exams and otherwise at age 14 (North Bierley Guardians' Minutes 3/2/1886; 26/9/1888). The 1870 Education Act made provision for the establishment of School Boards across England, which would oversee the construction of schools where they were necessary, while also supporting voluntary schools established by religious denominations. In 1893, the Guardians transferred the children who had been attending local schools to Clayton Board School (North Bierley Guardians' Minutes 18/10/1893).

By the end of the nineteenth century, the North Bierley Guardians were enquiring into alternative accommodation for children, looking to remove them from the workhouse. Like attitudes towards the elderly, attitudes towards children had evolved at North Bierley. This was in tune with the treatment of children at other nearby workhouses like Bradford. The Guardians' Minutes record instances of children boarding out in the local community (North Bierley Guardians' Minutes 11/10/1899). In 1911, the Guardians decided to provide separate facilities for workhouse children, but unlike the Bradford and Leeds Guardians, who opted to remove children from the workhouse site entirely, the North Bierley Guardians just removed children from the main workhouse building to a separate block on site (North Bierley Guardians' Minutes 25/10/1911).

By the start of the twentieth century and in line with general practice elsewhere, North Bierley Union provided a separate facility for the treatment of children. In North Bierley, plans for a children's home resulted from the evolution of attitudes towards the accommodation of child paupers around the turn of the century. The home, for which plans were drawn up in 1911, was located south-west of the workhouse site, away from the main workhouse and materially separating its inhabitants from the mainstream workhouse population.

Initially the children's home at North Bierley was intended simply to remove children from the main workhouse building, but as the overall focus of the workhouse site shifted towards treatment of the sick, the focus of the children's home shifted as well. As more and more children were boarded out or apprenticed, on-site facilities for children became increasingly devoted to serving the sick. Platt reported that the building had, by 1930, been designated a hospital. He further noted that it was 'occupied almost entirely by Mental Defective children' (Platt 1930, 53). The children's hospital was the on-site facility best equipped for the care of children who required special attention, and their long-term accommodation in the building likely resulted from the permanence of their condition. Consequently, sick children who were not mentally ill were likely accommodated in the general infirmaries.

North Bierley's Children's Hospital is the only documented facility examined as part of this book that was designated predominantly for children with mental disorders. The building's name – the Children's Hospital – does not accurately reflect its use, which calls into question the actual use of other children's facilities on workhouse sites in the region.

Platt's record is the only indication that North Bierley's children's home was devoted to children with mental infirmities. None of the other urban or outer-urban workhouses in the West Yorkshire area are included in Platt's 1930 survey because they were all infirmaries by the end of the Poor Law era, so it remains unknown where and how the mentally ill children of other Unions were accommodated. The majority of the North Bierley Children's Hospital building was single-storey. Staff rooms included a scullery, storeroom, duty room and larder. Accommodation included a thirteen-cot ward, a fourteen-cot ward with an open veranda, a sixteen-bed ward and several bathrooms, all of which featured wooden floors and central heating. Provisions for children outside of the wards included a day room with a flagged floor and an open fireplace. Since the abolition of the Poor Laws, the Children's Hospital has been demolished.

The rural and outer-urban workhouses in Yorkshire took their cues on practice and facilities from the larger unions like Leeds and Bradford. The Leeds Moral and Industrial Training School was an institution constructed by the Poor Law Union that evidenced the Leeds Guardians' commitment to educating children. Pulling children from what was seen as a cycle of poverty was a singular concern among lawmakers and reformers alike in the New Poor Law era (Hulonce 2016). The Leeds Moral and Industrial Training School was constructed in 1848. Its construction at this early date indicates that the Leeds Guardians intended to prevent poverty and improve the lives of child paupers from this early stage. Although the Poor Laws prioritised the treatment of able-bodied adult paupers, Leeds Guardians clearly defied this legislation by prioritising new buildings for the education of pauper children. The construction of industrial schools was not common; however, other northern cities, such as Manchester and Liverpool, also constructed pauper schools in the 1840s (Morrison 1999, 138). It seems that paternalistic attitudes towards pauper children were more pronounced in northern industrial cities where poor living and working conditions increased the numbers of pauper children. London had its own system of education for poor children from the 1870s, with the establishment of the London School Board, which provided primary education for working-class and poor children (Weiner 1994, 28). This led to a proliferation of schools in London at the time, many in ornate Queen Anne Revival style to reflect domestic middle-class architecture of the period (ibid., 86). The northern cities had no such cohesive system of education, and thus it fell to Poor Law Unions like Leeds to devise education solutions for poor children.

The Leeds Guardians believed it was their responsibility to educate pauper children to prevent those who 'might otherwise become prey of the abandoned and the profligate' (Pennock 1986, 134). The Industrial Schools

Act of 1857, which enabled magistrates to remove problem children to industrial schools across England, challenged the general principles on which the Leeds Moral and Industrial Training School was based. The Leeds Guardians rejected the Act as it was 'injurious to the spirit of the school' (Leeds Guardians' Minutes 15/5/1857). The refusal of the Guardians and the Industrial School to accept the Act demonstrates not only the limited power of the authorities over the Guardians, but also the considered importance of separating children from pauperism.

The design of the Industrial School was crucial in conveying the Guardians' attitudes and values (see Figure 4.1). The Guardians used the exterior and interior design of the school 'to banish from the minds of the inmates all idea that the institution partakes in any degree of the character of the workhouse' (*Leeds Intelligencer*, 17 Oct 1846). The school was designed by William Perkin and Elisha Backhouse, who also designed Ripon Workhouse and Leeds Prison, in similar styles. The exterior of the school conveys both the paternalistic attitude of the Guardians towards poor children and the corresponding civic importance of education. Its external appearance was intended to assert the civic pride of the city. In contrast to the classical, utilitarian style of contemporary workhouse buildings, the school

Figure 4.1. Leeds Moral and Industrial Training School, north-east elevation (photographed by Charlotte Newman).

adopted a grand Elizabethan (or Jacobean) style evoking images of earlier charitable institutions and reflecting a greater attention to ornamentation and aesthetics. The building's exterior style aimed to inspire civic order and improvement through its architectural detail. The three-storey building was constructed of red brick with stone detailing and had a Welsh slate roof. The main entrance was through an arched doorway surmounted by a fanlight in the central block in the east elevation. Above the entrance a stone reading 'Moral and Industrial Training School 1848' was set into the façade. The school's name clearly states the Guardians' principles. A three-storey, sixteen-pane window above the entrance provided light to the stairwell beyond. Three-storey bay windows either side of the entrance were flanked by stone, octagonal turrets and were surmounted by Dutch gables. Either side of the central block was a nine-bay wing. Like the central block, the end bay of both wings was set with bay windows, octagonal turrets and Dutch gables, which feature a small window light. Seven of the eight bays had windows with stone surrounds. One bay differed slightly, featuring a rounded French-styled window, which would have provided access to balconies that have since been removed. Some windows featured stained glass, presumably dating from the 1930s as they were not in the original design. A parapet along the roofline centred on a Dutch gable over the fifth bay. Ornamental ridge tiles capped the roof, which featured four chimneys of varying date for each wing.

Numerous modern additions to the south elevation obscure the original fenestration. Additions included a footbridge from the second storey to a new building. The style of the west elevation has been simplified, although the windows still featured stone surrounds at the time of survey. The south end of the elevation has been rendered, which conceals the original fabric and alterations. However, the numerous window styles and sizes used in this elevation suggest that many alterations have been made. The north end of the elevation features modern additions, which also obscure much of the original fabric. Like the south elevation, the north elevation features three bays and windows with stone surrounds. Although the main elevation retains its original appearance, modern additions have clearly altered the appearance of the other elevations and the central range and rear building have been demolished. A date-stone (1904) signifies the beginning of these alterations, when much of the school was converted for use as an infirmary (as discussed in Chapter 1).

The interior plan of Leeds Moral and Industrial Training School was designed to reflect the Guardians' priorities in educating children and in turn shaped the day-to-day experience of the children (see Figure 4.2). Originally the building conformed to a courtyard plan with a central range. The plan of the building reflected the importance of segregation by gender

98 • Poverty Archaeology

Leeds Moral and Industrial Training School

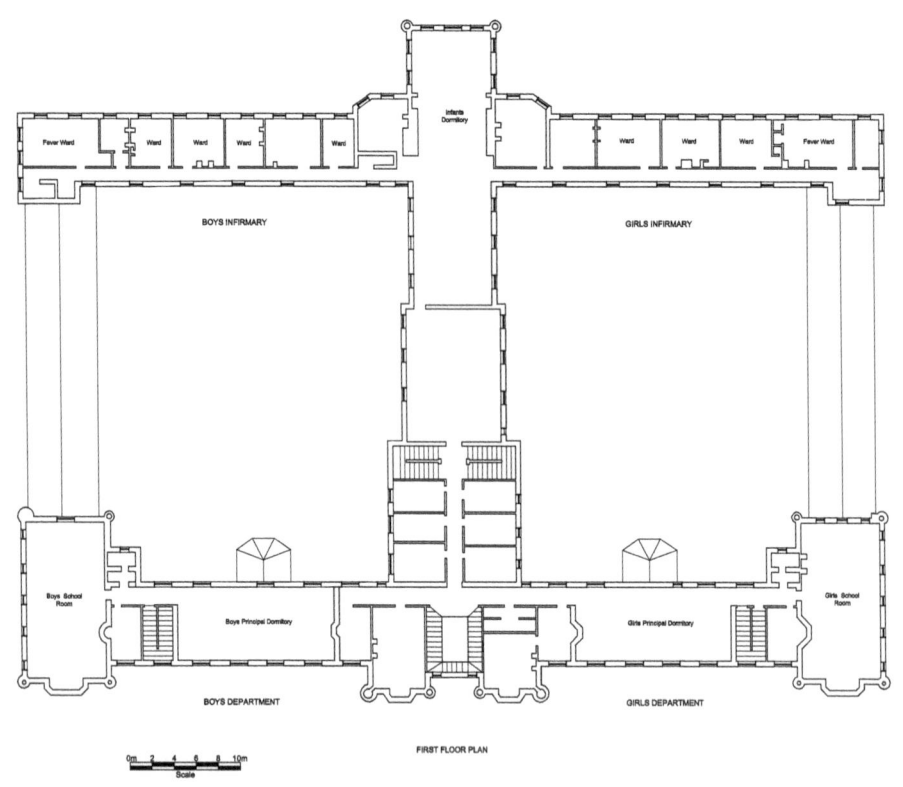

Figure 4.2. Leeds Moral and Industrial Training School, ground- and first-floor plans (digitised by Charlotte Newman).

to the Guardians. The boys were located in the north wing and girls in the south wing. The allocation of rooms indicates further segregation based on age. The children were divided into the following age groups: 2 to 6 years, 6 to 10 years and 10 to 16 years (Pennock 1986, 138). However, the census records indicate that some female inmates remained in the school for longer. These inmates who remained may have helped with the care of younger children when work was not found for them elsewhere. Allowing inmates to remain at the school illustrates the Guardians' desire to prevent their return to pauperism (which would result in them becoming a further burden on the state as adults).

The placement and accommodation of staff at Leeds Moral and Industrial Training School contributed to reinforcing the Guardians' authority in the institution. Staff numbers fluctuated over the years, but generally the

Guardians employed a master, matron, nurse, porter, cook, servant, laundress, seamstress and a number of teachers. As at Skipton Union Workhouse, the master occupied the central area. This arrangement created an authority laden symbolic barrier that maintained segregation and control over the children. The master was allocated an office and a sitting room, suggesting that he received visitors and socialised in the school. The teachers' common room and stairs to the first floor were also located in the central block. The centrality of staff within the building facilitated access throughout the school. Employing effective staff at the school appears to have been a continual problem for the Guardians. Poor pay and demanding conditions drove staff to desperate measures, but also resulted in neglect of their duties. The first three masters were dismissed for drunkenness, fighting and generally ineffective behaviour (Pennock 1986, 140). Teachers were also reprimanded for beating children and drunkenness. Staff turnover was high, and the Guardians' Minutes report staff dismissals on several occasions (Leeds Guardians' Minutes 28/10/1863; 27/4/1892).

Religion appears to have been a crucial part of the children's education and daily routine. The school chapel was located in the central block, and a chaplain was immediately appointed for the chapel after the school's opening (Leeds Guardians' Minutes 7/6/1848). Examples of religion in the children's daily routine included the ringing of the six o'clock bell every evening to signal boys to prayer and hymn recital. Such activities were overseen by the school staff, and if the children were well behaved, they would be given a Bible. Religious activities were not just observed in the chapel but also in the dormitories, presumably because the chapel was too small. There is little indication that children attended the workhouse chapel once it was constructed, which suggests that strict segregation was maintained between the school and the workhouse site. Provisions were also made for non-Anglican children. Catholic children were sent to St Mary's Orphanage, suggesting that the Guardians respected the differing religious needs of the children (Leeds Guardians' Minutes 9/8/1871). Working together with a religious institution also relieved some of the state's burden of support.

The children in the school spent the majority of their time in the wings of the building. Although the wings of the main block were similar in plan, room use differed. The ground floor of the girls' wing featured a clothing store, a bathroom and a day room where they would have undertaken activities such as sewing. The ground floor of the boy's wing also featured a day room and bathroom, but other rooms included a dairy and larder. The day rooms were a particularly contentious issue among staff, as having over one hundred boys occupying a room for several hours resulted in a foul odour that staff argued was not good for their health. Each wing featured a separate staircase, which provided access to the first floor and second floors (Pennock 1986, 169). Facilities on the second floor included dormitories for boys and two for girls. Each dormitory had a room for a teacher, which allowed thorough surveillance and control of the children. Each wing had a toilet. The stores were located in the central area between the wings.

The Leeds Guardians' enthusiasm for education is reflected in the educational facilities they provided. Elementary education was provided in the schoolrooms located on the first floor. Schooling reportedly took place in the morning. Rooms featured equipment such as maps and books, including the *History of England* (Leeds Guardians' Minutes 27/10/1857). Some children were part of the school band, which occasionally performed for audiences outside of the school, and were permitted to attend concerts. By 1880, many Unions were choosing to send pauper children to the local Board Schools, which reduced costs and integrated the children into society. Leeds Guardians followed this trend, and the children remaining in the Industrial School were sent to the local Board School (Pennock 1986, 144). The Guardians aimed to conceal the children's pauper identity through the provision of everyday clothing and by allowing the children to walk themselves to school (Humble, cited in Leeds Guardians' Minutes 22/7/1885).

The central range connected the main block to the rear block. The kitchen, scullery, dining hall and infants' schoolroom were located within the central range. The kitchen and dining facilities reveal further acts of defiance against the stringent recommendations of the New Poor Law. The children's diet of American pickled pork was reportedly unauthorised by the Local Government Board (Leeds Guardians' Minutes 24/9/1873). The Guardians appear to have cared little for many of the Poor Law Commission's recommendations, and intervention from central government later was not appreciated. As Guardians, they took their paternalistic role and civic duties very seriously, believing they knew what was best for the children.

Education also involved outdoor and extracurricular activities, privileges not enjoyed by other inmates or poor children outside Leeds Moral and Industrial Training School. The range divided the playground between the two blocks, dividing the boys' and girls' exercise yards. The outer walls of the courtyard plan created a covered walkway, so the children could exercise in the rain. Exercise was evidently an important aspect of the children's daily routine and included activities such as cricket (Leeds Guardians' Minutes 24/5/1871). The children were taken on extended walks outside of the school twice a week. Allowing children out of the school reiterated the Guardians' attitude of disassociating the school with the workhouse; the children were not to be regarded as inmates, or at least not in the same way as the denizens of the workhouse proper. As the school became more established, further trips were organised to places such as Harewood House and the theatre (Leeds Guardians' Minutes 31/12/1873). Education clearly went beyond that delivered in the school, and the children would have greatly benefited from these experiences, which many poor children in Leeds never had. In 1922, the children were permitted to attend a holiday camp for pauper children (Leeds Guardians' Minutes 10/5/1922). Facilities for the children under the New Poor Law improved greatly in comparison to those provided for other pauper classes. However, reports of the children's outings in the Guardians' Minutes reveal that control over the children was not always maintained. On several occasions reports were made to the Guardians of the children's poor behaviour on excursions. The moral education provided by the school clearly broke down on these occasions in acts of rebellion by the children against the values of the school. Evidently the children did not always consider themselves as having any kind of privileged position within the workhouse.

The two-storey rear block of the courtyard plan featured rooms for the infants and workrooms where the children took part in industrial activities. The central area, which divided the boys' and girls' wings, was used as an infant schoolroom and day room. Separating the infants from the other children protected the 'innocent' from the influence of the older children. The master and mistress's sitting rooms were also located in this area. Separate staff for this class of children also provided them with extra care, as there were never many children of this class resident in the school. The ground-floor wings of the rear block were used for the industrial training of the children, which aimed to promote future employability and ensure that they would not become burdens on the Union into adulthood. The majority of the girls' wing was used as a washhouse, preparing them for work in laundries. Laundry work was one of the avenues of employment open to women of this social class. Women were also employed largely in domestic service. By the end of the nineteenth century, there were nearly 1.8 million women working as domestic servants in England (Goose 2007, 9). As such, girls in the Leeds Workhouse were prepared to enter this growing occupation. To facilitate their training, the girls participated in domestic duties around the school, and sewing. These skills enabled many girls to work in services once of age to gain employment. A shoemaking workshop and a tailor's workshop, as well as a bakehouse and a flour store that could also be used as workshops, were located in the boys' wing. Industrial training for the boys was more diverse, reflecting the wider employment opportunities available to them, and provided them with skills to enter many trades in Leeds. The Leeds Guardians' Minutes frequently mention the apprenticeship of children. The Guardians continued to monitor the children once they were apprenticed, suggesting that the well-being of the children was more important than providing a living.

The health of the children was also a priority for the Guardians. An infirmary was located on the first floor of the rear wing. The workhouse employed qualified nurses to staff the infirmary, suggesting that the Guardians demanded a high quality of care for sick children. Outbreaks of sickness were damaging to other children and the reputation of the school. One Guardian even rented private lodgings for children outside the city, which improved recovery, whereas children with specific mental illnesses were sent to specialised institutions (Pennock 1986, 141). Improvements were also made to the building. For example, stone flags were replaced with boards to prevent the children developing chilblains (Allen papers, cited in Pennock 1986, 169). Changes to the interior of the building suggest that health was considered key to the success of the school.

The removal of children from the Industrial School to other facilities was gradual at Leeds, likely due to the comprehensive educational provision that was already available at the workhouse. As in neighbouring Unions, apprenticeships were sought. In some cases, children were sent to Canada, and others entered the scattered home scheme. In 1883, the expansion of infirmary facilities incorporated parts of the Industrial School's rear block. Further expansion in 1887 meant that the number of children in the institution halved and the remaining children were housed in the main building of the school (Leeds Guardians' Minutes 25/7/1888). Plans to modernise the infirmaries' facilities meant that in 1902 the entire school was converted into an infirmary, and the remaining eighty-seven children left the workhouse for the newly opened Roundhay Children's Home. In keeping with the initial intentions of the Industrial School, the Leeds Guardians sought to completely disassociate the children from the Poor Law institution.

At Bradford, provision was less comprehensive, reflecting inconsistency even in this small geographical area. Although workhouse inmates were strictly segregated by class, the basic classification system failed to account for the complexities of pauper identity. Some paupers met the criteria for more than one class of inmate, which complicated the enforcement of segregation, even of children from the rest of the population. The Bradford Guardians' Minutes report one occasion on which a boy was found in the men's dormitory (Bradford Guardians' Minutes 21/7/1869). Although his age classified him as a child, his occupation as a shoemaker prior to entry into the workhouse also put him into the category of an able-bodied worker. The Guardians ruled that his presence in the able-bodied ward was not appropriate, reinforcing the illusory distinction between childhood innocence and able-bodied labour, a hypocritical gesture in the context of an industrial city that relied heavily on child labour.

The treatment of children in Bradford reflects their privileged status among paupers. Like other West Yorkshire workhouses, Bradford endeavoured to maintain workhouse children's health. Healthy children were less likely to incur additional expense and more likely to leave the workhouse employable. The medical officer was permitted to alter the children's diets to improve their health, and the Guardians ordered extra bathtubs for the children's wards to ensure hygiene and cleanliness (Bradford Guardians' Minutes 6/6/1855; 27/6/1855; 3/10/1855). In addition, in keeping with regional trends, Bradford removed children from the workhouse whenever possible, either through adoption, emigration, apprenticeship, transfer or out-relief. On one occasion, the Guardians financed the removal of a blind child to a designated facility, and the minutes record several cases of children leaving the workhouse to start apprenticeships in the textile and ironworking industries (Bradford Guardians' Minutes 11/6/1852; 15/2/1839; 11/10/1839; 5/7/1854; 30/8/1854).

Children's workhouse experiences were characterised primarily by education. Ashworth (1982) describes the Poor Law era education of workhouse children in Bradford as a drastic improvement upon the limited instruction they received in workhouses of the old Poor Laws. Though it was not as spatially specialised as the school at Leeds, there was a commitment to education at the Bradford Union. The Guardians employed a schoolmaster and schoolmistress to teach the children subjects including history and geography. The quality of teaching was improved through the 1850s with the purchase of books and maps for the schoolroom (Bradford Guardians' Minutes 4/11/1853; 22/11/1854). Soon after the opening of the workhouse in the 1850s, inspector of schools Thomas Browne recorded 'good schools in the workhouse for both boys and girls' (Anderson 1980, 94). Unlike their attitude towards other pauper classes, the Bradford Guardians' attitude towards children was progressive. Although the Poor Laws dictated that workhouse conditions should be inferior to those of the poorest labourer outside the workhouse, Bradford Guardians did not apply this guideline to education or children. In many cases, before the 1870 Education Act workhouse children received better education than the independent poor (ibid.). From 1885, the Guardians employed an industrial trainer intended to improve the employability of workhouse children on their departure from the workhouse (Bradford Guardians' Minutes 9/9/1885; 9/12/1885). Despite this and other educational and industrial-training measures, Bradford's facilities for children remained inferior to those offered at the purpose-built industrial school at neighbouring Leeds

Workhouse. Bradford's unstable early nineteenth-century economy rendered such a facility unfeasible.

Discussion

The location of buildings and the accommodation of inmate classes within the Ripon Union workhouse complex reflects a more charitable and generous attitude towards certain inmates, which created a hierarchy of care and control within the institution. For example, the children's block was located furthest from the entrance, away from the 'detrimental' influence of the adult paupers and vagrants. The children's accommodation was reportedly of a better standard, featuring wooden floors throughout, and they were provided with a schoolmistress, indicating that their education was a priority. By 1930, staff accommodation was located in the children's ward. The close proximity of staff to children may indicate the superior care and control intended for this pauper class. Furthermore, documentary evidence shows that children received relief outside the workhouse, an indication that the Guardians sought to spare them the stigma of pauperism associated with entry into the workhouse.

From the outset, urban Unions endeavoured to be more specialised. Leeds Union opted to construct specialised facilities for the accommodation of children. Unlike other West Yorkshire Unions, in which the first New Poor Law building was a general workhouse, Leeds constructed an industrial school, Leeds Moral and Industrial Training School, before a general workhouse. Leeds's decision to distinguish between children, who were deemed deserving, and other paupers so early in its application of the New Poor Laws created a distinct hierarchy among recipients of relief, one that became more complex in later phases. The construction of Leeds Moral and Industrial Training School offered children the chance to improve their lives through work, education and the removal of poverty's perceived negative, immoral and contagious influences and stigma. The reformative and preventative goals of the institution illustrate the value placed on removing paupers from the Poor Law workhouse system in the long term and the overriding ambition to promote the civic order and pride of Leeds as a rapidly developing industrial city. These aims are reflected in the geographical location and architectural style of Leeds Moral and Industrial Training School. Typical of early Poor Law institutions, the Industrial School was positioned away from the centre of town but in a prominent area of the city, next to the corporation graveyard. Its grand, Elizabethan style reflected the Guardians' aspirations of civic pride and paternalism. Like other nineteenth-century workhouse buildings, Leeds

Moral and Industrial Training School adopted a courtyard plan, which promoted segregation by age and gender. The plan also facilitated education, religion and industrial activity, illustrating the importance of morality, civic order and work ethic to the Guardians.

At the same time, an outer-urban institution like the North Bierley workhouse differed in subtle but meaningful ways from its fellow outer-city workhouses. It lacked the facility for the elderly provided at Wharfedale Union and featured a designated building for children, unlike either Wharfedale or Bramley. In its unique use of a T-shaped plan and its unique interpretation of national guidelines, it affirms the regional difference traced throughout this book and undermines the validity of broad, general typologies for understanding workhouse buildings.

Children in West Yorkshire Poor Law workhouses received more specialised treatment than other pauper classes. In most instances, the Guardians employed schemes to remove children from the workhouse and the New Poor Law system. Education was regarded as fundamental to a child's successful future. Uniquely among the case studies, Leeds built an industrial school, which removed children from the workhouse. This institutional facility provided education and industrial training, which aimed to prevent long-term pauperism. The efforts of the Leeds Guardians to invest in the education of children reveals that they fought strongly against the more stringent aspects of the New Poor Laws, to remove children from the perceived negative influences of pauperism. The Guardians' rejection of the Industrial Schools Act, which would have allowed criminal children into the Industrial School, confirms their paternalistic attitude towards poor children, whose treatment reflected an outlook that suggested that poverty was their circumstance but not their fault. The Guardians acted to prevent criminal children from contaminating the perceived morality of the institution. The Leeds Moral and Industrial Training School's architectural design arguably inspired civic order and ideas of social improvement, which attracted the support of neighbouring rural Unions, who occasionally opted to send suitable children to the school. Still, it is important to note that despite the innovation of the Leeds Guardians in providing an industrial school, facilities were far from perfect. Overcrowding, poor staffing and rebellious behaviour plagued the institution, and facilities were constantly being reassessed and improved.

Despite the lack of an industrial school in other urban and outer-city workhouses discussed here, schooling and education featured significantly in the children's workhouse routine more broadly. In fact, workhouse children received a better education than many non-workhouse children, who often worked in the local factories of industrialising towns and did not frequently attend school. In Bradford, for example, the Guardians' Minutes note that workhouse children were probably receiving a better education than their counterparts outside the workhouse. Ultimately, Bradford, Bramley and North Bierley aspired to aims similar to those of Leeds and, accordingly, appointed schoolmistresses. Like Leeds's, Bradford's Guardians also appointed an industrial trainer, which was a preventative measure against long-term poverty. Despite the lack of specialised facilities for children, poor children in Bradford's urban areas received significantly better education than they had prior to the New Poor Law. The increasing number of specialised teaching staff at Bradford suggests that the prioritisation of education increased over the course of the Poor Law era. The economic constraints of outer-city workhouses are again reflected in the educational provisions offered by such workhouses for pauper children. Although the Guardians employed schoolmistresses and sent suitable children to the local school, at times school inspectors found provisions negligible, especially at North Bierley.

Like the urban examples, Skipton, Ripon, Great Ouseburn, Wetherby and Pateley Bridge all appointed a schoolmistress at some point. Schoolmistresses provided children with an education and a higher level of personal care than other workhouse inmates received. In addition to the employment of a schoolmistress, at Great Ouseburn, Wetherby and Ripon, children also attended the local school, were apprenticed or were sent to specialised institutions, such as Leeds Moral and Industrial Training School. Such provisions had always been available in some rural areas, such as Ripon, Great Ouseburn and Pateley Bridge. The tradition of providing education for the poor emerged from rural charities and the priorities of Gilbert Unions, which were well established in rural regions under the old Poor Laws. Post-1834 Poor Laws' educational schemes illustrate the continued importance placed on integrating children into society and making them self-sufficient so as not to perpetuate the cycle of poverty. Ultimately, education aimed to remove the stigma of pauperism from this pauper class and to present them to society as worthy individuals.

Children were further distinguished from other pauper classes in the way they were treated in the workhouse. In urban and rural workhouses, children received special treats, such as toys, and went on excursions away from the workhouse. Some Union workhouses note instances of children receiving specialised healthcare. At Leeds Moral and Industrial Training School, children were allocated a specialised infirmary within the school. At Bradford, the medical officer was permitted to alter children's diets to improve their health and order extra bathtubs to improve hygiene. Examples of specialised medical attention for children are also noted in some of the rural case studies, where documentary evidence records children leaving the workhouse to received specialised healthcare. For example, Great

Ouseburn's children went to Harrogate to see the dentist. By maintaining the children's health, the Guardians rendered them more employable. High standards of physical wellness thus advanced the institution's aim of preventing long-term pauperism.

Although children in need of extra care or attention are relatively invisible in workhouse architecture and are frequently generalised under terms like 'defective' in the historical record, the interdisciplinary approach to the urban workhouse offered here illuminates the ways in which children with mental or physical impairments were managed spatially in the workhouse. In addition to providing a children's infirmary, Leeds provided specialised facilities (a rented holiday cottage) for mentally ill children. North Bierley's children block, built in 1911, provides the only other example of specialised facilities for mentally ill children. This research raises questions regarding the treatment of the mentally ill and their presence in the workhouse more generally that beg further research. However, the available evidence suggests that, when necessary, the Guardians provided separate facilities for these children, acknowledging their increased needs and vulnerability. Separating the children from the mainstream workhouse population also prevented the 'moral contamination' of children and the disruption of order in the workhouse.

Although there were similarities in the treatment of children among rural and urban West Yorkshire workhouses, children's accommodation also varied widely from one Union to the next. As previously discussed, children at the Leeds Union were not accommodated in the workhouse. Instead, they entered Leeds Moral and Industrial Training School and were eventually transferred to a children's home located away from the workhouse site. In contrast, in Bradford, North Bierley and Bramley, children were initially accommodated in the main workhouse building. Eventually, all three workhouses devised schemes to remove children from the workhouse. At Bradford, children's homes were erected throughout the city, and a specialised children's home was constructed for 'delicate children'. However, despite the attempt to introduce such schemes at outer-urban workhouses, outer-urban children remained in the workhouse until the end of the Poor Law era. This is yet another indicator of the economic constraints facing the Guardians of outer-urban workhouses.

Accommodation for workhouse children in rural areas varied to a greater extent than in urban areas, possibly due to greater variation between Unions in terms of economy, culture and embedded traditions of makeshifts and charity carried over from the time of the old Poor Laws. Ripon, for example, was the only workhouse to provide separate accommodation for children in the initial workhouse design, reflecting the Union's paternalistic nature and accurate expectations of pauper need. Similarly, at Great Ouseburn, high-quality, more comfortable accommodation was reserved for the children. This is likely due to the Union's previous Gilbert Union status. Developing New Poor Law ideals in Skipton led to the construction of a separate block in 1928, much later than in surrounding Unions.

During the later years of the Poor Law era, rural workhouses found children alternative accommodation to the workhouse whenever possible. Examples of children boarding out or emigrating are found at all Unions addressed here. Children's removal from the workhouse was a priority for all Unions, and very few children resided in workhouses at the end of the Poor Law era.

Chapter 5

The Mad

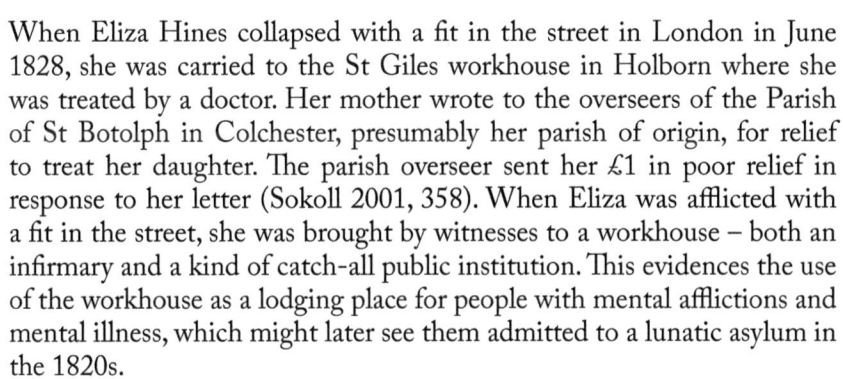

When Eliza Hines collapsed with a fit in the street in London in June 1828, she was carried to the St Giles workhouse in Holborn where she was treated by a doctor. Her mother wrote to the overseers of the Parish of St Botolph in Colchester, presumably her parish of origin, for relief to treat her daughter. The parish overseer sent her £1 in poor relief in response to her letter (Sokoll 2001, 358). When Eliza was afflicted with a fit in the street, she was brought by witnesses to a workhouse – both an infirmary and a kind of catch-all public institution. This evidences the use of the workhouse as a lodging place for people with mental afflictions and mental illness, which might later see them admitted to a lunatic asylum in the 1820s.

As a discrete class of pauper, for whom the public lunatic asylum was not an option due to the chronic nature of their condition or for other reasons, lunatics were common enough in workhouses before the New Poor Law to warrant their separate classification and housing. This chapter will examine the spaces dedicated to lunatics in the workhouses, focusing first on rural workhouses before going on to discuss in detail two urban Unions and their responses to demand to accommodate lunatic inmates. These examples are both typical of and distinctive in the care and management of the lunatic class of pauper. Leeds and Bradford, two industrial cities in West Yorkshire, were heavily industrialised in the second half of the nineteenth century, and were cities where most of the population was poor, while the pauper class were distinctive in their extreme poverty. The cities were served by two county lunatic asylums by the end of the nineteenth century, and even so, both Poor Law Unions were compelled to provide dedicated, separate accommodations for lunatic inmates. Their two Unions, despite being very close geographically and similar in terms of the populations they served, were quite different in their approaches.

Poverty and Mental Illness Before and After the New Poor Law

The poor, along with the criminal, the sick and the insane, were social categorisations subject to mass institutionalisation by the middle of the nineteenth century. The discourse of social malleability and 'improvement' that predominated in the nineteenth century resulted in the development and construction en masse of dedicated building types for control and reform (Tarlow 2007, 136). Poverty, as a social problem, could be managed; lunacy, as a social problem, could be managed in the same way. That this process of management frequently occurred in the same place is not coincidental. Peter Bartlett (1999, 32) argues that lunacy and poverty were inextricably linked in the nineteenth century, stating that the roots of asylum reform were in the Old Poor Law, and that 'throughout the nineteenth century [the asylum] remained an institution directed towards the poor'. A not-inconsiderable proportion of the workhouse population of England in the mid-nineteenth century was comprised of 'lunatics' and 'idiots', catch-all categories for anyone with mental illness. Before public asylums were widespread across the English landscape (from the late 1840s onwards), workhouses were a cheaper solution to housing pauper lunatics considered non-dangerous (Smith 2013, 107) or with chronic conditions. Workhouses, despite intentions regarding their use for short-term relief of the poor specifically, succumbed to the process that Foucault discussed as 'confinement' – a workhouse became an 'amalgam of heterogenous elements' (Foucault 2001, 41).

There is already significant established scholarship on this inmate category in workhouses (see, for example, Driver 1993). What this chapter contributes to that existing scholarship is a regional view, focused on the material spaces of the workhouses themselves. Indeed, regionality in the actions of Guardians with regard to lunatics in their charge has underpinned reassessments of the history of the Poor Law system, a notable example being Forsythe et al.'s (1996) study of the Devon Asylum and its relationship to the local Poor Law Union. The high regionality in the administration of the Poor Law extended to the buildings themselves and is evident in their architecture. Given the significant regionality in the architecture and organisation of workhouse spaces, this regional approach will shed light on how individual institutions responded to the accommodation of inmate classifications for which they were not conceived to handle.

Dedicated wings and dormitories for lunatics were commonplace in workhouses before the New Poor Law and were eventually incorporated into those constructed after the 1830s. The New Poor Law formalised the confinement of lunatics in workhouses 'licensed' for their reception and provided for their confinement in workhouses that were also serving as county lunatic asylums. However, the law was very clear that no 'dangerous lunatic, insane person, or idiot' be detained at a workhouse for longer than two weeks (Poor Law Amendment Act 1834, n.45). As Felix Driver (2004, 106–7) argued in *Power and Pauperism*, his examination of the Poor Law system in the mid-nineteenth century, a significant number (over a quarter between 1859 and 1884) of paupers deemed insane were confined in workhouses. Workhouses across the United Kingdom constructed lunatic asylum wards and separate accommodations dedicated to separating the insane from the sane poor. Given that this rise in pauper insane in workhouses was concurrent with the expansion of the public lunatic asylum system under the Commissioners of Lunacy, the construction of dedicated lunatic wards in workhouses led to clashes between the Guardians of Poor Law Unions and the Commissioners of Lunacy. In a report in 1859 addressing the increasing numbers of lunatics in workhouses, the Commissioners of Lunacy recommended an expansion of the district asylum system to cater for this demand, a suggestion for national relief that local workhouses undermined by their endeavours to expand their own individual accommodations to allow for classification of inmates (Driver 2004, 109–10).

At this point, it is important to clarify that the designations 'lunacy', 'idiocy' and 'insanity' were catch-all terms for multiple classifications of mental illness and physical impairment that could impact the mind. As the nineteenth century wore on, where possible this very broad classification of inmate was moved to specific institutions for mental illness (asylums) (Tarlow 2007, 145). Unprecedented demand for places in lunatic asylums meant that the insane – a broad classification often applied to anyone with a mental illness in a workhouse (Morrison 1999, 161) – often ended up in workhouses. Where workhouses did not have specialised accommodation for their reception, they were generally mixed into the rest of the inmate population. As workhouses were not intended for the reception of the insane in the first place, further classification and subdivision according to the nature of their maladies was not common. As such, when we account for lunatics in the workhouse populations discussed below, it is worth pointing out that where possible, lunatics were sent to local asylums.

In the early to mid-nineteenth century, the discourse surrounding the treatment and management of mental illness was focused on *cure*. Notable asylum reformers like William and Samuel Tuke at the York Retreat, for instance, wrote on and advised authorities regarding the creation of physical spaces and management practices that could cure the mentally ill of their affliction (Fennelly 2019, 35–36). Acts in 1808 and 1845 provided for the construction of county lunatic asylums for paupers, but these were quickly overcrowded as unprecedented demand was placed on institutions as they were built. Ultimately, the mission of reformers like the Tukes and other lunacy reformers like John Conolly – to 'manage' lunacy through the facility of a curative environment and facilities that reflected an ordered and therapeutic environment, or 'moral management' – was overtaken by demand for places. In spite of the ideals that typified the early purpose-built pauper asylums, they were ultimately forced to expand beyond the dimensions of their original buildings (Piddock 2007, 105–6). Workhouses, as sister institutions often under the remit of the same groups of Guardians and magistrates, were forced to support demand. Though legislation formalised the removal of the most acute cases of lunatic inmates to county asylums in 1862 (Driver 1993, 109), demand only increased and the burden of meeting it fell on workhouses. Incurable cases could often find themselves admitted to the workhouse for lack of better accommodation, and workhouses responded individually to their own regional demands. The response to unprecedented demand on lunatic wards, resulting in the construction of dedicated wings, separate buildings and even new institutions, was not consistent across England, as each Union implemented their own strategies as they saw fit.

Lunatics in the Workhouse

Provision for lunatics varied by Union, depending on demand and the local authority. While the 1862 Lunacy Acts Amendment Act required workhouses that would receive lunatic inmates to construct appropriate and separate facilities for their accommodation, the Commissioners of Lunacy had no authority to compel workhouses to improve conditions (Cox and Marland 2015, 276), even as overcrowding in asylums required them to make use of the workhouse. Reception of inmates was in the gift of workhouse Guardians, not all of whom agreed with the policy of using the workhouse for asylum overflow. As such, provision across England was inconsistent; workhouses in the countryside and workhouses in cities interacted differently with their local asylums. As such, the reception of lunatics and other categories of inmate bears a closer examination on a case-by-case basis.

At Skipton, the building itself bore no evidence of dedicated, separate facilities for the insane, but there is archival evidence of their being housed at the workhouse. This was apparently a cause of some concern as, by the early twentieth century, the Guardians sought increasingly to remove the mentally and physically impaired paupers from the workhouse (Skipton Guardians' Minutes 15/8/1915; 30/6/1906). These are broad categories, and included inmates who were deaf or epileptic, who were sent to special colonies, while 'imbeciles' were sent to the local county asylum. This latter policy was in line with the 1913 Mental Deficiency Act, which provided for the removal of 'imbeciles' and the 'feeble-minded' from asylums and workhouses to dedicated institutions. Skipton Union frequently received letters from neighbouring Unions requesting that it receive 'imbeciles' into its infirmary, suggesting that the practice was relatively common elsewhere. The Guardians at Skipton, however, always refused. Their consistent refusal suggests that the Union did not consider their workhouse equipped to handle the needs of the mentally ill, who were sent to local asylums instead.

At Wetherby, the workhouse building remained in use for the accommodation of the mentally handicapped after the Poor Law was abolished in 1930. This suggests that there was a standing population of insane and mentally handicapped in the workhouse before this. Wetherby Union had a reputation for trying to keep their Poor Law rates low, even at the cost of inmate welfare. Wetherby was one of the Unions particularly resistant to the New Poor Law in the 1830s and 1840s, which is possibly why it worked to maintain low rates. As they already had a Gilbert Union in place, Wetherby was also eligible to opt out of the New Poor Law (Evans and Jones 2014, 117). Keeping this class of inmate in the workhouse rather than sending them to be maintained in the asylum would have been more cost-effective. Many Unions did commit to sending inmate classes that fit other institutions away from the workhouse, in the interest of keeping inmate numbers low. Pateley Bridge's New Poor Law workhouse, for example, was the administrative centre of the Pateley Bridge Union, but was not considered by its Guardians to be the central solution to relief. The able-bodied were kept out of this workhouse, through out-relief, public works programmes and incentivised emigration programmes. The mentally ill who sought relief at Pateley Bridge Union were sent to Menston Asylum outside Leeds, keeping the numbers in that inmate class down.

Around the city of Leeds, the benefit of the proximity of a large institution like Menston is seen in smaller accommodations for the insane.

The demand on that institution, however, meant that the workhouses in the area were pressed for space when the asylum could not accommodate the number of potential patients. At North Bierley on the outskirts of the city, the Union workhouse was incapable of accommodating the number of lunatics in need of institutional relief, though they were still pressed to accommodate those pauper lunatics who could not get a place at the county asylums. Like other sizable workhouses outside cities, such as nearby Wharfedale and Bramley, North Bierley did not construct an entirely separate facility for its lunatic inmates. Initially, those paupers who could not be sent to the county asylums were accommodated in the workhouse infirmary – a relatively common practice – and, when possible, those lunatics and 'idiots' who were considered harmless occupied empty rooms in the main workhouse buildings (North Bierley Guardians' Minutes 25/1/1849; 5/6/1861). This indicates that there was some form of classification, albeit very general, in the separation and accommodation of lunatics and idiots in the workhouse. Facilities for lunatics and idiots in North Bierley were far from ideal. The minutes in the mid-1860s, a period of intense demand on workhouse accommodations, indicate that male patients were accommodated two to a bed (North Bierley Guardians' Minutes 10/11/1864). As with many West Yorkshire workhouses, North Bierley Union's early attempts to accommodate this separate class of pauper resulted in overcrowding and occupation of inappropriate facilities and spaces, as well as a lack of specialised staff for the care of these inmates.

In consequence of the 1862 Lunacy Acts Amendment Act, and the Poor Law Board's recommendations regarding lunacy in 1864, which included the removal of idiots and imbeciles from the institutions, the Guardians at workhouses like North Bierley were 'desirous to carry out every provision of the Act' (North Bierley Guardians' Minutes 10/11/1864) and took measures to improve the workhouse experience for the lunatics in their charge. The outside areas of the workhouse, the yards reserved for this class of pauper inmate, were considerably extended, and trees were planted to provide proper walks for the inmates. Late though this was, the planting of trees and the extension of outdoor space was very much in line with the mid-century rhetoric of notable asylum reformers like John Conolly, who recommended landscaped airing courts and sufficient space for outdoor recreation in his ideal asylum (Piddock 2007, 62). Within the North Bierley workhouse, the wards were also extended to provide more accommodation and space for patients. Contemporaneous hospital reform, spearheaded by people like Florence Nightingale, underpinned the opening-up of wards for ventilation and personal comfort (Taylor 1991, 56–57). Tables, books and illustrated and pictorial periodicals were provided for the inmates' entertainment, marking a significant shift towards the importance placed on personal comfort and entertainment for this pauper class. When the master considered it appropriate, inmates of this classification were given light work (for example, in the laundry) to occupy their time (North Bierley Guardians' Minutes 10/11/1864; 29/1/1902).

Like the other Unions in West Yorkshire, North Bierley endured a continuous increase in the number of lunatic and idiot paupers seeking accommodation throughout the nineteenth and into the twentieth centuries. After the construction of a new infirmary at the workhouse in 1878, the original infirmary was given over entirely to the accommodation of this class of inmate. Within this new lunatic wing, mentally ill paupers were segregated by gender into separate wards. The entrance provided access to a central hallway, which featured a flagged floor and the door to a nurse's room. Male accommodation on the ground floor featured a dining room, bathroom and four-bed ward. Female accommodation consisted of a duty kitchen, a bathroom, two day rooms and an attendant's bedroom. The first-floor male accommodation featured a twelve-bed ward, an eleven-bed ward and two staff bedrooms. In contrast, the first-floor female accommodation featured smaller wards. As demand for accommodation for each sex was not always equal, this may reflect less demand for female accommodations. In the female accommodation, a ten-bed ward, two six-bed wards, a four-bed ward and a two-bed ward, as well as five toilets, were provided for inmates (Platt 1930, 52). Open fireplaces in the wards were the only source of heat. By the end of the nineteenth century, the Guardians had ensured that there were specialised on-site facilities to accommodate lunatic inmates, but they continued to remove lunatic paupers from the workhouse to the asylum as a priority whenever possible. (North Bierley Guardians' Minutes 25/7/1894; 7/8/1895). Even so, the Guardians employed trained staff to attend to the wards (North Bierley Guardians' Minutes 6/12/1883), but when the West Yorkshire Asylums Committee proposed the transfer of 'chronic harmless lunatics from the County Asylum to the workhouse' in 1897 (North Bierley Guardians' Minutes 17/3/1897) in order to reserve asylum beds for those patients deemed curable, the North Bierley Guardians objected strongly. The Union 'opposed any scheme in extension of the system of treating imbeciles and lunatics in the workhouse', arguing that an increase in the number of lunatics in the workhouse would have strained resources and thus compromised the general but deliberate classification and separation of the lunatic inmates' experience of the workhouse from the experience of the ordinary pauper. The Guardians' resistance towards increasing the number of lunatic paupers in the workhouse indicates some level of compassion and consideration for this inmate class, as well as economic concerns. That the North Bierley Guardians, and the Guardians of other outer-urban workhouses, became more sympathetic to the lunatic poor in the early twentieth century is supported by entries like those in the North Bierley Guardians' Minutes that documented gestures of kindness and consideration towards lunatic paupers. In 1901, for example, the lunatic wards were painted in 'cheerful colours' (North Bierley Guardians' Minutes 25/9/1901, and in 1903, lunatic inmates were granted leave of absence at Christmas to visit their families, without losing their place at the workhouse, while various entertainments were also occasionally provided (North Bierley Guardians' Minutes 16/12/1903; 3/8/1910). The particular mention of these actions indicates that at North Bierley, at least, lunatic inmates were treated differently to other pauper inmates by the start of the twentieth century.

In general, by the 1890s, workhouses had specialised, separate facilities for inmates who could be classified as separate (such as lunatics). The main workhouse building was meant to accommodate the able-bodied, the elderly and vagrants, though vagrants more often had their own block away from the main building. In practice, how the main workhouse building was used varied from institution to institution. In the urban workhouse at Leeds, by the 1890s the main workhouse building accommodated mostly elderly inmates and those infirm and lunatic inmates who could not be accommodated in the designated separate, specialised facilities due to overcrowding.

The Leeds workhouse housed very few able-bodied inmates in these years, as many able-bodied paupers were offered out-relief or encouraged to emigrate. Large portions of the Guardians' Minutes were given over to relaying the apportionment of out-relief to able-bodied paupers (Leeds Guardians' Minutes 1887). In the 1891 census, the only census to record the basic classification of inmates, out of 387 inmates at Leeds Workhouse, only thirty were classed as able-bodied. However, given the commitment at Leeds to keeping able-bodied inmates out of the workhouse, we suggest that a few able-bodied inmates who did enter the workhouse probably had some form of disability but did not require the level of care administered to patients in asylums, or were not acute enough to be designated 'lunatics' and were thus not accommodated in the workhouse's Lunatic Block. As such, these inmates were capable of undertaking labour in the workhouse, were technically 'able-bodied' and were thus not classed as lunatic inmates. This assessment is supported by a photograph of inmates published by Bedford and Howard (1985) entitled 'able-bodied paupers', which depicts individuals with physical attributes often associated with disability. The classification system was, perhaps, too rigid in the case of Leeds to allow for nuance like this.

The Leeds Guardians had, throughout the nineteenth century, endeavoured to send lunatic paupers to the county asylum where possible. However, densely populated and increasingly industrialising and urbanising Yorkshire placed significant demand on the pauper lunatic asylums. The first West Riding asylum at Wakefield was built to house 150, and after rapid expansion and extension, housed around fourteen hundred by 1889 (Ellis 2008, 282). A second West Riding asylum was opened at Menston near Leeds in 1888, while two other asylums to serve the north and the south of the county were constructed at Sheffield in 1871 and Clifton in 1847. These asylums were generally oversubscribed, however (Leeds Guardians' Minutes 21/5/1845; 17/9/1845; 29/9/1847). In 1862, a new workhouse was constructed at Leeds that provided for separate accommodation for lunatic paupers in the main workhouse building from the outset. Accommodating lunatic paupers in a separate facility in the same building as the workhouse both created an association and distinguished between lunacy and poverty. The shared building emphasised the common aspect between all inmates – poverty. There were some distinguishing features and special treatments. The work that lunatic paupers undertook in the workhouse was not physically demanding and included tasks such as sewing and laundry duties, and some attended church twice a week, on Sundays and Tuesday evenings. Further privileges included receiving friends in the airing courts (Leeds Guardians' Minutes 29/10/1862). Their daily routine suggests that although accommodation was insufficient compared to what was expected by lunacy reformers of the period, this inmate class was nevertheless offered some care.

Despite their efforts to provide separate space for lunatic inmates, however, the demand on these in-house facilities was significant. As such, the separate lunatic ward commenced construction in 1862 (see Figure 5.1). The block was constructed to relieve stress on the overcrowded county asylum at Wakefield and provide better facilities for the classification and management of lunatic inmates at the workhouse. Located next to the infirmary and surrounded by a small garden, the lunatic ward assumed a similar style to the earlier infirmary. It was constructed of red brick, with ten bays and two stories, with stone dressings and a slate roof with Dutch gables and a parapet. The south-facing entrance led to a central corridor that ran the length of the building with wards on either side that could accommodate sixty-two inmates. This design for a lunatic ward was in line with contemporaneous pavilion-plan hospitals and asylums. Hospital-reform advocates like Florence Nightingale were, at this time, advising and corresponding with the architect Thomas Worthington on the design of the workhouse infirmary at the Chorlton Union workhouse in nearby Manchester (Butler 2013, 94). Therefore, this was far from being a local or provincial concern; the Leeds lunatic wards must have been part of a broader movement in progressive social architecture in the period. That

118 • Poverty Archaeology

Figure 5.1. Leeds Workhouse lunatic ward (1862), north (photographed by Charlotte Newman).

such an attempt was made at Leeds evidences the Union's concern with keeping abreast of the latest concerns in healthcare. Such a concern at a Yorkshire workhouse is not surprising given the widespread opposition in the region to the New Poor Law in the first place; maintaining a progressive stance may have soothed public opinion towards the Union in general.

In 1864, the Poor Law Board reported favourably on the lunatic ward conditions at Leeds. Overall, the workhouse was praised for its treatment of lunatic paupers, and particularly the actions of the master and matron. Lunatic inmates at the Leeds Union continued to receive special treatment, including fortnightly entertainment in the wards (Leeds Guardians' Minutes 17/5/1871). The Guardians also suggested that the lunatic inmates be provided with beer – which they believed would promote good health – but the Poor Law Board rejected this request as it was considered an unnecessary expense (Leeds Guardians' Minutes 12/6/1872). Visits to the inmates from family and friends continued to be permitted by the Union, and inmates were occasionally granted short periods of leave from the workhouse to visit home, without fear of losing their place at the workhouse (Leeds Guardians' Minutes 28/9/1864). The lunatic wards did present some problems to the Board and the Guardians, however. The Poor

Law Board report in 1871 highlighted the difficulties faced by staff on the ward (Leeds Guardians' Minutes 17/5/1871). The wards were overseen by an employed nurse, who was assisted by six inmates. The inmates who assisted the nurse received clothing and food for their work, which elevated their status within the inmate hierarchy (Leeds Guardians' Minutes 28/9/1864). In other contemporaneous institutions for lunatics, the social and power hierarchies – staff-to-patient relationships – were maintained through materiality in this way (Fennelly 2019, 23). For lunatic asylum staff, this was possession of keys and uniform; for the inmate-assistants of the workhouse lunatic ward, this was better clothing and access to better food than their fellow inmates. Nursing workload was considerable, so these assistants were necessary. The nurses worked from 6:30 a.m. until 7:30 p.m., but they could also be called upon out of these hours if they were needed. On one occasion, the nurse on duty was attacked and almost overpowered by three inmates (Leeds Guardians' Minutes 17/5/1871). The amount of work demanded of one dedicated member of staff was enormous, so it is unsurprising that getting people to fill these roles was difficult. Even so, the Poor Law Board considered the conditions in the lunatic wards to be favourable despite inadequate staffing. Orderliness and hygiene were valued over care and specialised treatment, so this is not surprising, but it is jarring. The standard for acceptable conditions and treatment must have been low indeed.

The number of lunatic paupers continued to increase at Leeds, and by the early 1870s, the specialised facilities constructed for their separation as an inmate class were overcrowded. Lunatic paupers were once again housed in the main workhouse building and the infirmary, whose accommodations were unsuitable for any kind of specialised management. Nonetheless, conditions were still considered by the Guardians to be adequate. The Local Government Board noted that inmates were 'kept clean in their person, and tidy in their dress' (Leeds Guardians' Minutes 19/3/1890). Rather than being encouraging, however, this reflects an approach to the treatment of lunatic paupers that had not evolved beyond appearances and basic management, regardless of changes in approaches to lunatics elsewhere. Improved understanding regarding the needs of lunatics housed in county asylums – the development of psychiatry, movement beyond moral management – was clearly not entering workhouse practice at this time. By the end of the century, though, advances in the management of lunatics and the mentally unwell in general had reached the workhouse, even as they were implemented at the nearby pauper lunatic asylum High Royds. The Leeds Guardians' Minutes in 1896 record that lunatic paupers were housed throughout the workhouse, in the school, the infirmary, the general wards and the designated lunatic wards. Designated for 62 patients, the lunatic wards at this time accommodated 76 (Leeds Guardians' Minutes 22/1/1896). The problems of overcrowding and lack of separation of inmates were persisting. As such, a new lunatic block was planned.

The new lunatic block consisted of three separate wards connected by a corridor. It was constructed behind the workhouse proper, near the north boundary wall, and was demolished later in the twentieth century. The building was constructed primarily of brick, featuring bay windows and stone detailing, and a parapet-ornamented slate roof with numerous decorative chimneys. This was in keeping with the neo-Gothic aesthetic of other institutions – hospitals, asylums, prisons. However, the styling of the Leeds lunatic wards was especially ornate, while more economical styles were adopted at other workhouse sites in the period. The use of ornate stylings in the aesthetic design of the lunatic wards was something of an anachronism by 1900. An ornate design, which was in keeping with the earlier buildings on the site (rather than the contemporaneous functionality of other institutions in the period), suggested an importance placed on civic order and grandeur over practicality. The Leeds Guardians appreciated the visual impact of architectural style on the pauper experience.

The provision of a new and specialised facility for lunatic inmates improved provision for lunatics in the workhouse, but the new block did not compare to the scale of the county asylums of the period. Facilities aimed at curative management were constructed in the asylums that went beyond the wards and day rooms of their predecessors. The new asylums had ballrooms and theatres and hosted productions that were aimed at entertaining the patients, for whom extensive, landscaped grounds were maintained for exercise. In contrast, the workhouse lunatic block was very basic. The new ward at Leeds was necessary to accommodate the overflow of patients from country asylums as, regardless of their elaborate facilities, pauper places in asylums were constantly in demand. The workhouse lunatic wards were never intended as long-term alternative accommodation to the local asylum and could not house all of the Union's lunatic inmates. As such, even after the construction of the lunatic block, Leeds Union still paid for five hundred of its lunatic paupers to be accommodated in county asylums (Leeds Guardians' Minutes 8/5/1901) to ease the burden on the workhouse.

The plan of the Leeds workhouse lunatic wards was strategic. It was constructed in such a way as to allow for further extensions as needed, evidencing the Guardians' expectations that the number of lunatic paupers would continue to increase. This view was likely informed by the constant demand on county asylums, which showed no sign of abating by the start of the twentieth century. The Guardians proved correct, as later alterations and extensions to the building indicate. The lunatic ward's central block was used for administrative purposes, and included an entrance block, a waiting room, receiving wards, a secure room, a dining room and apartments for staff. Male and female patients were divided into the two-storey wings. The connecting corridors were wide enough to be used as day rooms (*The Builder* 8/2/1896). The building was extended in the 1910s, with an additional floor on each wing. Five verandas and two two-storey extensions were also added, and are visible in the 1900s and 1910s Ordnance Survey maps of the site. An additional two-storey dining hall was also added, featuring bay windows and a hipped roof. This was added in 1923 (*The Builder* 5/10/1923, 545), suggesting a response to rising demand and, probably, the inadequacy of previous facilities, such as the use of the corridors for day rooms. All additions were of brick and had stone detailing.

At the nearby Bradford Union, the Guardians prioritised segregation of the infirmary and the lunatic ward by gender. Scarring on the external walls of the surviving buildings and evidence of removed railings indicate that the area between the infirmaries – the yard – was divided. The height of the scarring suggests that the wall obstructed vision between the yards. Cartographic evidence confirms that the area was divided into two, maintaining gender segregation spatially for those inmates capable of walking and outdoor exercise. The Guardians' Minutes also record the commissioning of a wall between the infirmary and the lunatic ward (Bradford Guardians' Minutes 9/8/1865). Later, a large iron structure was constructed linking each floor of the two pavilion-plan infirmaries. Architectural differences between the wards in the pavilion wings, though subtle, suggest that they were put to different uses. The central two wards and the two outer wards all conform to open, pavilion-style plans popular in hospital and institutional design towards the end of the nineteenth century, but there is a difference in size and design between the inner and outer wards. Now demolished, the outside west block conformed to an L-shaped plan. The extant outside east block featured a large doorway in the north elevation surmounted by a fan-light window, set within a stone surround. The gable-ends feature ornamental triplet windows. Although it is not clear from the architecture which pauper class occupied which block, certain distinctions are documented. *The Builder* records the construction of an 'Imbecile Block' in 1870, and a separate building for female 'imbeciles' in 1892, confirming that there was separation between the physically infirm and lunatic and other inmates at least (Local Government Board 1880 XXVI.I 402, cited in Royal Commission of Historical Monuments of England 1983).

As at Leeds Workhouse, lunatic inmates at Bradford were accommodated separately from the rest of the workhouse population, with specialised staff to oversee their management. Although the most severe cases were still referred to the county asylums, many were accommodated in the workhouse. As mentioned above, overcrowding was a constant problem at the county asylums, so less severe cases remained in the workhouse if they could be managed. By 1900, lunatic inmates were recorded as having been treated to entertainments, such as performances by the Temperance Band and *Punch and Judy* shows (Bradford Guardians' Minutes 30/5/1900). The link between charitable movements and concerns such as Temperance Bands or friendly societies in entertaining the public (and, here, the poor) is well established. Engaging in communal efforts for public benefit was one of the ways that working-class men engaged in the increasing number of friendly societies demonstrated community and respectability (Prom 2010, 904). Both the Leeds and Bradford Unions provided separate facilities and entertainment for lunatic paupers, but accommodations differed substantially. Leeds's ornamental, Elizabethan-style E-shaped-plan lunatic wards, which were segregated from the workhouse by landscaped gardens, lent a degree of separation from the workhouse proper, as opposed to Bradford's pavilion-style accommodation, which formed part of the main workhouse complex and was architecturally indistinguishable from the rest of the workhouse buildings.

Despite the extended facilities for the sick and mentally ill, doubts remained among the management, the Guardians and the public as to the adequacy of the system in place for lunatic paupers. This stood in contrast to provision for the sick in the workhouse, which was generally far better. By the end of the nineteenth century, the infirmary at the workhouse was superior in its treatment of sick paupers to the facilities available to the independent poor outside of the workhouse. It was far more likely that a sick individual would recover from illness in the workhouse than outside, considering the living conditions in heavily industrial Bradford for the working class and the poor outside the workhouse. The medical officers at the workhouse campaigned for patients to be admitted to it from a wider section of society, regardless of their level of poverty (Ashworth 1982, 96). Even so, many of Bradford's poor chose to stay at home rather than enter the workhouse, even for medical treatment. Large numbers of the poor did not judge the Bradford Union by its superior and specialised medical facilities, but regarded the workhouse as a symbol of humiliation, defeat and shame (ibid.). By the end of the nineteenth century, many of those medical officers who had championed the workhouse infirmary became disillusioned by the system. The Guardians' Minutes record the resignation of numerous medical officers, indicating that the demands of the position were too great for some (Bradford Guardians' Minutes 1899). Even so, the Bradford Guardians invested in the improvement of medical provisions on the workhouse site with largely positive results for the population therein, though the new facilities did not encourage all sick paupers to seek help at the workhouse or enter it for treatment. The same could not be said of facilities for the lunatic poor.

Care for lunatic paupers at the Bradford Union was far less sophisticated than that for sick inmates. Like at Leeds, the Bradford Union provided separate accommodations, and operated on the basis of only accommodating those who could not be accommodated at the county asylum. Frequent mentions of lunatic inmates in the Guardians' Minutes suggest that they demanded a significant amount of attention from the staff and the Guardians. Prior to the construction of separate facilities, the lunatic inmates were housed in the main workhouse building. Though Leeds provided separate accommodations from 1862, at Bradford, separate specialised facilities were not mentioned by the Guardians until 1879, relatively late in comparison. Prior to this date, the Guardians focused efforts on improving provision for the lunatic poor in the workhouse, but care centred primarily around cleanliness and comfort, for instance purchasing combs and brushes for the physical cleanliness of the inmates (Bradford Guardians' Minutes 2/5/1866), rather than the deployment of any kind of formal treatment or management. Separate wards like those at Leeds and Bradford were the target of considerable criticism from the Commissioners of Lunacy in their inspection of workhouses after 1845, as they saw the expansion of facilities and accommodations for the lunatic poor in workhouses as a block to any expansion of the much-pressed county asylum system, which they were concerned with expanding to meet considerable demand (Driver 1993, 109). Even so, they made recommendations on the treatment of lunatic inmates and the furnishing of lunatic wards. The Bradford Guardians adopted many of the Commission on Lunacy's suggestions for the improvement of their facilities, such as papering the walls, boarding floors and providing books, papers and games (Bradford Guardians' Minutes 2/5/1866).

In spite of their efforts to improve conditions for lunatic inmates, the Guardians' Minutes also record major lapses in the care of this pauper class in the middle of the nineteenth century. Insufficient staffing and the aforementioned demands on time pressured nurses into mistakes, negligence and occasional cruelties (Bradford Guardians' Minutes 1/4/1869). Visiting committees reported major overcrowding in the lunatic wards, as the workhouse provided only 122 beds – 47 for males and 75 for females – which were always in demand; at one point in 1851, the workhouse accommodated 135 lunatic inmates (*The Builder* 9/6/1851, 379). In an attempt to maintain control over such a large number of inmates, staff sometimes took crude and drastic measures. On one occasion in 1865, staff placed nails in the floors to prevent inmates from transgressing their segregated spaces or escaping (Bradford Guardians' Minutes 13/12/1865). In 1866, an assistant nurse was accused of negligence and lack of control over the lunatic inmates in her care. The master reported of the inmates that 'many of them have become filthy, both in their clothing and bedding', and urged that 'these poor creatures shall be strictly attended to, both with respect to kindness and cleanliness' (Bradford Guardians' Minutes 3/1/1866). Such incidents indicate that the workhouse was inadequate and unsuitable to the needs of the lunatic inmates. The recording of these incidents reflects an awareness, however, of the shortcomings of housing inmates with care needs in a workhouse.

Like Leeds and other workhouses, the Bradford Union was not built to support long-term housing of lunatic inmates. Those inmates who were resident at the workhouse were never supposed to stay long-term. The lunatic wards and imbecile blocks constructed by the workhouse were not supposed to replace the county asylum, but to support demand where the asylum fell short, whether due to overcrowding, demand on places or in less acute cases. However, in contrast to the Leeds Guardians, who continued to invest in facilities for their lunatic inmates on the workhouse site into the twentieth century, the Bradford Guardians invested in a different direction, commissioning a separate colony for lunatics and the 'feeble-minded' in 1912 (Bradford Guardians' Minutes 13/12/1912). The Bowling Park Colony was a separate institution. The Bradford Guardians recognised the need for a dedicated facility specialising in the treatment, management and care of this pauper class. The removal of lunatic inmates from the workhouse in 1912 meant that the site could be given over entirely to the housing of the sick. In its separation of Poor Law institutions before 1930, the Bradford Union engaged in a truly ambitious policy of specialised management that was not repeated anywhere else in West Yorkshire.

Discussion

From the implementation of the New Poor Law throughout England in the 1830s and 1840s, demand on workhouse facilities grew exponentially. Lunatic inmates comprised a significant portion of the workhouse population right from the start, driving demand for the construction of dedicated lunatic asylums for paupers. This was codified in law with the passing of the Lunacy Acts in 1845, which provided for the construction of a lunatic asylum for paupers in every county in England and Wales. The West Riding of Yorkshire already had a lunatic asylum at Wakefield near Leeds, and this was gradually expanded until a new asylum was constructed at

Menston in 1888. Both of the urban institutions discussed in detail in this chapter expanded their facilities for the accommodation of lunatic inmates at the same time, leaving the original workhouse building or the main buildings for the use of able-bodied inmates, or the elderly and infirm, who made up a significant part of the workhouse populations.

Throughout the nineteenth century, after the New Poor Law came into effect, the number of lunatic inmates accommodated in workhouses increased, despite several Lunacy Acts, notably in 1845 and again in 1890, refining the system for mental health treatment in England, and the construction of county asylums around the country. These concerns were not limited to the urban Unions, either. What was happening in the cities was reflected in the countryside on a smaller scale. The economic limitations on small rural workhouses made it difficult for them to finance dedicated facilities to provide specialised care for lunatic paupers. As such, they relied on cooperation with the local county asylums. The Guardians' Minutes from the rural Unions of Skipton and Great Ouseburn, for example, document close links with county asylums to facilitate transfers. However, most Unions still housed lunatic inmates. Less severe or chronic patients, for instance, occupied an ambiguous category of inmate in both the workhouse and the lunatic asylum, as their conditions did not necessitate their long-term institutionalisation in an asylum, but they were still of the pauper class. This class of inmate moved back and forth between the asylum and the workhouse. The movement of inmates back and forth between the different institutions suggests that over time the Guardians of Poor Law Unions refined their methods of classification, as inmate numbers increased and the process of diagnosis improved. This improvement in the process of diagnosis towards the end of the nineteenth century was concurrent with a broader, politically motivated discourse surrounding the importance of early treatment of mental disorders, which drove the reform of professional practice in asylums in 1890 (Takabayashi 2017, 261). There were economic concerns, too, as accommodating lunatic paupers in the workhouse long-term strained resources. These inmates demanded more attention from staff and specialised management, as Guardians noted at the time, and in workhouses where specialised accommodations were not available, this was only exacerbated. The Guardians' Minutes of rural Unions occasionally record the receipt of letters from the Guardians of other nearby rural Unions requesting transfer of lunatic inmates. Such requests were always refused, reflecting the inadequacy of rural workhouses to the needs of lunatic inmates and the Guardians' desire to keep the number of inmates of this class down.

The urban Unions, despite having more specialised accommodations, still struggled to facilitate large and ever-increasing numbers of lunatic paupers throughout the nineteenth and into the twentieth century. Although both examples discussed in this chapter, Leeds and Bradford, expanded facilities for housing and caring for lunatic inmates or built strategies for this into the general workhouse building or the infirmary, they both financed the accommodation of lunatic inmates in nearby county asylums, too. Asylums had their own concerns regarding overcrowding, and were a more expensive option for Unions, so often the less disruptive or chronic cases remained in the workhouse. At Leeds, lunatic inmates who could manage it undertook light work and were allowed to receive visits from friends while at the workhouse. Overall, their privileges as a pauper class in the workhouse made them better off than able-bodied paupers. At Bradford, documentary evidence indicates that there was a focus in that institution on the cleanliness and comfort of lunatic inmates, in line with the recommendations of Lunacy Commissioners. However, the Guardians' Minutes and the haphazard, non-standardised and often inadequate architectural provision for the accommodation of lunatic inmates demonstrate that neither effective treatment nor cure was within the ability or even the mission of workhouses. This is not to suggest that the inadequacy of provisions reflects a lack of understanding regarding the needs of this pauper class. Indeed, many of the Union Guardians would have also overseen the local asylums. Rather, as Driver (1993, 108–10) suggests, too successful a workhouse system that accommodated lunatic paupers was not encouraged by the Lunacy Commissioners either, who were concerned with reforming and improving the asylum system rather than relying on workhouses to pick up the burden of care.

Whatever the reason, the lack of initiative on the part of Unions to implement a more sympathetic or effective system of treatment for lunatic paupers resulted in many inefficiencies, inadequacies and even cruelties within workhouse walls, which blighted the experience of lunatic paupers. At North Bierley Union, for instance, lunatic paupers reportedly shared beds. Overcrowding also impacted the effectiveness of staff in maintaining order. Often, one untrained and overworked staff nurse monitored large numbers of lunatic inmates in the general workhouse. At the Bradford Union, staff used nails to maintain control over space and segregation among a particularly challenging group of inmates. It is unsurprising that mortality rates among the lunatic pauper class were high, particularly at Bradford and North Bierley workhouses. In the early years of workhouse development, after the New Poor Law came into effect, separate accommodations were almost non-existent, such that the needs of this class of inmate were often unmet. As the nineteenth century went on, and the numbers of lunatic inmates increased exponentially, the Guardians of Union workhouses more often reacted to demand than proactively addressed the situation. The Guardians' Minutes at Leeds report incompetence among staff, high death rates and frequent overcrowding, even after the construction of the new facilities there in 1862. Yet even though the Leeds Guardians' Minutes themselves report poor conditions in the wards for lunatic inmates, reports from the Poor Law Board before 1871 on the same institution's provision for lunatic patients were favourable. Discrepancies in reports like this suggest that the bar for acceptable treatment of the lunatic poor at a national level was low indeed.

By the 1860s, legislative amendments regarding lunatic paupers, workhouses and asylums promoted a change in how Poor Law Unions approached mental illness. Although Unions continued to transfer acute cases to county asylums as advised by the Commissioners of Lunacy and the Lunacy Acts of the 1860s, Leeds (in 1862), Bradford (throughout the 1870s) and North Bierley (in 1878) commissioned separate facilities for the specialised accommodation of lunatic paupers. This was part of a wider drive towards the reform of workhouses and medical facilities therein more generally. There were a number of widely publicised scandals relating to health in the workhouse system more generally. For instance, reports of the employment of inmates in labour that was damaging to their health, such as carpet-beating, and negligence towards infirm inmates arose in the pages of the British Medical Association journal *The Lancet*, and as a result of the active charitable practice of workhouse-visiting (Brundage 2002, 98–99). As such, a spotlight was on workhouses in the late 1860s and into the 1870s to improve. When management of the workhouse system was passed to the Local Government Board with the disbandment of the Poor Law Board in 1871, workhouse management was more centrally overseen. At a local level, changes and improvements can be seen in the archival record. At North Bierley, archival evidence indicates that the whole workhouse experience was improved, not just the building or provisions for one class. The exterior grounds were extended to include more trees and proper walks. This expanded the recreational area for lunatic paupers. Many workhouses also recorded the purchase of provisions including books, pictures and entertainment for lunatic inmates. Lunatic inmates were also employed in light work where the workhouse deemed it appropriate, and at workhouses like Leeds, lunatic inmates were permitted to leave the workhouse for short or weekend visits to family and friends. This unusual privilege suggests that the challenges of relieving lunatic paupers inside the workhouse resulted in an entirely different workhouse experience for this pauper class. A greater number of lunatic inmates moved in and out of the workhouse with greater frequency than other inmate classes, whether to homes or to other institutions. However, despite the new facilities in place in many workhouses, inadequacies in treatment and management endured.

At the start of the twentieth century, urban Unions again expanded their facilities for lunatic paupers. This was likely prompted by concurrent developments in hospital and asylum design and reform in patient treatment, as well as the reorganisation of workhouse provision and the workhouse system during this period. Even so, the ever-increasing demand on asylum places meant that, in spite of overcrowding pressures at workhouse facilities, asylums continued to send non-acute patients back to the workhouse. The primary problems facing urban Unions were the sheer numbers of lunatic paupers seeking relief, the long-term nature of their residency in workhouses or persistence in the system of transferals between the workhouse and the asylum, and the expense incurred in providing and maintaining specialised accommodation that was suitable and appropriate to the needs of this pauper class. The New Poor Law workhouse was initially conceived of as a deterrent against poverty, and in the later years of its history increasingly focused on medical treatment and care for the poor. Both functions relied on the transience of resident populations, a constant turnover of inmates to ensure that the system could perpetuate itself. In direct opposition to this mission were the needs of lunatic paupers, whose conditions frequently required permanent or long-term care, thus undermining the function of the institution. Architectural evidence from Leeds and Bradford suggests that the two Unions took very different approaches to lunatic paupers, indicating that their perceptions of the needs of this pauper class differed significantly. Leeds opted to construct a separate facility on the workhouse site, in the same architectural style as the original workhouse building, but assuming a domestic character. The adoption of this style aligned the sentiments of the Guardians with thinking on the importance of homely comforts in the arrangement of asylum buildings and interiors. Beyond comfort, domestic furnishings in an institutional setting may also be read as a means of imposing a kind of social control on workhouse inmates, communicated through interiors imposing an environment of politeness to 'encourage the niceties of etiquette' (Hamlett 2015, 20) through domestic furnishing. Although the Leeds Union anticipated the continued increase in demand on its lunacy wards and made allowances for future extensions, it continued to support the accommodation of up to five hundred mentally ill paupers at the local county asylums. Even so, the provision of an extensive dedicated facility for the accommodation of lunatic paupers altered the dynamic of the institution over time. It may be because the Bradford Union Guardians wished to avoid a dramatic change in the dynamic of their facility that they opted to remove many of the mentally ill accommodated in Bradford Workhouse to a separate, specialised facility.

The position of lunatic inmates and other inmates with specific care requirements in the workhouse was extremely complex, and their experiences varied dramatically between workhouses. The development of specialised facilities in urban Unions especially indicates that the classification of the mentally ill in an individual workhouse was dependent on the demographics and challenges faced by that Union, or their interpretation of the needs of their inmates. In consequence, lunatic inmates accommodated in workhouses endured particularly harsh conditions in the early years of the New Poor Law, as staff struggled to cope with demand and all official discourse was aimed at removing inmates to the already crowded county asylums. However, as thinking on the institutional treatment of lunatics developed, especially through the last quarter of the nineteenth century, some workhouses – especially those in urban areas – attempted to adapt or develop facilities to reflect a more 'moral' approach to treatment, in the parlance of the reformers of the period. Even so, workhouse facilities were still somewhat limited in their provision of accommodations for lunatics compared to the extensive and expanding county asylums. A comparative study of treatment in the two institutions would necessarily be highly regional, but presents an interesting avenue for further study.

Chapter 6

The Workers

Much has already been written about the behaviour of staff towards inmates in workhouses in the Victorian and Edwardian periods. The role of staff in high-profile scandals in the 1830s and 1840s at workhouses like Andover, for instance, led to the dissolution of the Poor Law Commission and the closer inspection of workhouses under the Poor Law Board. As such, staff – their behaviour and their competence – have always been a key concern in the top-down management of the workhouse. The situation of staff within the workhouses is less frequently considered, however. Even as staff managed workhouses, workhouse access or the wards themselves, they were also frequently resident in the workhouse. As such, staff form a separate but distinctive class of staff-inmate in the Poor Law workhouse.

This chapter moves away from considering the actions of individual staff members in their duties and rather looks towards spatialising staff within the workhouse complexes. While the masters of workhouses are easy to locate in their centralised accommodations and offices, and the inmates for whom the institution was constructed are clearly located in wings and wards, the location of the other distinctive class of semi-inmate – mid-level staff – is less visible and obvious and varies considerably from place to place.

The People

There were several different classes of worker in a workhouse, though the staff hierarchy was not as complex as in some other institutions. As some of the labour of the workhouse – laundry work, or joinery, or even assistant nursing – was carried out by the able-bodied inmates themselves, separating the staff from the inmates in the day-to-day running of a workhouse is not always straightforward. The workhouse staff, frequently denizens of the workhouse themselves, can be considered part of an inmate population, albeit occupying a different kind of institutional hierarchy than the paupers, for whom the workhouse had a more direct dichotomy and over whom the staff had authority. Crucially, the difference between the pauper inmates and the staff of the workhouse was that the staff's position enabled them to participate in economic life outside of the workhouse as consumers. The paupers who 'worked' in the workhouse were provided for in terms of food and accommodation by the institution – their needs, in Goffman's (1961, 20) words, were 'planned for'. By contrast, the staff who worked there as nurses or porters, or the master and matron, had access to a wider economic and social life beyond the workhouse and outside its control, in a *de jure* if not always a *de facto* sense.

There were resident and non-resident staff in a workhouse, the daily experience of the former being far more contingent on the rigours of the workhouse schedule than the latter. The medical officer, the clerk to the Guardians and the chaplain visited the workhouse, while the resident staff included the master and the matron (frequently a married couple), the porter who managed access to the institution, and in infirmaries at least, one nurse, and in the larger Unions a schoolmaster or schoolmistress. Low pay, especially compared to that of other institutional workers such as prison guards, long hours and stringent rules about leaving the institution meant that in most workhouses there was a high turnover of staff (Longmate 2003, 105–6). As outlined below, the staff of the workhouse faced material issues in the spaces they had to operate in, and power and hierarchy systems that were rigid in similar ways to those faced by the people they were tasked with managing. The blurring of staff lines in workhouses and the frequent association between staff and the workhouse paupers who assisted them in various tasks make the staff–inmate dynamic at workhouses unique compared with other institutions of the same period.

Spaces for Staff

The location of staff within the workhouse plan was a crucial aspect of functional institutional surveillance and control, but it also reflected the status of subsets of workers within the wider workhouse hierarchy. As with other large-scale institutions like asylums, the workhouse master, who oversaw the operation of the workhouse and acted as a bridge between the Guardians, who held the purse, and the institution, was almost always centrally located. The central location of the master reflected his position of authority and made him more 'visible' to the rest of the workhouse staff and inmates alike. This idea of visibility was sometimes architecturally reinforced. This is true of the Union workhouse at Skipton, where the master was located conspicuously in a central hub visibly signifying his elevated power. In urban workhouses such as Leeds and Bramley, the master was centrally located in the T-plan of the main buildings, a physical buffer between the two wings that segregated inmates according to gender. Despite the central location of the master at smaller workhouses, such as Great Ouseburn, his minimal accommodation did not make his presence as visually obvious, which lessened his authoritative position.

There were strict hierarchies in place for the placement and situation of inmates. Similarly, strict hierarchies among the staff were also spatialised. Many workers lived in the workhouse like the inmates. Specialised staff were granted accommodations in more privileged locations, separated from the main workhouse. The porter, for instance, was frequently located in the entrance block or in a separate porter's lodge and was responsible for controlling admissions into and out of both the workhouse building and the wider workhouse site. At Bramley, the porter was allocated an entirely separate porter's lodge, suggesting that this role was afforded particular prestige and singularity in the workhouse hierarchy from early in the Poor Law era. Towards the end of the nineteenth century, nurses were increasingly provided with separate, often architecturally elaborate nurses' homes, symbols of their professionalism in institutions that were becoming more intensively medicalised. Often these facilities were built to encourage nurses to work in the workhouse and to prevent high staff turnover (a point discussed in more detail below).

Not all workhouse employees were accommodated in separate areas of the workhouse. Instead, some staff were integrated into the main workhouse building near the inmates for whom they were responsible. Schoolteachers at the Leeds Moral and Industrial Training School on the workhouse site, for instance, were allocated bedrooms near the children's wards. Although this increased an environment of institutional control over the children, it granted staff very little privacy, and their close proximity to their charges meant they were essentially always working.

In contrast to the rural Unions at Ripon and Skipton, Great Ouseburn Workhouse had limited facilities for administration and staff, which illustrates how workhouse designs could be economised and that the architectural form of the workhouse varied according to the means of the Union. The master's quarters at Great Ouseburn did not dominate the plan of the building, which suggests that the hierarchy of power within the workhouse was not as clear as at Skipton and Ripon. The relationship between staff and inmates would not have been so politically and socially charged.

Like the location of workhouse staff, the extent of staff facilities and privacy also reflected an employee's role and status within the workhouse. The extent of the master's facilities was largely determined by the scale of the Union, the Guardians' institutional values and the Union's economic constraints. In larger, rural workhouses, the master and matron (frequently a married couple as noted above) were allocated extensive accommodation, which included a dining room and bedrooms. At Ripon, the master's accommodation occupied the front of the central block and consisted of a living room and a dining room that doubled as an office. The provision of a dining room for the master implies either that he did not always dine with the inmates or that he received guests in the workhouse and this area was also used for social purposes. There were also two bedrooms, one bathroom, a pantry and a matron's store (Platt 1930). In contrast to the masters and matrons of other rural and urban Unions, the master and matron of Ripon Workhouse stayed in their posts for a substantial amount of time, with only two consecutive masters between 1854 and 1922 (Chadwick 2008). Clearly, the Guardians at Ripon created a constructive working environment for the master and matron. A long-serving master and matron created stability within the workhouse for both staff and inmates.

Not all workhouses provided the master and matron with substantial, separate accommodation. The master's and matron's accommodation at smaller workhouse plans, such as Great Ouseburn and Pateley Bridge, was closely integrated with inmates' accommodation, which afforded the master less privacy, but the lesser extent of their facilities also meant they had less personal space. Unlike Ripon, Pateley Bridge could not retain a master for long, and several were dismissed. The Local Government Board considered Pateley Bridge Workhouse to be in bad repair by the beginning of the twentieth century, which resulted in its closure in 1914. Examples of primitive facilities can be found in the Guardians' Minutes. For example, it was reported that no facility had been provided for the drying of clothes in the receiving wards. The Guardians' answer to this problem was to light a fire (Pateley Bridge Guardians' Minutes 18/5/1878). It is likely that the poor facilities and conditions of work at Pateley Bridge did not encourage experienced and capable staff like those attracted by larger settlements. In 1877, the Guardians of Pateley Bridge constructed a new vagrants' ward. The vagrants' ward has a similar form to the main building, constructed from stone with a slate roof and gabled to the east side. The gables feature oculi within pointed relieving arches, and the windows have shouldered lintels. The ground floor contained the master's accommodation, which was comprised of bedrooms, a sitting room, an office and a bathroom, each of which featured boarded floors, sash windows and painted or papered walls (Platt 1930). This implies that even the master would not take accommodation in the workhouse building proper. The location of the master in the vagrants' wards as opposed to the main building is a rarity and was not encountered in the other workhouse examples considered as part of this study. Living within close proximity to vagrants dramatically reduced the master's position of superiority in comparison to workhouses such as Ripon and Skipton, where separate facilities were provided.

Like larger rural workhouses, urban workhouses afforded the master and matron several rooms, which significantly separated their work space from their private space. The facilities in the master's and matron's quarters clearly distinguished them from the rest of the workhouse. Both Bradford and Leeds, for instance, provided large, open fireplaces and elaborate architectural details such as cornices and wallpaper. At Bradford, the central area of the first floor was plastered, painted and entirely segregated from the rest of the building, suggesting that the master and matron were accommodated here. In contrast to the master's facilities at Leeds, which were connected to the workhouse wards, the master's facilities at Bradford were enclosed, restricting his surveillance of the inmates' wards but offering increased privacy and separation from inmates. However, despite efforts to provide the master and matron with comfortable facilities, Bradford and the outer-urban workhouse at North Bierley struggled to employ proficient or reliable personnel. At Bradford, the Guardians' Minutes record several examples at both Unions of masters' and matrons' dismissals for unacceptable behaviour. A master was suspended in 1851 for habitual drunkenness and immoral conduct (Bradford Guardians' Minutes 26/12/1851), and the succeeding master and matron were dismissed in 1852, for incompetence (Bradford Guardians' Minutes 7/12/1852). Later masters were also accused of drunkenness, among other inadequacies (Bradford Guardians' Minutes 17/11/1884; 11/3/1885). At North Bierley, for example, a master was dismissed for cruelty and directly disobeying Guardians' orders (North Bierley Guardians' Minutes 9/8/1860). Such behaviour may reflect the Guardians' employment criteria. Bradford experienced periods of regional unrest throughout the nineteenth century – anti-Poor Law sentiment and Chartism went hand in hand in this part of the county in the mid-century (Brundage 2002, 82) – so the Guardians at both North Bierley and Bradford sought masters with experience in prison management so as to pre-empt any violence within the workhouse (Ashworth 1982, 97; Local Government Board MH 26/1/1860). An equivalence between the poor and the criminal in this case attests to the Guardians' ambivalence between care for and control of the region's poor, though the frequent dismissal of these masters for unacceptable behaviour evidences some oversight on the part of the Guardians regarding the actions of the masters.

Aside from the master's and matron's facilities, staff facilities varied between Unions and correlated to employee status. In rural workhouses, a limited staff hierarchy emerged, drawing distinctions based on workhouse roles. General staff, such as the porter, cook, schoolmistresses and laundress, were all granted better-quality rooms than inmates, but these were not comparable to those of the master and matron. As previously discussed, in the majority of workhouses accommodation for general staff was integrated among the inmates' accommodation. At Wharfedale, for instance, staff bedrooms were located through the general wards, and at Great Ouseburn the labour master was located in the vagrants' wards. Like at Great Ouseburn, at Wetherby, staff shared facilities with inmates and were dispersed throughout the workhouse. As a result, differentiation between inmates' and staff's space was minimal. The workhouses' trying conditions and lack of privacy severely diminished staff's sense of self-worth and motivation, which likely caused the high staff turnover experienced by these workhouses throughout the New Poor Law era. A more complex staff hierarchy developed in urban Unions because they required a substantial number of staff. However, there are similarities between staff facilities in rural and urban workhouses. For example, both rural and urban workhouses integrated staff accommodation into the inmates' wards, although staff accommodation was distinguished from inmate accommodation through increased architectural details. At Bradford, for instance, the interior decor differentiates between staff and pauper areas of the workhouse. In contrast to the decorated entrance lobby, the central corridors feature stone floors and painted brickwork walls. The extant corridors have altered very little since the Poor Law era.

In contrast to the staff who were housed in the main workhouse building, accommodations for porters employed in larger rural workhouses clearly distinguished them from the former group of staff. In Skipton, Ripon and Wharfedale, the porter was granted separate facilities, including an office, bedroom and general living space, in the entrance block. The distinction of the porter from other staff reflects his complex role in the broader aims of these Unions. As well as overseeing admissions into the workhouse and the vagrants' wards, the porter was involved in inmate training programs. At Ripon, for instance, the porter was housed in the stylised Elizabethan entrance block similar to earlier almshouses. The architecture of this entrance block reflected Ripon's more paternalistic (and somewhat antiquated by this time) attitudes towards the poor. A porter was appointed to receive inmates into the institution, but he was also required to have a trade, such as shoemaking, indicating that he was also partly employed to teach the inmates skills it was believed would ultimately improve their character (*Ripon Gazette* 18/3/1869). Teaching inmates a trade was also intended as a measure to lessen the burden of support from the state in the future. An inmate with a trade was more employable when they left the workhouse. At Ripon, the porter's accommodation comprised a sitting room, a W.C. (Platt 1930) and later a bedroom (Ripon Guardians' Minutes 1865). Limited sanitary facilities were provided for the porter, but his area did have separate offices for the master of the workhouse and a registrar (Platt 1930, 24; Ripon Union Workhouse Letter Books 10/1860, 132).

The porter in urban workhouses, like those in larger rural examples, was granted more facilities than the general staff, which increased his level of privacy and status, reflecting his significant position in the workhouse routine. The only workhouse in this study area to provide a completely separate building in the workhouse site plan for the porter was Bramley Union. At Bramley, the porter was provided with an entirely separate porter's lodge. Constructed as part of the first phase of development, the porter's lodge is a small, single-storey brick building with stone detailing and a slate roof. Originally the plan of the building was a cross-plan. The building's principal elevation features a bay window, and access is gained via a doorway set within an arched frame. Access was also gained through the rear elevation, but this was blocked during a later phase. Each elevation features large sash windows, which permitted the maximum amount of natural light to enter the building. Within the building, the lobby provides access to two main rooms, which provided working and living space for the porter and portress. At Bramley, the importance of the porter's role within the wider workhouse hierarchy was directly reflected in his architectural provision.

The porter was clearly considered separately to the rest of the workhouse general staff. This is in common with contemporaneous asylums, where the position of the porter was entirely separate from the hierarchy that operated in the asylum itself, though the porter in his management of access and egress held some authority over the general staff (Fennelly 2019, 102). Workhouse staff who resided in the workhouse were, like inmates, largely under the institutional control of the master and Guardians. Long working hours and residing in the workhouse meant that the lives of workhouse staff were closely connected to their work. At Bramley in 1903, for instance, the laundress had to ask permission to remain away from the workhouse overnight. However, she missed her train back to the workhouse after visiting her mother. She telephoned the master, and her explanation was considered satisfactory. 'I was satisfied that she had not wilfully missed the train and I told her to stay with her mother for the night and return first train in the morning which she did' (Bramley Guardians' Minutes 7/6/1903). Instances such as this demonstrate the level of control the workhouse had over employees' personal lives. In some cases, employees' families lived in the workhouse, so their entire domestic social lives were contained within the institution. That families of staff often lived in the workhouse reveals a class of workhouse inhabitants who were neither staff nor inmates. At Wharfedale, an engineer used a ground-floor ward in the original infirmary. He attended to the block and was provided with a sitting-room and kitchen. It was reported that his whole family lived in the block and that his child slept in a screened-off section of the first-floor female ward (Platt 1930, 38). In many cases, workers were clearly institutionalised by the workhouse buildings and their employers.

Discussion

Throughout the Poor Law era, Guardians sought increasingly specialised nursing staff to attend to the specific needs of sick inmates. In the years immediately after the construction of the New Poor Law Unions, urban Unions, including Leeds, for example, employed one nurse and trained able-bodied pauper inmates to undertake nursing tasks. Despite the expansion of Leeds's infirmary facilities, which accommodated four hundred paupers by 1880, the workhouse only employed fourteen nurses. Owing to the conditions of work, the Guardians' Minutes of all West Yorkshire Unions stress the difficulties of employing experienced nursing staff. Nurses opted when possible to work in voluntary hospitals, where the pay and conditions were considerably better than in the workhouse, so their employment at the latter was usually short-lived (*The Hospital* 3/11/1894, 85). However, exceptions occurred, illustrating the importance of individual personalities in the running of the workhouse. At Bramley, for instance, one nurse was employed to care for fifty-five patients, a ratio characteristic of the unreasonable conditions nurses generally sought to avoid. However, this nurse was undeterred; census data indicates that Nurse Ann Greaves remained in position for decades. Evidently, Bramley was able to retain staff despite poor conditions, suggesting that staff morale in the institution remained high.

Due to the increasing medicalisation of workhouses and the adoption of medical advances, Unions increasingly sought trained staff. More and more medical facilities appeared on workhouse sites towards the end of the nineteenth and into the twentieth century. The building survey and analysis carried out here reveal that in West Yorkshire two approaches were adopted by Guardians to solve the problems in workhouse nursing: training programmes and nurses' homes. The analysis of room use at Leeds and Bradford reflects the fact that these workhouses developed their own training programmes rather than relying on nurses' receiving training elsewhere. Training schemes reflect the scale of Leeds's and Bradford's institutional demands. Although the smaller scale of outer-city workhouses meant that training nurses was not as viable, North Bierley's Guardians sent their nurses to Bradford to receive additional training (North Bierley Guardians' Minutes) and maintained a small lecture room in the workhouse for additional on-site training. By 1930, the lecture room and quiet room were located in the basement of the nurses' home and featured central heating and two open fireplaces (Platt 1930). These spaces provided a comfortable environment for educational activities and promoted professional development. The urban case studies suggest that training programmes increased nurses' professionalism, which accordingly increased their sense of worth and status.

Qualified, professional nurses sought respectable accommodation reflective of their position, and Unions aimed to attract experienced nurses to the workhouse through the provision of nurses' homes. The elevated status of professional nurses was displayed through the separate, comfortable facilities with which they were provided. The designation of separate facilities completely disassociated the nurses from the inhabitants of the workhouse and reflected their privileged status within it. At Leeds and Bradford, for instance, the nurses' home faced away from the workhouse and featured numerous architectural ornamentations creating a sense of grandeur, which was intended to inspire and attract nurses to work for the Union. Constructed in 1897, Bradford Nurses' Home consists of a nine-bay, three-storey stone building assuming an E-plan (see Figure 6.1). It consists of a main block with a series of connected projections to the rear and wings either side (see Figure 6.2). The principal elevation centres on bay five, which features an arched entrance surmounted by decorative stonework with the letters 'NH' (nurses' home), with bay windows either side lighting the nurses' communal rooms behind. Decorative stonework is repeated above the second-floor window. Further decorative features include stone-string courses, detailed keystones and window surrounds. Bay windows on the second floor ornament the roofline. Like Bradford, in 1893/94 Leeds Union also constructed a building to encourage employment through its modern plan and style (*The Builder* 23/12/1893, 475; see Figure 6.3). The building in Phase 1 assumed an E-plan with a single-storey central block and two two-storey wings. Constructed from red brick with stone detailing and a Welsh slate roof, the building assumed a style comparable to the rest of the workhouse complex. In 1903, ornamental details were added to the building through an additional storey extension, such as turrets on the gable end. Ornamental details were mirrored internally

Figure 6.1. Bradford Workhouse nurses' home, principal western elevation (photographed by Charlotte Newman).

with highly ornamental staircases in comparison to those in the workhouse or infirmary. Nurses were given individual bedrooms, sanitary provisions and access to recreational facilities, which at Leeds also included a tennis court, where tournaments were organised for the staff (Leeds Guardians' Minutes 14/9/1898; see Figure 6.4). For workhouse nurses, life did not focus on workhouse duties, like it did for staff accommodated within the workhouse. As medical facilities expanded, so did nurses' homes, their scale reflecting the size of the institution for which they were constructed. Later extensions aimed to improve facilities. For example, at Leeds, Bramley and Bradford, covered walkways were erected between buildings to protect the nurses from adverse weather.

Although many workhouses located in large towns and on the outskirts of cities provided separate nurses' homes by the start of the twentieth century, not all of these nurses' homes matched the superior facilities offered to nurses at Leeds and Bradford. At Bramley, for instance, the nurses' accommodation adopted a plain architectural style and was located at the centre of the workhouse site. Furthermore, the nurses' accommodation shared a block with administrative facilities, so it did not entirely separate the nurses from workhouse activities. Such accommodation reflects the

140 • Poverty Archaeology

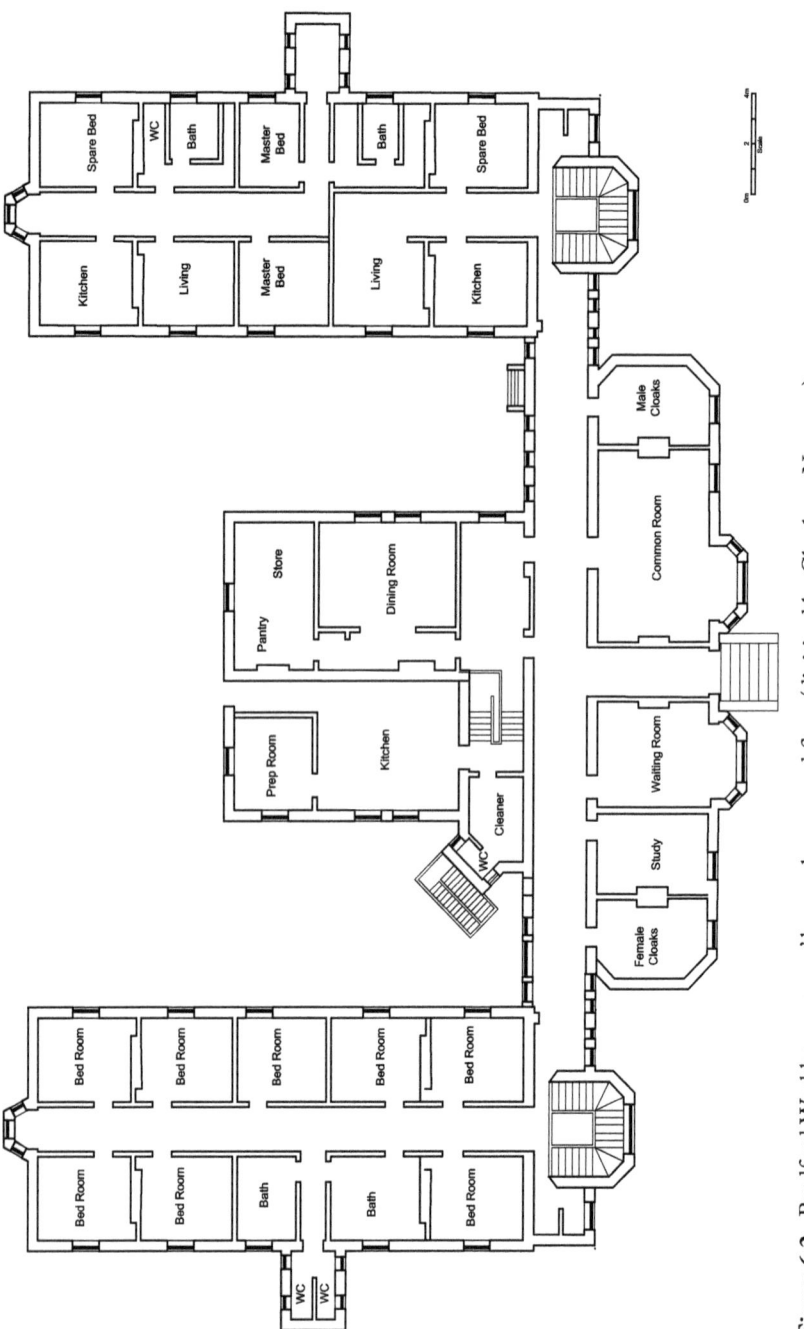

Figure 6.2. Bradford Workhouse nurses' home plan, ground floor (digitised by Charlotte Newman).

Figure 6.3. Leeds Workhouse nurses' home, L-plan extension, north-east (photographed by Charlotte Newman).

continuing economic constraints of outer-city workhouses. Since Bramley bordered the city of Leeds, nurses may have commuted from the city rather than moving into the workhouse. At North Bierley, conversely, nurses had no choice but to live on site due to the continually isolated location of the workhouse. Constructed in approximately 1900, North Bierley's nurses' home was more extensive than Bramley's, but not as elaborate as Leeds's or Bradford's. Located at the rear of the workhouse site, the three-storey, sixteen-bay, simply styled nurses' home was extended several times during the Poor Law era to accommodate the increasing numbers of nurses required. Staff accommodation in general featured a higher level of comfort than inmate accommodation. Facilities for the nurses consisted of a sitting room, dining room and sanitary facilities with central heating and some open fires (Platt 1930). Although located away from a city proper, like in Bramley, the nurses of Wharfedale Poor Law Union were housed in the central block of the workhouse. The nurses were provided with a sitting room, dining room and kitchen, with additional facilities for the head nurse, but they lived among administrative facilities and in close proximity to inmates. Wharfedale's nurses' provision reflects its position between ru-

142 • Poverty Archaeology

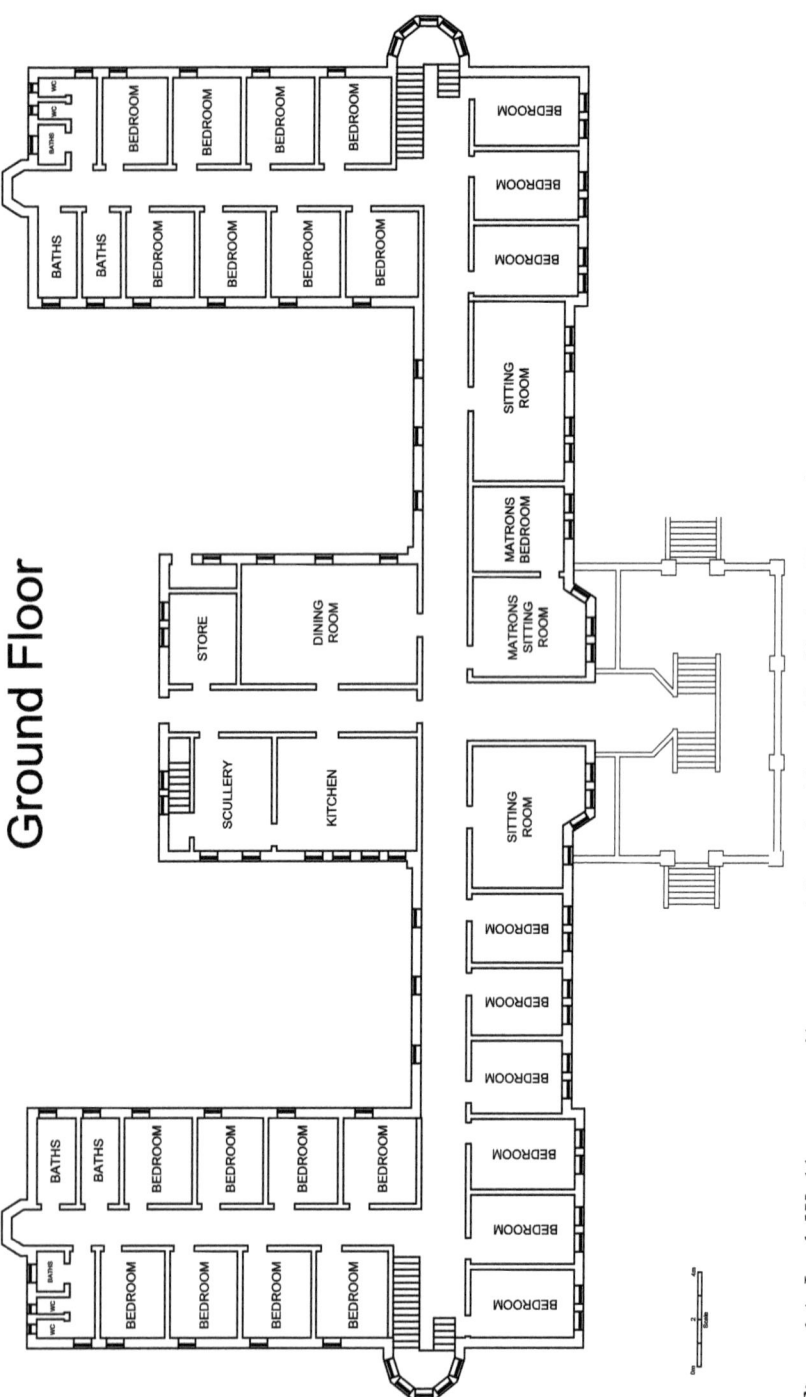

Figure 6.4. Leeds Workhouse nurses' home, ground-floor plan (digitised by Charlotte Newman).

ral and urban traditions, clearly influenced by modernising urbanism and medical advances.

The increasing number of qualified nurses in urban workhouses by the end of the nineteenth century resulted in a chain of command based on qualification and experience. At Leeds nursing staff were overseen by two matrons located in the central block, who were granted additional facilities, including private sitting rooms, which afforded them an increased level of privacy and comfort. At North Bierley, staff were overseen by a sister nurse. Her central location in the building allowed her to survey and control the behaviour of the other nurses. Her accommodation consisted of a private sitting room and bedroom. In larger nurses' homes, such as those at Bradford and Leeds, nurses were also distinguished from probationary nurses, who were granted separate common rooms and kitchens. Providing separate facilities created a clear hierarchy of status among nursing staff, which may have encouraged quality in the work of nurses motivated to gain promotions and additional benefits.

Unlike large, urban workhouses, small, rural workhouses could not justify the expense of training nurses, so they relied on attracting qualified staff. In rural Unions, the extent and nature of the workhouse largely dictated the number of nursing staff employed. Once an infirmary was added to the workhouse, residential nurses were employed. Great Ouseburn and Pateley Bridge, small workhouses, employed a single nurse who was responsible for the care of all the workhouse's sick. Like in early urban Unions, the nurse was supported by able-bodied inmates. Whereas Pateley Bridge and Great Ouseburn accommodated their nurses in the workhouse, Wetherby provided separate accommodation for the night nurse above the vagrants' wards.

Larger Unions with more substantial infirmary facilities, such as Ripon, Skipton and Wharfedale, required additional nurses. Skipton eventually provided an entirely separate nurses' home in the original infirmary to attract experienced staff to the workhouse, but its facilities were reportedly in poor condition. Platt (1930, 16) considered the nurses' home insufficient for providing the comforts deemed 'very necessary if the nursing staff are to attain a high standard of efficiency'. The front entrance led to a hall with a stone staircase, which rose to a half-landing. Originally, each floor had a tall, two-bay ward on either side of the central staircase. These were heated by stacks at either end of the building. The rear wing featured paired, narrow windows, suggesting that it housed sanitary facilities. The passage between the two rooms likely led to kitchen facilities on the ground floor and staff accommodation and a sitting room on the first floor. At Skipton, the insufficient facilities did not encourage high-quality work from staff; standards of care likely suffered. Staff nurses are consistently mentioned in the documentary records. In the early twentieth century, rooms were converted to provide extra staff quarters, and uniforms including shoes were purchased (Skipton Guardians' Minutes 28/9/1912; 23/11/1912). Such provision, however, was clearly deemed inadequate by the nurses. The turnover of nursing staff was high. Nurses' positions were occasionally terminated after their probationary period, and it was reported in the minutes that staff had been accused by the press of inappropriate behaviour and treatment on multiple occasions. In contrast, Ripon accommodated nurses in the infirmary or children's block, and they had to share sanitary facilities with maternity cases, which offered a complete lack of privacy and comfort for anyone involved. Records from the Guardians' Minutes indicate that Unions in rural areas struggled to employ qualified, experienced nurses throughout the course of the Poor Law era. The Marquise of Ripon employed temporary Nightingales because so few nurses would work in the infirmary (Ripon Union Workhouse Masters Report Book 1/6/1893). Often the limited number of staff was required to care for large numbers of sick and mentally ill paupers, which created an extremely challenging and stressful working environment. Furthermore, rural workhouse nurses were not permitted the same luxuries as those in urban Unions. Therefore, rural Unions did not attract the best staff.

Analysing the workhouse from the perspective of the workforce offers an alternative story of an institution that is primarily associated with the pauper. Bringing the worker to the fore highlights the complexities of staff hierarchies and variations in living conditions among workers. The examples outlined in this chapter indicate that shared spaces between workers and inmates contributed to the blurring of boundaries that the workhouse architecture itself sought to maintain. As such, the very mission of the workhouse to create designated, separate spaces for paupers was never as rigidly adhered to by necessity of having to house staff within the workhouse. At Wharfedale, the close proximity of workers and inmates resulted in attempts to create privacy for the family of workhouse staff through erecting screens. The makeshift screen offers an architectural response to a unique circumstance, but also suggests that privacy for workers and their families was difficult to achieve. Like at Wharfedale, the rest of the case studies in West Yorkshire illustrate how regional diversity impacted workhouse provisions and how they evolved throughout the Poor Law era. The professionalisation of medical occupations is directly reflected in the institutions' architectural form, but this vastly differs within urban and rural areas, as well as between them. For those employed and residing within the West Yorkshire workhouse, provisions were embedded within the institutional form, reflecting the values and aims of a rapidly industrialising region.

Concluding Thoughts

The next point is to determine what ought to be the size of a hospital; in other words, how many beds it can contain with safety. But from what has been said, it will be observed that this question resolves itself into the previous one, viz., what should be the size of each hospital pavilion? because, if a pavilion of healthy construction is obtained, it is evident that the only limit to the size of the hospital will be an administrative one. A hospital may be constructed for any number of sick, until a point is arrived at, when some portion of the administrative arrangements, material or personal, has to be provided in duplicate. Any further extension beyond this ceases to be economical.
—Florence Nightingale, *Notes on Hospitals*

The halls were of different sizes but most either accommodated 125 or 250 beds, this was like the modular tented camp designs that the British Army use on operations. The scalable and modular camps are 125, 250 and 500 person camps that just need to be fitted into the space available. This idea of having scalable wards of around 25 beds per ward was used to design one of the smaller halls and the requirement could then just be scaled up into the larger halls.
—Claire Smith, 'Building the Nightingale Hospitals: Engineering on the Fast Track', *Nursing Times*, 23 June 2020

Writing this book during the COVID-19 pandemic has provided an interesting parallel from which to examine our historic buildings. Where the concerns of the nineteenth century were administrative – the ability of hospitals to manage reasonably certain numbers of patients –concerns about scalability emerged when it came to the short-term so-called Nightingale hospitals constructed across England in 2020. Rather than administration, the concern there was with managing hygiene and space while providing for as many patients as demand required. Hospital design is far from refined in 2023, and the COVID-19 outbreak demonstrates the ways in which the concerns of large institutions in the nineteenth century continue to play a part in debates about the balance between spatial concerns and meeting demand for services.

Many hospital buildings in the United Kingdom began as workhouses or workhouse infirmaries, or developed out of local government concerns for public health that emerged as pressure on workhouses highlighted the need for a centralised, general hospital system. *New* hospitals, that is, purpose-built hospitals constructed for the express purpose of admitting patients with general health concerns, were rare at the end of the nineteenth century, leading to a significant amount of architectural innovation. Workhouses began to expand their infirmaries and main buildings to focus more explicitly on healthcare between the 1890s and the end of the Poor Law era in 1930. The principles of reformers like Florence Nightingale, and her *Notes on Hospitals* (1863), which promoted ventilation and light in hospital design, were expressed in the new pavilion-plan hospitals that proliferated across England and Wales in the late nineteenth and early twentieth centuries, often on the sites of older Poor Law infirmaries. Juxtaposing these pavilion-plan hospitals promoted by Florence Nightingale with the new COVID-19 triage centres that bore her name evidences how experimental hospital design still is. Constructed to accommodate patients with a highly infectious disease, these hospitals applied all the technology and sanitary concerns of modern medicine with almost none of the architectural finesse and style of their predecessors. Indeed, these emergency Nightingale hospitals were, in some ways, more comparable to the rapidly expanded infirmary facilities at workhouses – built to respond to emergency demand, applying principles of light and ventilation and separation as far as reasonably practicable within the confines of a building that was never meant to be a hospital. In the case of our workhouses, these might be an infirmary annexe or children's ward; for the Nightingale hospitals, these were venues like the ExCeL arena in London. Adaptation, regional need and the response of individual architects to demand have, it seems, been fundamental aspects of healthcare provision in England going back to the start of the Poor Law era.

In this book we have accounted for the architectural provision for different classes of inmate at New Poor Law Union workhouses in one part of England in the nineteenth century. The study of variance in one regional context evidences the broad interpretations of the Poor Law even between Unions that abutted each other. Rather than a monolithic and homogeneous principle of social improvement, Poor Law provision was highly varied in its uptake and execution. Despite regional and national government attempts to standardise practice and provision at various points during the Poor Law era, provision on the ground was dictated by the individual workhouses themselves. As such, there were as many interpretations of how the Poor Laws ought to be applied as there were workhouses.

From an archaeological perspective, we have presented here a methodology that accounts for the mitigations encountered in studying working, abandoned or demolished institutional buildings. By asking archaeological questions of the material culture, the architecture and the documentary evidence, we address the ways in which material spaces were adapted for the changing demands, shifting political sands and gradual developments in civic management and medicine over the course of the Poor Law era. This archaeologically informed approach provides insight into the ways in which workhouses were used, accounting for discrepancies between what was intended and what was built, between how spaces were *supposed* to be used and the ways in which they were used on a day-to-day basis and modified for the needs of the class within. Those for whom the workhouse was built were not a homogeneous 'poor' but multiple classes, each of which demanded different things of the spaces they inhabited.

The sick in Poor Law Union institutions began as one of the unavoidable classifications of inmate that Guardians expected but did not anticipate accommodating in great numbers. Guardians soon found their Unions to be the inevitable resort of paupers who, through injury, infirmity or illness, found themselves unable to work. As such, infirmaries in workhouses expanded faster and more substantially than accommodation for other classes. As Local Government Boards became increasingly concerned with public health going into the twentieth centuries, workhouses expanded their facilities to meet ongoing demand and alleviate overcrowding. Urban Unions were more likely to build substantial infirmary buildings, some very substantial, as they had the rates to support these kinds of projects. Engraved stones bearing the word 'Hospital' evidence the intention of the Guardians to underscore the separation between these new buildings and the sense of public shame and fear that had surrounded the workhouse system. In parts of the country like Yorkshire, where opposition to and fear of the Poor Law had been most intense in the mid-nineteenth century, distancing the workhouses from hospitals intended for the reception of the general public was key.

Though many workhouses were overwhelmed by the number of sick inmates applying for accommodation, this is not to suggest that workhouses were intended specifically for the reception of the able-bodied. Indeed, the able-bodied poor only made up one class of inmate in the workhouse. The dichotomous separation of the poor into deserving and undeserving has become something of a generalisation in discourse on the Poor Law, but the elderly were one class of inmate whose treatment reflects a more favourable consideration of certain classes over others. In many workhouses, the elderly were provided with accommodations that set them apart from other inmates. These favourable treatments included entertainments, but also permission to leave the workhouse and take tea outside of it, as well as the provision of some material comforts or aids to mobility, such as handrails. In some cases, married couples were accommodated together. Provisions such as these in even the smallest regional Unions evidence a more favourable eye on this class of inmate. However, an increasing number of elderly people in the workhouse also speaks to a wider problem in the England landscape, that is, an increasingly urban population and a breakdown of the support networks that would traditionally have cared for the elderly. In an industrialising economy where worth was increasingly tied to contribution to society through work, elderly people were afforded less social value. Interestingly, the workhouse was one place where age alone was enough to be elevated in the social ranking.

In some workhouses, the elderly inmates were accommodated alongside or sometimes together with other classes of 'deserving' inmate. These included children. The treatment of children from the start to the end of the Poor Law era changed considerably, concurrent with legislation on education and social conceptions of childhood. Education and moral well-being emerged as the most important aspects of state management of children, over employability and deterrence to dependence. The urban workhouses like Leeds, which constructed dedicated schools for education and training, were early expressions of these ideas. Most workhouses were, in general, determined to remove children from the workhouse as much as possible. Workhouses worked with philanthropic organisations, schools and industries for apprenticeship, and in some cases encouraged emigration. Initially intended as a means of breaking a cycle of poverty by training children in skills and behaviours so that they would not be burdens on the state as adults, workhouse provision, or at least attitudes towards children in the workhouse, became increasingly humane towards the end of the Poor Law era. In most cases, children – like the elderly and lunatic inmates – were offered small treats for good behaviour, evidencing some interest in their comfort.

Despite the stringent Poor Laws, which dictated what kinds of inmates should be permitted accommodation in workhouses, inmate classes like children, the sick and the mentally ill proliferated in these institutions. This was due to a dearth of specialised institutions for the poor of these social classes, especially in the regions – foundling hospitals for children, general hospitals for the sick and lunatic asylums for the poor were more common towards the end of the century, but this was a response to demand rather than pre-emptive. Indeed, the need for a more comprehensive and dedicated system for the management of the insane was clearly evidenced by the overcrowding of small lunatic wards at Union workhouses throughout England, especially in the nearly two decades between the passing of the Poor Laws and the uptake of counties to construct pauper lunatic asylums after the 1845 Lunacy Acts. Even as the Poor Law Commission and later the Poor Law Boards struggled to standardise provision for the accommodation of the insane in their hundreds of workhouses, Lunacy Commissioners and advocates for more comprehensive institutional frameworks for lunacy were attempting to expand their own system. As such, workhouse facilities for the accommodation of the insane were limited and highly varied between institutions.

The final class of inmate studied in this book is the staff of the workhouse themselves. Workhouses were built to accommodate different classes of pauper inmate, to put people to work or to manage pauper classes who could not manage themselves. Overseeing all of this was a hierarchy of staff, with the master who ran the institution at the top and the porter who controlled access and egress, to middle-level staff and nurses, to the inmates themselves. These workers were, in many cases, resident in the workhouse too. The workhouse was carefully spatialised to accommodate workers residentially and in dedicated working spaces. These working spaces, like the common accommodation of the master at the centre of the building, were strategically placed to support the power hierarchy within the institution. In many cases the lower-level workers worked alongside the paupers whom the workhouse was constructed to accommodate, and were assisted by the able-bodied inmates. As the workhouses focused more and more on medical care through the nineteenth and into the twentieth century, the workers too became more specialised and better trained. By the early twentieth century, workhouse nurses were accommodated outside the main workhouse building, in nurse's homes and in small houses near the workhouse. Workhouses, in this way, contributed to their local economy as employers and residences, as well as acting as venues for the creation of staff-based communities. The working and everyday life of the staff of workhouses is one avenue that merits further study beyond this work.

Future Directions

Workhouses are complex, heterogeneous and – it is our conclusion – understudied given the rich histories that can be tapped from even individual examples. The history of poverty is tied to the history of capitalism, industrialisation and the urban development of the English landscape, but it is not exclusive to these things. The ways in which poverty was managed and mitigated in the nineteenth century speak to a wider conversation about civic and moral improvement for the people who found themselves in workhouses, but also stand as an experiment in cultivating a wider sense of social responsibility among the public of all classes. The 1834 Poor Laws evidence an interest on the part of the state to create institutions and frameworks to support an approach to poverty management that would satisfy the social guilt that accompanied urbanisation and industrialisation. Whether or not this mission succeeded is a bigger question.

In this book we have spatialised the experience of different classes of inmate in the New Poor Law workhouse, highlighting the different ways that workhouses organised internal and external space according to their own individual demands. While West Yorkshire evidences the scale of regionality in responses to the New Poor Law, the ways in which different workhouses mitigated challenges are broadly representative of practice around England, though there is more study to be done on the different regions of the country. That said, workhouses and the construction of Poor Law-style institutions were not confined to England. In Ireland, for instance, where the architecture of the workhouses built after the 1837 Poor Law was far more homogeneous, being the brainchild of a single architect, George Wilkinson, a comparative architectural study with a region like West Yorkshire would be valuable.

Comparison with a dataset like Ireland, where the architecture of the New Poor Laws was relatively standardised, would draw out the merits and drawbacks of a more centralised system, as was envisaged but never actually implemented in England. Ireland, though part of the same overarching state as England in the 1830s, faced vastly different circumstances in Poor Law implementation. A largely rural population, no heavy industrialisation and a famine within a decade of the 1837 Act meant that the system that was envisaged for Ireland was beset by very different challenges from the outset. As such, it is worth considering the Irish Poor Laws and the response of the Union Guardians architecturally (similarly to what is discussed here) to assess the efficacy of a countrywide policy on an issue as regional and ever-changing as poverty.

Beyond Ireland, analogues and echoes of England's Poor Laws were implemented worldwide, in colonies, former colonies and beyond. A transnational study on the architecture and material culture of institutions for public welfare could draw together the comprehensive archaeological approaches to welfare institutions that continue to be undertaken in places like Australia and North America and the more architecturally focused institutional studies of the British Isles. One of the authors has already undertaken study on welfare institutions in New York City and the way in which migrant populations from the British Isles availed themselves of services in an urban environment entirely divorced from their origins, yet similar enough in welfare provision to be navigable (Fennelly 2022). Given that a significant percentage of new migrants to cities like New York, Chicago and Sydney in the mid-to-late nineteenth century were British and Irish in origin, a wider transnational study on the ways in which welfare institutions were materially conceived of is potentially valuable.

The archaeology of poverty and welfare presents many avenues for future study and collaboration. The situation of the poorest and the means by which the state and the people in power manage, mitigate and sometimes obscure them is an avenue to understanding how society deals with crisis at any given time. Writing this book at a time of global crisis, when the institutional and systemic issues that impact people in our own society are laid bare, has made us consider how far the state has come from the legislation and language of reform that threatened to overturn British society back in the 1830s. Anti-Poor Law sentiment, reflected in how parishes implemented the Union system and in the architecture and ongoing management of the institutions of the Poor Law era, evidence how the concerns of one period of history can have long and lasting consequences for future generations.

Unlike that of asylums and prisons, the architecture of the Poor Law seems to have had less of an impact on our immediate built historic environment. Former workhouses are harder to spot than prisons and asylums constructed in the same period, hidden as they are behind the new façades of current hospital buildings and sites, or demolished completely. Workhouse gate lodges, walls or chapels form part of anonymous housing estates or apartment complexes, business parks or healthcare facilities, their original purpose only disclosed through street names. Workhouses are imbued with less of the macabre mystique of a ruined mental hospital or a prison that is still in use, so are less frequently the subject of urban exploration or thematic conversion. It is surprising how ubiquitous they were, given how seamlessly they have been built around and incorporated into our current built environment, but they are there. This archaeology of poverty is an examination of a regional case study, but demonstrates the potential of these buildings and their remains to tell a story about the people who used them, who were as varied in need and background as in any institution of the nineteenth century.

References

Anderson, Philip. 1980. *The Leeds Workhouse Under the Old Poor Law 1726–1834*. Leeds: Thoresby Society.
Ashworth, David. 1982. 'The Treatment of Poverty', in J.A. Jowitt and D.G. Wright (eds), *Victorian Bradford: Essays in Honour of Jack Reynolds*. Bradford: City of Bradford Metropolitan Council, Libraries Division, pp. 81–100.
Bartlett, Peter. 1999. *The Poor Law of Lunacy: The Administration of Pauper Lunatics in Mid-Nineteenth Century England*. London: Leicester University Press.
Baugher, Sherene. 2009. 'Historical Overview of the Archaeology of Institutional Life', in April M. Beisaw and James G. Gibb (eds), *The Archaeology of Institutional Life*. Tuscaloosa: University of Alabama Press, pp. 5–13.
Baxter, G.R.W. 1841. *The Book of the Bastiles; Or, The History of the Working of the New Poor Law*. London: J. Stephens.
Bedford, P., and D.N. Howard. 1985. *St James's University Hospital Leeds, a Pictorial History*. Leeds: Hospital Trustees.
Beresford, Maurice. 1980. 'Demographic Change, 1771–1911', in Derek Fraser (ed.), *A History of Modern Leeds*. Manchester: Manchester University Press, pp. 46–71.
Booth, Charles. 1892. *Pauperism: A Picture; And the Endowment of Old Age, an Argument*. London: Macmillan.
Botelho, L.A. 2004. *Old Age and the English Poor Law, 1500–1700*. Woodbridge: Boydell and Brewer.
Boyer, George R. 2019. *The Winding Road to the Welfare State: Economic Insecurity and Social Welfare Policy in Britain*. Princeton, NJ: Princeton University Press.
Bradford Union Workhouse Guardians' Minutes (available at West Yorkshire Archive, Bradford).
Bramley Union Workhouse Guardians' Minutes (available at West Yorkshire Archive, Leeds).
Brundage, Anthony. 2002. *The English Poor Laws, 1700–1930*. London: Palgrave.

Buchli, Victor, and Gavin Lucas. 2006. 'The Archaeology of Alienation: A Late Twentieth-Century British Council House', in Victor Buchli and Gavin Lucas (eds), *Archaeologies of the Contemporary Past*. London: Routledge, pp. 158–67.

Butler, Stella Vera F. 2013. '"A Model for the Country": Letters from Florence Nightingale to the Architect, Thomas Worthington, on Hospitals and Other Matters 1865–1868', *Medical Humanities* 39(2): 91–97.

Casella, Eleanor Conlin. 2007. *The Archaeology of Institutional Confinement*. Gainesville: University of Florida Press.

———. 2012. 'Little Bastard Felons: Childhood, Affect and Labour in the Penal Colonies of Nineteenth-Century Australia', in Barbara L. Voss and Eleanor Conlin Casella (eds), *The Archaeology of Colonialism: Intimate Encounters and Sexual Effects*. Cambridge: Cambridge University Press, pp. 31–48.

Casella, Eleanor Conlin, and Katherine Fennelly. 2022. 'Social Welfare Institutions', in Eleanor Conlin Casella, Michael Nevell and Hanna Steyne (eds), *The Oxford Handbook of Industrial Archaeology*. Oxford: Oxford University Press, pp. 619–34.

Chadwick, A. 2008. *Guardians and Staff at Ripon Workhouse*. Ripon: Ripon Museum Trust.

Cook, G.C. 2002. 'Henry Currey FRIBA (1820–1900): Leading Victorian Hospital Architect, and Early Exponent of the "Pavilion Principle"', *Postgraduate Medical Journal* 78(920): 352–59.

Cox, Catherine, and Hilary Marland. 2015. '"A Burden on the County": Madness, Institutions of Confinement and the Irish Patient in Victorian Lancashire', *Social History of Medicine* 28(2): 263–87.

Crompton, Frank. 1997. *Workhouse Children*. Stroud: Sutton.

Culley, Amy. 2019. '"A Journal of My Feelings, Mind & Body": Narratives of Ageing in the Life Writing of Mary Berry (1763–1852)', *Romanticism* 25(3): 291–302.

Dickens, Charles. 1838. *Oliver Twist; Or, The Parish Boy's Progress*. London: Richard Bentley.

Doyle, Barry. 2010. 'Labour and Hospitals in Urban Yorkshire: Middlesbrough, Leeds and Sheffield, 1919–1938', *Social History of Medicine* 23(2): 374–92.

Driver, Felix. 1993. *Power and Pauperism: The Workhouse System 1834–1884*. Cambridge: Cambridge University Press.

Ellis, Robert. 2008. 'The Asylum, the Poor Law and the Growth of County Asylums in Nineteenth-Century Yorkshire', *Northern History* 45(2): 279–93.

Evans, Megan, and Peter Jones. 2014. '"A Stubborn, Intractable Body": Resistance to the Workhouse in Wales, 1834–1877', *Family and Community History* 17(2): 101–21.

Evans, Robin. 2010. *The Fabrication of Virtue: English Prison Architecture, 1750–1840*. Cambridge: Cambridge University Press.

Fairclough, Graham. 2008. '"The Long Chain": Archaeology, Historic Landscape Characterisation and Time-Depth in the Landscape', in Graham Fairclough et al. (eds), *The Heritage Reader*. Abingdon: Routledge, pp. 408–24.

Fennelly, Katherine. 2018. 'The Bedford Asylum: Building for the "Industrious Child" in Early-Nineteenth Century Dublin', in Jane Eva Baxter and Meredith A.B. Ellis (eds), *Nineteenth Century Childhoods in Interdisciplinary and International Perspectives*. Oxford: Oxbow, pp. 153–65.

———. 2019. *An Archaeology of Lunacy: Managing Madness in the Early Nineteenth-Century Asylums*. Manchester: Manchester University Press.

———. 2020. 'The Institution and the City: The Impact of Hospitals and Workhouses on the Development of Dublin's North Inner City, c. 1773–1911', *Urban History* 47(4): 671–88.

———. 2022. 'Mapping Poverty in Gotham: Visualizing New York City's Almshouse Ledgers from 1822 to 1835', *International Journal of Historical Archaeology*. https://doi.org/10.1007/s10761-022-00671-6.
Fennelly, Katherine, and Charlotte Newman. 2017. 'Poverty and Illness in the "Old Countries": Archaeological Approaches to Historical Medical Institutions in the British Isles', *International Journal of Historical Archaeology* 21(1): 178–97.
First Annual Report of the Poor Law Commissioners for England and Wales. 1835. London: W. Clowes and Sons.
Forsythe, Bill, Joseph Melling and Richard Adair. 1996. 'The New Poor Law and the County Pauper Lunatic Asylum – the Devon Experience 1834–1884', *Social History of Medicine* 9(3): 335–55.
Foucault, Michel. 1977. *Discipline and Punish: The Birth of the Prison*. London: Penguin.
———. 1989. *Madness and Civilisation*. Abingdon: Routledge.
———. 2001. *Madness and Civilisation*. Routledge Classics edn. London: Routledge.
Fowler, Simon. 2007. *The Workhouse: The People, The Places, The Life Behind Doors*. Richmond: National Archives.
Geber, Jonny. 2015. *Victims of Ireland's Great Famine: The Bioarchaeology of Mass Burials at Kilkenny Union Workhouse*. Gainesville: University of Florida Press.
Goffman, Erving. 1961. *Asylums: Essays on the Social Situation of Mental Patients and Other Inmates*. New York: Anchor.
Goose, Nigel (ed). 2007. *Women's Work in Industrial England: Regional and Local Perspectives*. Hatfield: Local Population Studies.
Great Ouseburn Workhouse Guardians' Minutes BG/OUG (available at North Yorkshire Archive, Northallerton).
Hamlett, Jane. 2015. *At Home in the Institution: Material Life in Asylums, Lodging Houses and Schools in Victorian and Edwardian England*. London: Palgrave.
Harvey, Ben. 2015. 'The Putative Fathers of Swinton, England: Illegitimate Behaviour under the Old Poor Laws, 1797–1835', *Journal of Family History* 40(3): 373–98.
Henriques, U.R.Q. 1967. 'Bastardy and the New Poor Law', *Past and Present* 37(1): 103–29.
Hey, D. 2005. *History of Yorkshire: County of Broad Acres*. Lancaster: Carnegie.
Higginbotham, Peter. 2021. The Workhouse: The Story of an Institution (website). Retrieved 21 March 2023 from http://www.workhouses.org.uk.
Historic England. 2017. *Health and Welfare Buildings: Listing Selection Guide*. Swindon.
Holtorf, Cornelius J. 2008. 'Is the Past a Non-Renewable Resource?', in Graham Fairclough et al. (eds), *The Heritage Reader*. Abingdon: Routledge, pp. 125–33.
Hufton, Olwen H. 1974. *The Poor of Eighteenth-Century France, 1750–1789*. Oxford: Clarendon Press.
Hulonce, Lesley. 2016. *Pauper Children and Poor Law Childhoods in England and Wales 1834–1910*. Rounded Globe. Retrieved 21 March 2023 from https://roundedglobe.com/html/3b3a9a73-0518-487e-86b0-98d4c10f9af5/en/Pauper%20Children%20and%20Poor%20Law%20Childhoods%20in%20England%20and%20Wales%201834-1910/.
Hurren, Elizabeth T. 2005. 'Poor Law versus Public Health: Diphtheria, Sanitary Reform, and the 'Crusade' Against Outdoor Relief, 1870–1900', *Social History of Medicine* 18(3): 399–418.
Hutton, Barbara. 1986. *Recording Standing Buildings*. Sheffield: J. Collis.
Johnson, Matthew. 1996. *An Archaeology of Capitalism*. Oxford: Blackwell.
King, Steven, and Alannah Tomkins (eds). 2003. *The Poor in England, 1700–1850: An Economy of Makeshifts*. Manchester: Manchester University Press.
Leeds Union Workhouse Guardians' Minutes (available at West Yorkshire Archive, Leeds).

Leone, Mark P. 1995. 'A Historical Archaeology of Capitalism', *American Anthropologist* 97(2): 251–68.
Local Government Board and Predecessors: Correspondence with Poor Law Unions and Other Local Authorities, MH 12 (available at The National Archives of the United Kingdom).Longmate, Norman. 2003. *The Workhouse*. London: Pimlico.
Looser, Devoney. 2008. *Women Writers and Old Age in Great Britain 1750–1850*. Baltimore: Johns Hopkins University Press.
Lucas, Gavin. 1999. 'The Archaeology of the Workhouse: The Changing Uses of the Workhouse Buildings at St Mary's, Southampton', in Sarah Tarlow and Susie West (eds), *The Familiar Past? Archaeologies of Later Historical Britain*. London: Routledge, pp.125–139.
Lynch, Linda G. 2014. 'Death and Burial in the Poor Law Union Workhouses in Ireland', *Journal of Irish Archaeology* 23: 189–203.
Malthus, Thomas. 1798. *An Essay on the Principle of Population*. London.
Mandler, Peter. 1987. 'The Making of the New Poor Law Redivivus', *Past & Present* 117: 131–157.
Markus, Thomas A. 1993. *Buildings and Power: Freedom and Control in the Origin of Modern Building Types*. London: Routledge.
McAtackney, Laura. 2014. *An Archaeology of the Troubles: The Dark Heritage of Long Kesh/Maze*. Oxford: Oxford University Press.
Morris, Richard K. 2000. *The Archaeology of Buildings*. Stroud: Tempus.
Morrison, Kathryn. 1999. *The Workhouse: A Study of Poor Law Buildings in England*. Swindon: Royal Commission on Historical Monuments.
Newman, Charlotte. 2013. 'An Archaeology of Poverty: Architectural Innovation and Pauper Experience at Madeley Union Workhouse, Shropshire', *Post-Medieval Archaeology* 47(2): 359–77.
———. 2014. 'To Punish or Protect: The New Poor Law and the English Workhouse', *International Journal of Historical Archaeology* 18(1): 122–45.
———. 2015. 'A Mansion for the Mad: An Archaeology of Brooke House, Hackney', *Post-Medieval Archaeology* 49(1): 156–74.
Nightingale, Florence. 1859. *Notes on Nursing: What It Is, and What It Is Not*. London: Harrison.
———. 1863. *Notes on Hospitals*. London: Longman.
North Bierley Union Workhouse Guardians' Minutes (available at West Yorkshire Archive, Keighley).
Ottaway, Susannah R. 2004. *The Decline of Life: Old Age in Eighteenth-Century England*. Cambridge: Cambridge University Press.
———. 2013. 'The Elderly in the Eighteenth-Century Workhouse', in Jonathan Reinarz and Leonard Schwartz (eds), *Medicine and the Workhouse*. Rochester, NY: University of Rochester Press, pp. 40–57.
Pateley Bridge Union Workhouse Guardians' Minutes BG/PAT (available at North Yorkshire Archive, Northallerton).
Pennock, P.M. 1986. *The Evolution of St. James's, 1845–94: LMITS, Leeds Union Workhouse and Leeds Union Infirmary*. Leeds: Thoresbury Society.
Piddock, Susan. 2001. '"An Irregular and Inconvenient Pile of Buildings": The Destitute Asylum of Adelaide, South Australia, and the English Workhouse', *International Journal of Historical Archaeology* 5(1): 73–95.
———. 2007. *A Space of Their Own: The Archaeology of Nineteenth Century Lunatic Asylums in Britain, South Australia, and Tasmania*. New York: Springer.
Platt, P.O. 1930. *Survey of the County Poor Law Institution*. County Council of West Yorkshire.

Poor Law (Amendment) Act 1834.
Prom, Christopher J. 2010. 'Friendly Society Discipline and Charity in Late-Victorian and Edwardian England', *The Historian* 72(4): 888–908.
Przystupa, Paulina F. 2018. 'Nineteenth Century Institutional "Education": A Spatial Approach to Assimilation and Resistance at Hoopa Valley Indian School', in Jane Eva Baxter and Meredith A.B. Ellis (eds), *Nineteenth Century Childhoods in Interdisciplinary and International Perspectives*. Oxford: Oxbow, pp. 166–78.
Reynolds, Jack. 1983. *The Great Paternalist: Titus Salt and the Growth of Nineteenth-Century Bradford*. London: M. Temple Smith.
Richardson, Harriet. 1998. *English Hospitals 1660–1948: A Survey of their Architecture and Design*. Swindon: Royal Commission on the Historical Monuments of England.
Richardson, Ruth. 2012. *Dickens and the Workhouse: Oliver Twist and the London Poor*. Oxford: Oxford University Press.
Ripon Union Workhouse Guardians' Minutes BG/R1 (available at North Yorkshire Archive, Northallerton).
Ripon Poor Law Union Register of Refusals of Admission (available at North Yorkshire Archive, Northallerton).
Ripon Union Workhouse Master's Report Book (available at North Yorkshire Archive, Northallerton).
Ripon Union Workhouse Letter Books (available at North Yorkshire Archive, Northallerton).
Royal Commission of Historic Monuments of England. 1983. 'St. Luke's, Little Horton Lane' (available at National Monuments Record Office, Swindon).
Royal Commission of Historic Monuments of England. 1993. 'Raikeswood Hospital, formerly Skipton Union Workhouse, then Skipton Institution, Gargrave Road' (available at National Monuments Record Office, Swindon).
Shapland, Michael. 2020. 'Capturing the Spirit of Singular Places: A Biographical Approach to Historic Building Recording', *Post-Medieval Archaeology* 54(1): 18–41.
Shave, Samantha A. 2018. '"Great Inhumanity": Scandal, Child Punishment and Policymaking in the Early Years of the New Poor Law Workhouse System', *Continuity and Change* 33: 339–63.
Skipton Union Workhouse Guardians' Minutes BG/SK (available at North Yorkshire Archive, Northallerton).
Slack, Paul. 1995. *The English Poor Law, 1531–1782*. Cambridge: Cambridge University Press.
Smith, Leonard. 2013. '"A Sad Spectacle of Hopeless Mental Degradation": The Management of the Insane in West Midlands Workhouses, 1815–60', in Jonathan Reinarz and Leonard Schwartz (eds), *Medicine in the Workhouse*. Rochester, NY: Rochester University Press, pp. 103–20.
Sokoll, Thomas (ed.). 2001. *Essex Pauper Letters 1731–1837*. Oxford: Oxford University Press.
Spencer-Wood, Suzanne M. 2009. 'Feminist Theory and the Historical Archaeology of Institutions', in April M. Beisaw and James G. Gibb (eds), *The Archaeology of Institutional Confinement*. Tuscaloosa: University of Alabama Press, pp. 33–48.
Spencer-Wood, Suzanne M., and Sherene Baugher. 2001. 'Introduction and Historical Context for the Archaeology of Institutions of Reform. Part I: Asylums', *International Journal of Historical Archaeology* 5(1): 5–17.
Takabayashi, Akinobu. 2017. 'Surviving the Lunacy Act of 1890: English Psychiatrists and Professional Development during the Early Twentieth Century', *Medical History* 61(2): 246–69.

Tarlow, Sarah. 2007. *The Archaeology of Improvement in Britain, 1750–1850*. Cambridge: Cambridge University Press.
Taylor, Jeremy. 1991. *Hospital and Asylum Architecture in England, 1840–1914: Building for Health Care*. London: Mansell.
Thompson, John D., and Grace Goldin. 1975. *The Hospital: A Social and Architectural History*. New Haven, CT: Yale University Press.
Thompson, K. 1989. 'Apprenticeships and the New Poor Law: A Leicester Example', *Local Historian* 19(2): 51–55.
Unwin, R. 1987. *Wetherby: A History of a Yorkshire Market Town*. Leeds: Leeds University Press.
Walkowitz, Judith R. 1992. *City of Dreadful Delight: Narratives of Sexual Danger in Late-Victorian London*. Chicago: University of Chicago Press.
Webb, Sidney, and Beatrice Webb. 1910. *English Poor Law Policy*. London: Longmans, Green and Company.
Webb, Sidney, and Beatrice Webb. 1927. *English Poor Law History: Part II; The Last Hundred Years*. London: Longman Green.
Weiner, Deborah E.B. 1994. *Architecture and Social Reform in Late-Victorian London*. Manchester: Manchester University Press.
Weisbrod, Bernd. 1985. 'How to Become a Good Foundling in Early Victorian London', *Social History* 10(2): 193–209.

Index

accessibility, 69, 80, 148
admission practices, 7, 73, 132, 135
almshouses, *viii*, 3, 5, 6, 34, 57, 61, 66, 78, 81, 82, 135
Anatomy Act, 1832 64
Andover. *See* Andover Scandal
Andover Scandal, 2–3, 4, 7, 9, 32, 86, 127, 130
Anti-Poor Law, 2, 28, 41, 61, 65, 76, 83, 134, 151
asylums, general, 3, 6, 8, 11, 12, 42, 110, 111–114, 116, 119–120, 122, 124–129, 131, 136, 149, 151
Atlantic World, 4
Australia, *ix*, 10, 16, 151

bastardy, 5, 84–85
Bentham, Jeremy, 4
Blackburn, William, 8
Booth, Charles, 81–82
Bowling Park Colony, 124
Bradford, 21–24, 26, 28, 47, 54–55, 56–60, 70, 75–78, 80–81, 93–95, 102–107, 109, 121–124, 126–128, 134–135, 138–141, 143
Bradford Union Hospital (B.U.H.), 55, 60
Bramley, 21–22, 24, 28, 41–47, 54, 57, 59–60, 68–69, 75, 80, 80–81, 90–93, 105–107, 114, 132, 136–137, 139, 141
Bristol Corporation of the Poor 1696, 5

Canada, 87, 102
Children's Act 1908, 88
Chorley, C.R., 50
Chorlton Union, 117
Clifton Asylum, 117

Commissioners of Lunacy, 7, 111–112, 123, 127
Conolly, John, 112, 114
Contagious Diseases Acts, 31
cook (position), 99, 135
COVID-19, *viii*, 145–146
Crabbe, 1
crime, 85

Daisy Hill Cottage Homes, 70, 81
deserving and undeserving poor, 7, 12, 19, 23, 32, 55, 62–65, 69, 70, 72, 75, 77, 80–82, 84, 86, 104, 148
development-led archaeology, 10, 14
Devon County Asylum, 110
Dickens, Charles, 4, 32, 50, 83
Dublin, 86

Edinburgh, 19
education, 11–12, 17, 51, 66, 86–91, 93, 95–96, 99–106, 138, 148
Elementary Education Act 1870, 12, 93, 103
Elizabethan Poor Law 1601, 5
emigration, 73, 87–88, 103, 113, 148

family, 19, 62, 66, 67, 84, 88, 91, 137, 144
First World War, 13, 88
Foucault, Michel, 4, 11, 27, 110
foundling hospitals, 84, 149

gender segregation, 8, 48–49, 54, 64, 65, 68, 70, 75, 77, 79, 90, 92, 97–99, 105, 121
Gilbert Scott, George, 8
Gilbert Unions, 6, 23, 34, 57, 66, 68, 78, 90–92, 106, 108, 113

Gilbert, Thomas, 5, 78, 82
Gilbert's Act 1782, 5–6
Great Ouseburn, 18, 20, 28, 34–37, 57, 66–67, 79, 90–92, 106, 108, 125, 132–133, 135, 143, 155
Grey, Charles, 1st Baron Grey, Earl Grey, 5

Hartley, James, 38, 40
Hartshead Moor, 65, 76
Head, Francis, 8, 27
Houses of Industry, 6, 86
Huddersfield, 65
Hull, 87
Humber Industrial School, 87
Hunslett Union, 52

improvement, *ix*, 4–5, 17, 27, 97, 105, 110, 147, 150
institutional archaeology, *x*, *ix*, 10, 14, 63, 151

Keighley, 26
Kempthorne, Sampson, 6–8, 20, 27, 65

Lambeth Union, 61–62
Lancet, 26, 29, 127
laundress (position), 99, 135, 136
Leeds Union Workhouse, 42, 45, 47, 51–55, 58, 69, 104, 107, 118, 120, 128, 138
Leeds Moral and Industrial Training School, 23, 51–52, 92, 95–98, 100, 104–107, 132
Leeds Prison, 96
Leeds Union Infirmary, 45, 50–51, 54
leisure pursuits, 37, 59, 70, 72, 75, 77, 79, 81, 87, 89, 93, 100, 101, 114–116, 118, 120, 122–123, 127, 148
Local Government Boards, 30, 37, 40, 51, 53, 60, 88, 91, 100, 119, 127, 133, 147
Lock Hospitals, 31
London, 19, 29, 31, 51, 53, 58, 60, 95, 110, 146
Lunacy Act 1808, 11, 112
Lunacy Act 1845, 11, 112, 124–125, 149

Lunacy Act Amendment Act 1862, 112, 114, 127
Lyddington Bede House, *viii*

Malthus, Thomas, 60, 84
Manchester, 32, 48, 95, 117
marriage in the workhouse, 64, 69, 70, 72–73, 80, 131, 133, 148
Master (position), 72, 99, 101, 115, 118, 124, 130–136, 149
Matron (position), 52, 99, 118, 131, 133–135, 143
Mental Deficiency Act 1913, 113
migration, 11, 22, 62, 73
Moffatt, William Bonython, 8

National Health Service, 15, 26, 53
New Poor Law. *See* Poor Law Amendment Act 1834
New York, 151
New Zealand, 8
Nightingale, Florence, 30–31, 35, 44, 114, 117, 146
Nightingale Hospitals, 145–146
Nightingale ward style, 35, 44, 74
nonconformism, 91
North Bierley, 21, 24, 59–60, 69–70, 80–81, 93–95, 105, 107, 114–116, 126–127, 134, 138, 141, 143
North Bierley Children's Hospital, 95
Northallerton, 26
nursing (profession), 31, 42, 50, 119, 131, 137, 143, 144

Oastler, Richard, 65
Old Poor Law, 9, 63, 66, 75–76, 78, 86, 103, 106, 107, 110
Oldham, 65
Oliver Twist, 4, 83
orphans, 17, 66, 84, 92, 99
Otley, 18–19
outdoor relief. *See* out-relief
out-relief, 5, 19, 23, 33, 46, 49, 57, 61–66, 82, 85, 90–91, 103, 113, 116

Pateley Bridge, 18, 20, 27, 32–34, 56, 66, 91–92, 106, 113, 133, 143

Poor Law Amendment Act 1834, 2–3, 6, 9, 18, 27–28, 30, 32, 49, 60, 61, 64, 75, 78, 84, 85, 92, 106, 111, 150
Poor Law Board, 6, 29–30, 48–49, 56, 58, 114, 118–119, 127, 130, 149
Poor Law Commission, 6–8, 18, 21, 27, 30, 64, 65, 66, 86, 90, 100, 130, 149
porter (position), 13, 99, 131–132, 135–136, 149
prisons, 1, 3, 6, 8, 13, 27, 86, 96, 120, 131, 134, 151

Quakers. *See* Society of Friends

regionality, *ix*, 2, 9, 13, 30, 32, 57, 60, 110, 150
religion, 19, 49, 50, 91, 99, 105, 117, 131
Ripon, 19–21, 28, 34, 46, 56–57, 59, 79, 88–90, 92, 96, 104, 106, 107, 132, 133, 135–136, 143–144
Roundhay Children's Home, 102
Roundhay Park, 72

sanitation and hygiene, 31, 37, 48, 54, 57–58, 73, 75–76, 81, 103, 106, 119, 136, 146
schoolmaster (position), 103, 131
schoolmistress (position), 89–90, 93, 103–104, 106, 131, 135
Second World War, 26
Sheffield Asylum, 117
Skipton Workhouse, 18–20, 28, 34, 37–41, 45, 56–57, 59, 65, 79, 87–88, 99, 106, 108, 113, 125, 132, 134–135, 143–144
Society of Friends, 5

Somerset House. *See* Poor Law Commission
St Bartholomew's Hospital, 31
St Giles Workhouse, Holborn, 29, 109
St Mary's Orphanage, 99
St Paul, Covent Garden, 5
St Thomas's Hospital, 31
standing building survey (method), 10, 24–25, 86, 114
Suffolk, 9
surveillance, 20, 24–25, 77, 100, 131, 134

Temple Newsam, 75
The Retreat, York, 112
Tuke family, 112

vagrancy, 20, 46, 73, 88, 104, 116, 133–135, 143

wallpaper, 134
Webb, Sidney and Beatrice, 1, 6, 29, 38
West Riding Asylum, Menston, 36, 110, 115, 117
West Riding Asylum, Wakefield, 36, 110, 115, 117
West Yorkshire Asylums Committee, 115
Wetherby, 19–20, 23, 34, 57, 59, 79, 91–92, 106, 113, 135, 146
Wilkinson, George, 150
Winn, Thomas, 52
Worcestershire, 9
workhouse plans, 6, 8, 18, 20, 27, 32, 36–37, 43, 50, 54, 66, 74, 77, 105, 117, 121–122, 132, 136, 138, 141
workhouse test, 7, 49, 63, 78
Worthington, Thomas, 17, 32

Milton Keynes UK
Ingram Content Group UK Ltd.
UKHW022308230424
441636UK00005B/111